D1429112

Phylogenesis
foa's ark
foreign office architects

390 **Towards a Non-Standard Mode of Production**
Patrick Beaucé, Bernard Cache

Phylogenesis: foa´s ark
Alejandro Zaera-Polo, Farshid Moussavi

The research that we present in this document has been produced
as a reflection after the fact on the work that FOA has completed
during its first ten years of practice, 1993-2003. In this exercise we
are trying to address general questions about the identity and the
consistency and the operativity of an architectural practice today.
It is a very specific reflection on the contemporary conditions of
production, and a work in progress consisting of a series of recent
exhibitions and publications in which we have been fortunate to
involve others – editors, curators, critics, friends... This book includes texts by some of these invited critics that address the work
in relation to a series of "external" topics, without necessarily describing it directly or commenting extensively on it; some have not
even been specifically written for the book, but appropriated from
other works of the authors. There is no overlay or articulation between both layers, but rather a sudden adjacency, a "direct cut", the
purpose being to exploit the resonance between the work and the
discourse without trying to bind them too directly or make them
immediately consequent.

As an organisation grown primarily from a speculative and academic milieu, we have spent our first ten years in the development
of a technical arsenal for the implementation of a certain approach
to the practice of architecture. This approach and its instruments
have been explored through a series of competitions, speculative
commissions, and lately some real projects, some of them already
completed, others still under construction. Through these exer-
cises, we have been developing an identity of the practice that is
now becoming more tangible, and so is starting to pose questions.
What do we need an identity for? Is it operative? How should it be
defined? What is its degree of stability and reactivity?

The question of identity has lately become crucial due to the increasing rate of globalisation of architectural practice, such that

the identity of an architectural practice is probably one of the most crucial considerations that a contemporary architect needs to make. The identity of a building or an architectural practice used to be determined either by the domain of operation – in the "contextual" mode – or by the particular "style" of the principal architect – in the "artistic" mode – in an oscillation between material and will: between the *Baukunst* and the *Kunstwollen*, between technique or material and interpretation or style. As the domains of operation for architects are increasing, both in terms of competences and territories, a contemporary practice needs to develop alternative forms of consistency, beyond the effective replication of verified local protocols or the deployment of a consistent "style." We belong to what we could call the second generation of architects operating within a globalised domain of practice. The previous generation developed what we can generally call a practice of stylistic consistency, as a vehicle to overcome the differences in raw materials and site specificities, and still be able to sustain a certain degree of "branding" regularity. But a faster pace of market evolution, increases in the rate of consumption, and the level of information and competition between locations has started to render stylistic consistency ineffective: some of the most advanced advertising agencies are now testing concepts like "mutant identity" and "local variation." Others have simply declared the end of "style" and claimed that location and matter are the critical factors in the synthesis of identity.

The ideas we propose in this document are aimed at the development of alternative forms of consistency in the practice of architecture, using our own practice and production as a case study.

The reflection that we propose here is an attempt to overcome both style and authorship without falling into servile and plain inconsistency – a quality that some architects are putting forward as pragmatic and realistic – but also without becoming captive to the material and the processes of production. We are part of a generation that grew interested in the manipulation of material, and that often has failed to produce any more comprehensive architectural statements. In the end, one cannot ground architectural achievements in the solution of demographic problems or sustainable performance, even if that is the material that we need to architecturalise. This classification of projects is an attempt to establish a certain benchmark, internal to our practice, that will at least map out the range of territories that we have explored so far, and that will allow us to position the future ones.

In order to make this reflection, we needed to run our practice for a few years: we needed to generate a population of projects with which to start developing a classification. This is not an a priori classification, but one that – like most classifications in the natural sciences – emerges from a population. By constructing our identity from a populational analysis of the projects, we are trying to avoid constructing it on the basis of idealistic or critical claims. We are constructing the consistency of our practice out of its own material, understanding our production as a non-arbitrary group of individuals that may or may not share features and therefore belong to a species. From this perspective, our practice may be seen as a phylogenetic process in which seeds proliferate in time across different environments, generating differentiated yet consistent organisms. The idea here is to try to describe a practice as a lineage of ideas that evolve through time and across different environments.

A practice is always determined by a series of repetitions and differentiations. Excessive repetition leads to sclerosis and inflexibility, and fails to exploit opportunities in new environments and to expand the practice's genetic potentials. On the other hand, excessive differentiation dilutes the internal consistency of the work, enslaves it to external conditions, making it purely local, purely contingent. The operativity of a practice depends on this balance between repetition and differentiation. Operativity is not only determined by the capacity to adapt to changing conditions, but also by its transformative capacity to purposefully alter environments. And that capacity is primarily developed through repetition, through the development of a specific culture of the practice. Techniques, protocols and handshakes are improved through testing, as certain operations or traits prove to be successful under certain conditions and become part of a practice's arsenal. The perspective of this publication is built by identifying repetitions in the work and trying to produce an evolving classification of traits, to try to understand the way in which they become mediators for a variety of materials. It is in these repetitions that we try to identify the consistency of the practice, to construct a kind of fingerprint, a DNA of our practice. We want to see the outcome of these first ten years neither as a series of contingent experiments, defined by their particular conditions, nor as the definition of a style, but rather as a consistent reservoir of architectural species to be proliferated, mutated and evolved in the years to come: a genetic pool.

By looking at the work in this way we are trying to distance ourselves from the naive idea, recently claimed commonly by architects, that a practice has no repetition and is driven exclusively by external forces to which it is infinitely pliant. A solid product can never be entirely constructed by the market; it needs to contain a high degree of internal consistency. A market is never constant – especially now – and that is why a typological approach is increasingly ineffective as an articulation between an environment, a program or an effect, and a particular material assemblage.

But neither is the equally traditional alternative of claiming that a "style" is able to provide internal consistency to the work under any circumstances: very often the traits of a style become irreconcilable with the material consistencies of the environment.

Our perspective here is aimed at dismantling the identity between the internal consistency of the projects and our authorship: through the identification of a phylogenetic lineage in our work we are trying to construct a kind of alienated and evolving authorship, able to accumulate effectively the various experiences that we have developed, the various characters that become part of the practice. Through the development of a phylogenetic tree of the projects we are aiming at establishing forms of congruence between the internal consistency of the work and its consistency with external processes. The need to construct an alternative approach to the classical opposition between the external and internal consistency of a production is probably grounded in the specificity of our nomadic practice: we had to learn to construct an argument that allows us to transfer knowledge across environments without losing our identity, while simultaneously being able to redefine our identity in response to the environment. This attempt to classify the work defines our practice as the culture of a particular set of species across time and space, with a very specific focus on their architectural content. The consistency of the practice is as a result grounded on the definition of consistent morphological diagrams rather than aesthetic, ethical or political preferences, which would have placed the consistency of the work outside architecture. Its progress does not depend therefore purely on its adequacy for future commissions or conditions, but rather establishes certain grounds to assess the evolution of the practice on its own terms.

Types are fundamentally constant in time and space and therefore their operativity is always local. Species are sets of consistent morphological relations that vary across time and space, and therefore offer a much more effective tool to operate within a constantly shifting environment. The "species" that we have developed through 10 years of practice had to be resilient enough to grow in multiple ecosystems. They constitute the "culture" of the office that we hope to grow further in the future, both in terms of the development of these species, but also in terms of other lineages to emerge from the current genetic pool. Seen in this light, projects are not something designed, but a breed of particular species. Design is a cultural activity, a task of translation and interpretation, even of psychological expression in the sense of Riegl's "will to art", but we are here much more interested in a Semperian re-encounter with matter, in the same sort of knowledge used to produce wines, horses or bulls: out of genetic pools and environments purposefully manipulated. This is not a simple bottom-up generation; it also requires a certain consistency that operates top-down from a practice's genetic potentials. Just as with horses and wines, there is a process in which successful traits are selected through experimentation and evolved by registering the results. Typologies were the traditional instrument by which groupings of traits and organisational features become part of disciplinary knowledge, reproduced and evolved. However, the belief that architectural typologies are eternal and static will only freeze the necessary evolution of the discipline to deal with the increased rates of environmental change that contemporary culture demands. This is where the concept of a species becomes relevant for the discipline of architecture, as a potential mediator between a top-down typological design process and a bottom-up parametric design approach. By defining an architectural practice, a location, a scale or a program as a lineage of consistent, evolving and non-contingent groups of organisms – as a particular genetic pool – we are able to establish an effective feedback between bottom-up and top-down construction processes. The series of projects included in this document describes the "cultures" of the office at a relatively early stage of development, not yet intensely mediated by the external conditions surrounding each project. It is a well-known process that as an architectural practice evolves it tends to suffer an increasing pressure from external factors that, while providing opportunities for proliferation, may also destroy its internal consistency. In this sense we feel that defining a reference system for future consistency is a necessary work to be done at this stage of practice.

There are probably several forms of description of the culture of a practice. We could have described the work of the office as a series of protocols or techniques that we apply systematically, a kind of methodology. That has also evolved in its own system of lineages, but would be the subject of an alternative analysis. Instead, this book aims to describe the genetic potential of the practice circa 2003 out of an analysis of the products themselves.

SURFACES

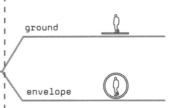

ground

envelope

The classification that we have made from the projects has the spirit of a scientific classification: we have tried to identify the genesis of the projects as the evolution of a series of "phyla" or abstract diagrams, actualised – and simultaneously virtualised – in their application to the specific conditions where the projects take place in time and space. The classification includes seven transversal categories of the plylogenetic tree, where the project species are formed. Those categories are:

Function
(ground - envelope)
This first differentiation divides the projects into two major lineages that relate obviously with the particular nature of our work. The manipulation of surface is a crucial trait of our work and therefore the first division relates to the predominant function of the surface. Projects are here classified into those which relate to the formation of enveloping surfaces, or surfaces whose primary function is the enclosure of space, and those whose primary function is the construction of a connective ground.

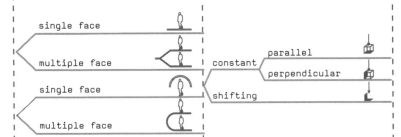

Faciality

(single face - multiple face)

A surface will have at least one face, depending on how many of its surfaces are inhabited.

For example, a monolith or a ground are experienced only on one of their faces, while usually a slab or a facade have an outside and an inside, or a floor and a ceiling. Depending of the number of layers into which the surface slices space, the order of faciality increases.

Balance

(constant: parallel/perpendicular - shifting)

This discriminator classifies surfaces in reference to the force of gravity, which becomes critical in establishing the relationship between the surface and the structure and drainage systems. This classification determines, in the first instance, whether the surface remains constant in its alignment to gravity, or whether it alternates orientation within the project.

If the surface remains constantly perpendicular to gravitational force, it will become mostly a ground or a roof. If it is constantly parallel, it will be mainly a wall or a facade.

If the surface shifts between being parallel and perpendicular to gravitational force, the building will be a blob or a shed, where the roof and the walls are continuous. Depending on this alignment the quality of the surface will vary substantially, in both its geometrical definition and its material qualities.

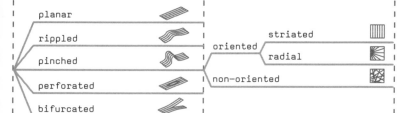

planar

rippled

pinched

perforated

bifurcated

striated

oriented

radial

non-oriented

Discontinuity

(planar - rippled - pinched - perforated - bifurcated)

This attribute of the species describes the typology of singularity that determines discontinuities on the surface, and is classified in a gradation depending on the intensity of the surface singularities. If the surface is continuous, does not have interruptions excepts in its limits, and does not have any surface singularities, it is planar. If it has some local deformations but no interruptions, it becomes rippled; if the singularities are more accentuated to the point where the tangent varies more than 90°, it is pinched. If it is locally interrupted, the surface is perforated. If it is locally interrupted but is continuous on a different level, layer or space, simultaneously establishing continuity and discontinuity, then the surface is bifurcated. Pierced organisations usually correspond to the resolution of specific connections between well-demarcated spatial segmentations, while bifurcations tend to be more common in projects that require loose spatial segmentations.

Orientation

(oriented: striated/polar - non-oriented)

This category divides surfaces with respect to the spatial ordering of their singularities. Independent of their nature, surface singularities can be organised following a consistent law, or they can be entirely contingent. The second category tends to correspond to organisations more dependent upon pre-existing traces or local singularities, responding to pre-existing focalisations of parameters in certain zones of space, while the first category corresponds more to organisations with a weak relationship to pre-existing fields and a more self-supporting scale or quality. Among those surface singularity fields that are oriented, they can be oriented following a striated distribution – that is, following a parallel order – or to respond to centres or poles. The striated variety is usually related to fields with a prevailing flow direction, while polar structures relate to either strong focal pre-existences or central or polycentric organisations of the project.

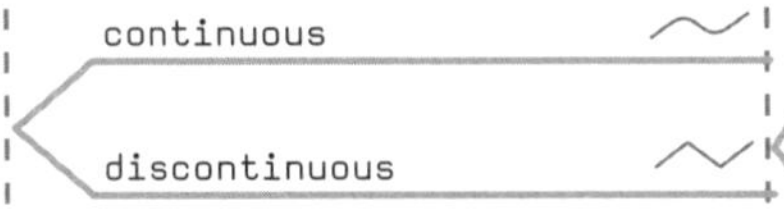

continuous ~

discontinuous ~

patterned ⬙

contingent ⬦

Geometry
(continuous - discontinuous)
The geometrical discriminator
refers to the geometrical
continuity of the surface. It
classifies the projects between
those which have a continuous
variation of the tangent, and
therefore produce a smooth
surface, and those which
have points of indeterminate
tangent to the surface at certain
moments, producing breaks in
the geometrical continuity of the
surface. Those projects produce
edges or ridges rather than
seamless discontinuities.

Diversification
(patterned - contingent)
Every branch of the phylogenetic
tree is split between those
projects where a patterned
system of discontinuities,
accidents or shift in orientation
occur on a regular basis across
the surface, and those where
they appear contingently based
on local specificity. Contingent
diversification responds usually
to organisations constructed
from the bottom-up or that
are highly responsive to local
specificities, while patterned
textures correspond to
organisations deployed from the
top-down, or where the scale of
the organisations is such that
the capacity of self-determination
is stronger than the local
singularities.

As with any form of classification, this system exerts a certain violence upon the elements it sorts, and it has raised several questions on the pertinence of a particular project to a particular phylum. Some projects belong to various lineages to a higher or lesser degree. Some projects belong to one lineage but inaugurate another, or suggest future evolutions, and have been placed according to what is more explanatory of the nature of the species that constitute now our practice. But this violence on the elements of the classification, the tension between projects and species, has in the process become enormously revealing of what we could call the embryological potentials of the practice, of the gaps that may be filled by future projects and the niches or opportunities to develop our current genetic potentials, of the correlation between certain phyla and certain ecosystems...

We are conscious that this is a very complex task and that we are just at the beginning of the process. Like every taxonomy, it has a certain degree of arbitrariness and remains in constant evolution. But our hypothesis is that the rigor of the classification will become productive by itself: through the process of mapping the lineages and developing the taxonomy, we automatically identify possibilities that we have not tried, repetitions of traces that survive in certain environments...

We are also very conscious that this classification is specific to our work, and it may not be adequate to classify other practices at this point. This experiment is not about establishing a classification of species for a generic practice, but to use speciation to understand the specificity and variability of our practice, and by doing so, to initiate a new domain of knowledge within the discipline of architecture. It is very important to point out the difference between the science we are proposing here and the models applied in biology, in the sense that this classification is not applied to organisations which reproduce, like animals or plants. Typological studies, dating more or less from the same age as the first classification of species, tend to presuppose that the purpose of classification is reproduction. It is true that material assemblages have a tendency to reproduce within architecture or urban science; however, the use value of these classifications are more prospective, and more directly linked to future production than the biological classifications. The use of this classification is not so much to generate arguments for repetition, but to identify areas of experimentation and to provide direction to the practice. To establish, finally, an evolving frame of reference able to tell us what we discover in every project in purely architectural terms, rather than as an external justification.

In this taxonomy, we have chosen to move away from the traditional functional classification of types – schools, residences, institutions, industrial – into a morphological one in which the prototype becomes a material mediator for a particular material assemblage. Typologies are an obvious reference for this method of naming architectural species, and in many ways this experiment addresses itself to redefining the subject of typology as an alternative to style or expression in establishing the consistency of an architectural practice. The assumption here is that traits of expression can be found in the deployment of particular organisations. One can easily identify how certain environments, scales and situations, particular species tend to be more adequate: for example, large infrastructural projects are more likely to adopt ground-like organisations and constant orientation to gravity than domestic structures...

As with any taxonomic effort there needs to be a level of repetition in the traces of the sample in order to make it possible, but that does not mean that a taxonomy necessarily leads to systematic repetition. On the contrary, hopefully it becomes, like language, a tool for the proliferation of reality.

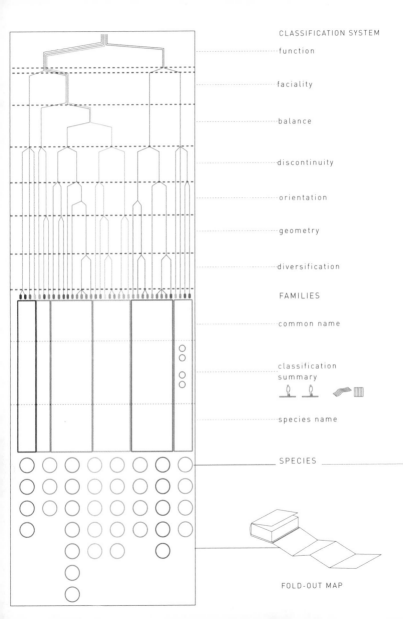

CLASSIFICATION SYSTEM

function

faciality

balance

discontinuity

orientation

geometry

diversification

FAMILIES

common name

classification
summary

species name

SPECIES

FOLD-OUT MAP

User´s manual

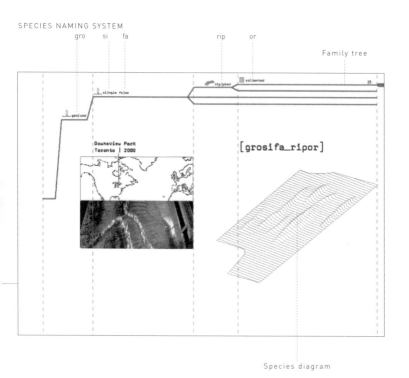

single face

ground

Downsview Park
Toronto | 2000

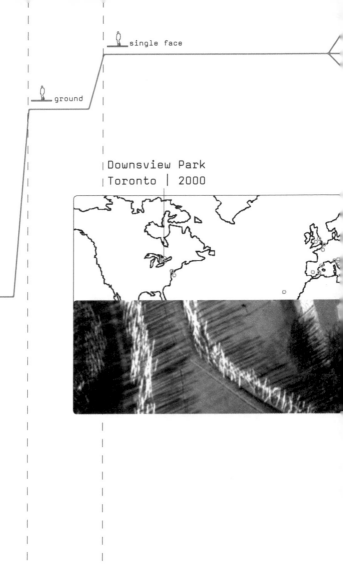

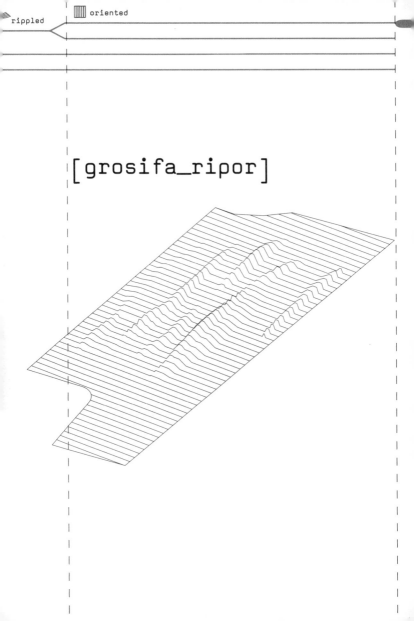

rippled

oriented

[grosifa_ripor]

More than ever before, the natural and the artificial are literally merging into each other. GM food, animal cloning, organic prosthetics, biological computers, the human genome... these are the indices of an era when the distinction between nature and artifice have become obsolete both to describe and to produce the environment of the 21st Century. Downsview Park presents a unique opportunity to explore and exploit the potential of these emerging artificial ecologies in the organisation of the territory, landscape and architecture. To succeed in its ambitions, Downsview Park will need to be able to synthesise and formalise the potential material organisation of its age, to give material consistency to the energies and the processes to operate in the park, to generate a new synthetic landscape through rigorous understanding and integration of its intrinsic and extrinsic systems: ecological, historical, cultural and social. Both the geometries and the programs of pure indetermination or pure linearity are a trace of the past, rather than a possibility for the future. This project provides the opportunity to overcome the technical barrier that resorts to contradiction as a form of complexity and to try to produce complexity through consistency, to generate organisation through a mediated, integrated addition of rigorous orders.

The suburban location of Downsview vis-à-vis the urban fabric suggests that it will neither operate as an urban park or as a natural reserve. In order to develop a national, and perhaps international, profile, Downsview will have to develop a dual behaviour, as a recreation area for the local community, but also as a thematic attraction able to draw people not only from the metropolitan area, but also from other cities and countries.

In order to produce this dual mode, our proposal is to turn this park into a world-famous location for extreme sports, as the thematic content of the park. Extreme use will evolve into lower-intensity sports and outdoor activities, to cover the full range of possibilities between a theme park and an urban park.

GENERATION OF
BERM GEOMETRY

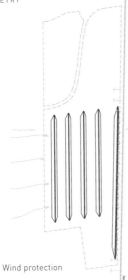

Wind protection

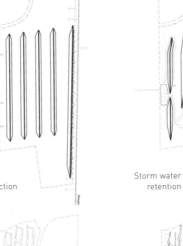

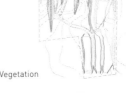

Storm water
retention

Activity fields

Vegetation

Downsview will become a park dedicated to the exploration of the relationships between the physical self and the landscape, from the most strenuous to the most soothing. The particular relationship that extreme sports have with landscape, as physical skills to exploit a field of accidents and material singularities, provides the argument to produce complex and differentiated landscapes with very specific programs.

The generative engine for the park is a large-scale topographical re-organisation able to incorporate and give consistency to all the programmatic and ecological processes that have been synthesised on the site. Two organisational structures for the land are proposed:

1. A function-based circuit system is used to generate the spatial structure of the site. This system compromises a network of different paths: walking, running, cycling, cross-country skiing, each with particular sectional requirements. Through manipulation of the topography, the physical level of difficulty of each path varies, and thematizes the sports and recreation program. The circuit system not only generates the topography but also negotiates with the existing one and with its own intersections, producing a systematic topography of accidents. If parks have traditionally imitated the urban grid, as a suburban park we have designed Downsview as a highway system.

2. A north-south corrugation pattern intensifying the geological striation of the glacial landscape is used to level the ground selectively to produce terraced horizontal planes of activity, while providing water-retaining barriers and wind shields for the resulting meadows and fields. The ridges also align the playing fields in the ideal north-south orientation and provide varying levels of slope for park circuits.

The precise geometry of both circuits and ridges emerges from the negotiation between the circuit layout and activity fields, the drainage/ retaining system, the vegetative system, the wind pattern, the sun path and the existing land forms.

Topography

1. AEOLIC AND SONIC PROTECTION

Typical section

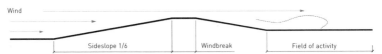

Wind

Sideslope 1/6 | Windbreak | Field of activity

Variation

Railway

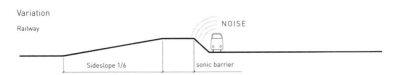

NOISE

Sideslope 1/6 | sonic barrier

2. RETENTION OF STORM WATER

Typical section

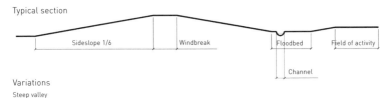

Sideslope 1/6 | Windbreak | Floodbed | Field of activity

Channel

Variations

Steep valley

Sideslope 1/2 | Floodbed | Field of activity

Marshy meadow

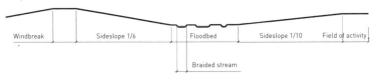

Windbreak | Sideslope 1/6 | Floodbed | Sideslope 1/10 | Field of activity

Braided stream

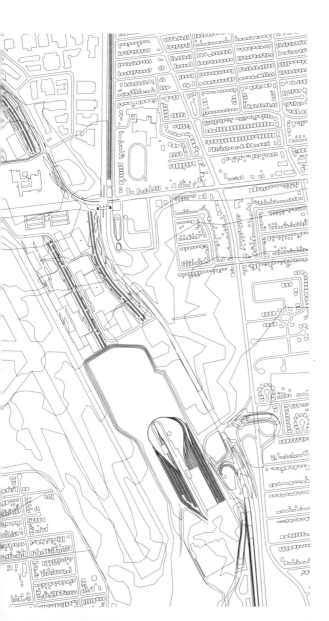

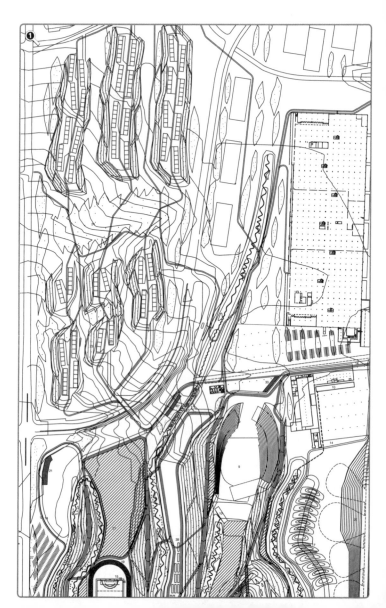

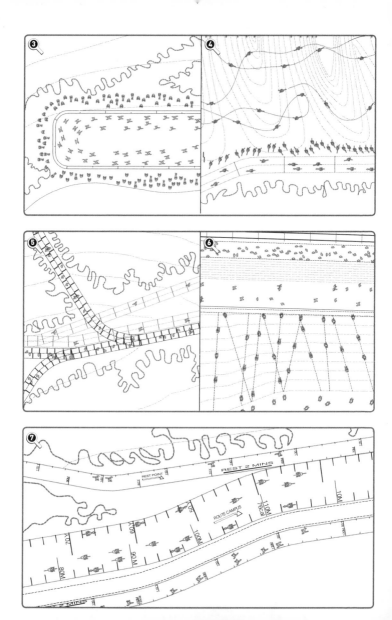

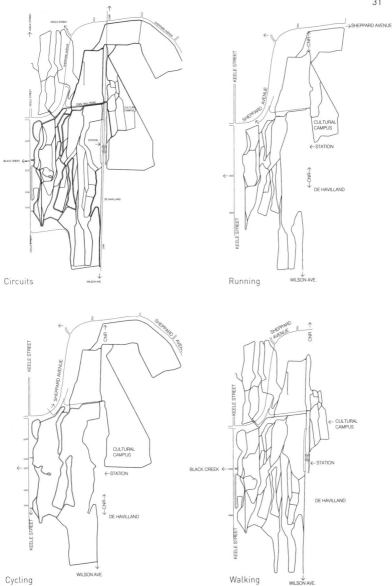

Circuits

Running

Cycling

Walking

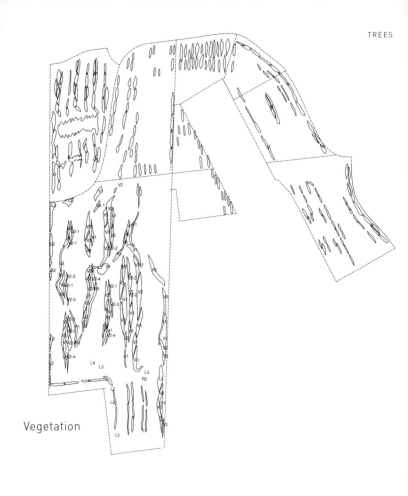

Vegetation

U1
UPLAND 1-WEST FACING,
DRY SOIL, FAST DRAINING
Type 1 (highest, most exposed)
Robinia Pseudoacacia
Rhus Typhinia
Type 2 (side slope, flowering)
Catalpa Speciosa
Crataegus Maollis
Type 3 (side slope, foliage)
Pinus Resinosa
Quecrus

U2
UPLAND 2-EAST AND NORTH
facing, mod. soil, fast draining
Type 1 (highest, most exposed)
Pinus Strotus
Liquidambar Styraeifhia
Type 2 (flowering magenta)
Cercis Canadiensis
Tilia Americana
Type 3 (flowering white)
Malus Ioensis
Liriodendron Tulipifera
Type 4 (foliage)
Populus Tremuloides
Gleditsia Triacantaus

R
RIPADIAN
Type 1 (wettest, most scouring)
Salix
Type 2 (big foliage)
Aesculus Glabra
Acer Rubrum
Type 3 (Pendulous)
Betula Nigra
Larix

L
LOWLAND
Type 1 (wettest)
Betula Papyrifrea
Larix
Acer Rubrum
Type 2 (driest, biggest)
Fagus
Quercus Palustris
Type 3 (flowering magenta)
Cercis
Liquidambar
Type 4 (flowering white)
Malus
Fraxinus

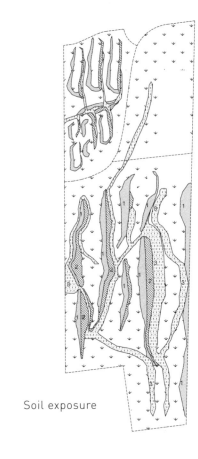

Soil exposure

▭ 1. UPLAND 1	west facing dry soil fast draining	▭ 3. RIPARIAN	wet soil mod/slow draining
▭ 2. UPLAND 2	east and north facing mod. soil fast draining	▭ 4. LOWLAND	level fields mod/slow draining

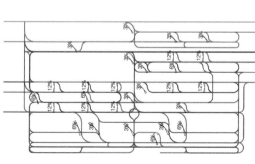

SLOPES GENERATIVE DIAGRAM
65% level - circuits with 0-3% slopes
20% semilevel - circuits with
3-6% slopes
15% hills - circuits with 6-12%
slopes for extreme sports.

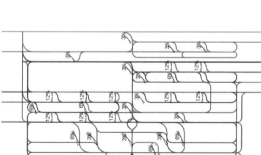

DISTANCES GENERATIVE DIAGRAM
Cross country, hiking, mountain bike:
4000 meters of circuits with bifurcations no more than every 400 meters.
Basic jogging, walking, cycling: 6000
meters of circuits with bifurcations
no more than every 200 meters.

GENERATING DIAGRAM FOR CIRCUITS
12000 meters of circuits with different
levels of difficulty:
4000 meters handship: 1; 3000 meters
handship: 2; 2500 meters handship: 3; 1500
meters handship: 4.

35

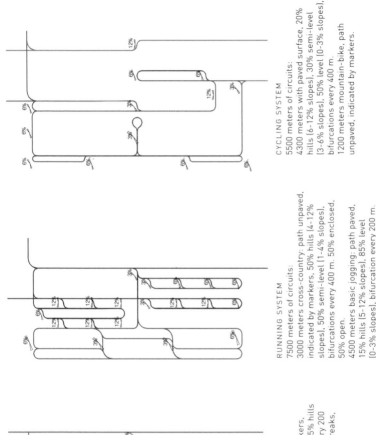

CYCLING SYSTEM
5500 meters of circuits:
4300 meters with paved surface, 20%
hills (6-12% slopes), 30% semi-level
(3-6% slopes), 50% level (0-3% slopes),
bifurcations every 400 m.
1200 meters mountain-bike, path
unpaved, indicated by markers.

RUNNING SYSTEM
7500 meters of circuits:
3000 meters cross-country: path unpaved,
indicated by markers, 50% hills (4-12%
slopes), 50% semi-level (1-4% slopes),
bifurcations every 400 m. 50% enclosed,
50% open.
4500 meters basic jogging: path paved,
15% hills (5-12% slopes), 85% level
(0-3% slopes), bifurcation every 200 m.

WALKING SYSTEM
9500 meters of circuits:
Path unpaved, indicated by markers,
85% semi-level (1-4% slopes), 15% hills
(4-12% slopes), bifurcations every 200
meters, 50% enclosed by windbreaks,
50% open across fields, hills.

Summer Sports
1. BMX
2. Soccer
3. Canadian football
4. Basketball
5. Flat multipurpose
sport areas
6. Bocce
7. Running track
8. Soccer and hockey
9. Baseball
10. Volleyball

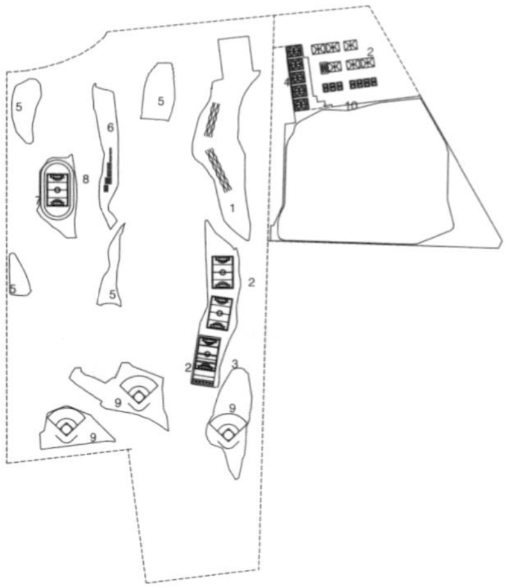

Winter sports
1. Tobogganing
2. Cross country
skiing
3. Skating

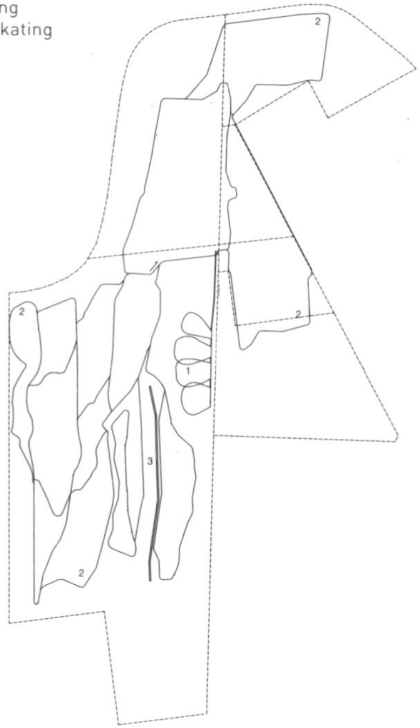

Picnic Areas
+ Service Areas
1. Picnic Meadow
2. Service Areas

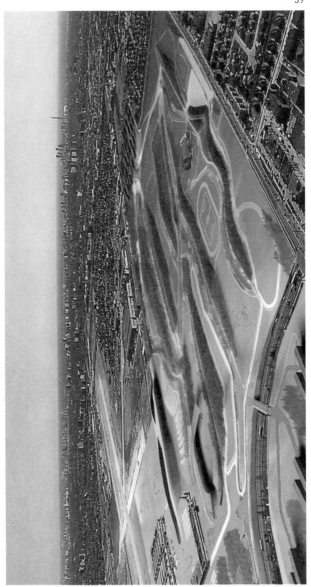

42

single face

ground

La Gavia Park
Madrid | 2003

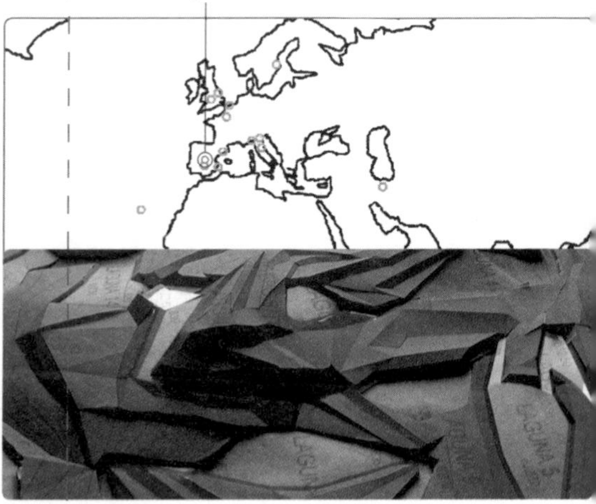

[grosifa_ripnonor]

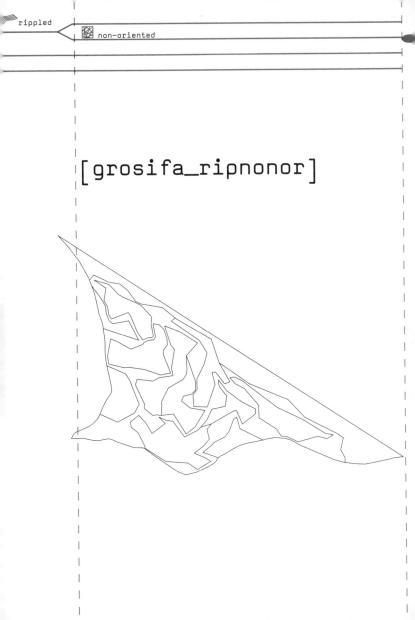

The strategy that we have used to generate the plan considers the 1.5 million of cubic meters of residue land which lay in one side of the site as potential to generate the new topography. As earth movements would be cheap and easy because of the lack of cohesion of the ground, we will manipulate them as the material that will constitute the new artificial landscape and condition all the other parameters that define the park.

This new topography is modelled according to five border conditions:

1. Acoustical protection. The park protects itself from the main roads which have a high noise pollution.

2. Protection or enhancement of visual connections. Some areas get hidden while others are emphasized creating high viewing points to enjoy the perspective of the whole park.

3. Perimeter flows. The topography is deformed to permit access to the park.

4. Winds. Topography behaves as a windscreen.

5. Program adjacencies. New programs are located to new similar existent ones, to reinforce continuity.

This new artificial topography is then occupied and modified by water, simulating an erosive system.

Water is considered not only as a decorative element of the park, but as a generator of landscape. Both purifying circuits (C1 and C2) are integrated into one single system; a necklace of lakes that cover and integrate the whole site. Instead of the streams suggested in the brief, our proposal is based on water films which are more effective for water oxigenization, and maximize their contact with the UV ray, fundamental for the second part of the circuit (C2). This lake system reaches its optimum state when water is in constant movement. For that reason lakes are constantly changing level, allowing water flow by gravity.

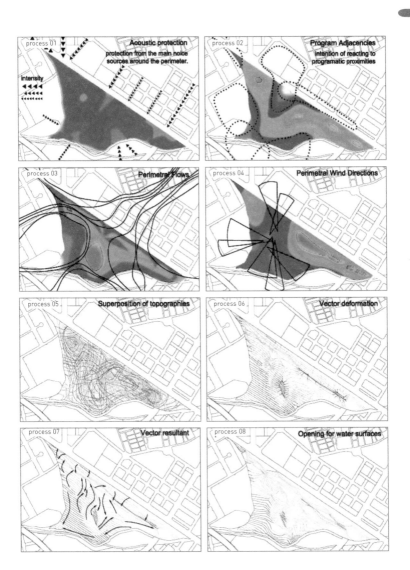

These lakes have different shapes and locations along the purification path. In the first stages (C1 and C2) water is clearly treated. Rock lagoons, lagoons with water lentils or breaking blocks appear, with a spiral section, to improve purification and sedimentation of suspended particles. After the end of circuit 2, lagoons are designed in relation to programs: boat lagoons, children lagoons, aquatic spectacles and so on are spread along circuit C3. Here the relationship between topography and water is intensified.

In order to generate the lagoon tissue, we decided to multiply the supply system in three points, for the following reasons:

-To divide the only supply circuit offers a more effective distribution of water along the park. Because of the characteristics of the land, from every point of the site water tends to get south direction, looking for the former Gavia stream.

-In terms of maintenance, the division of exit points offers more feedback capacity in case of accident. It would be possible to cut off one of the deposits without stopping the activity of the whole park.

-Dividing exit points also responds to the changes in volume of La Gavia Waste Treatment Plant. These volumes vary according to time and date. This tripartite division allows the absorption of the changes in volume. There are in principle two exits of 6500 m3/day, while the third one has a smaller volume, to be able to adjust to the changes mentioned before. At the same time, with these changes of level we are able to generate different landscapes based in water differences, from more humid ones (around deposits 1 and 2) to more dry (around deposit 3) ones.

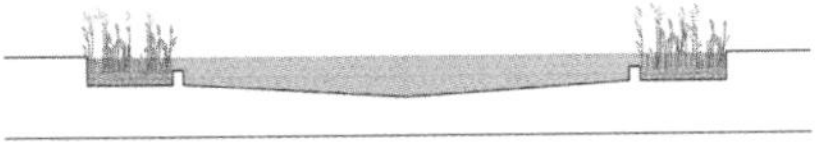

SQ
Lagoon sequence

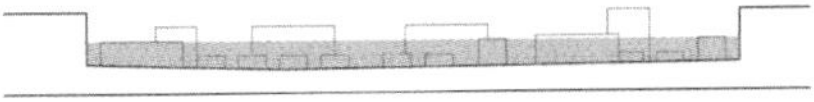

BW
Breaking water lagoon

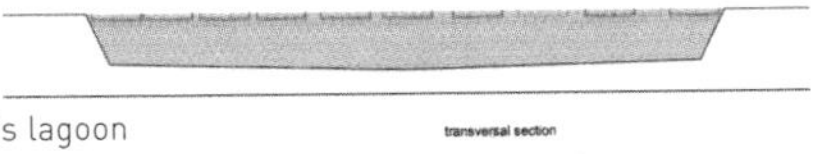

FP
Floating plants lagoon

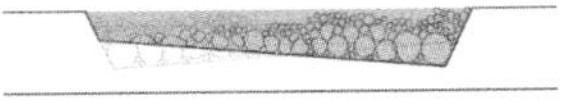

transversal section

BR
Bed rock lagoon

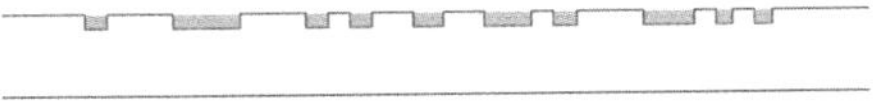

ML
Meander lagoon

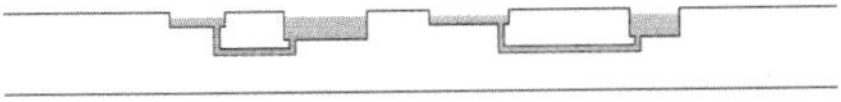

CL
Communicated lagoon

KL
Kids lagoon

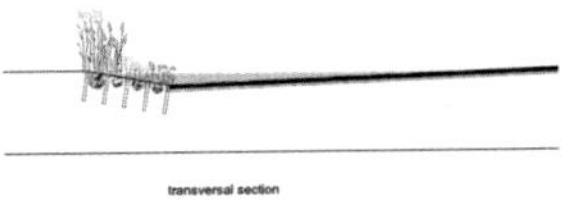

MX
Mixed lagoon

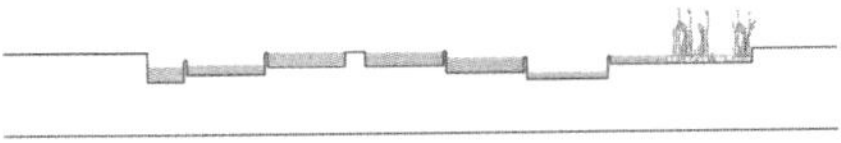

transversal section

CA
Cascade lagoon

PL
Plated lagoon

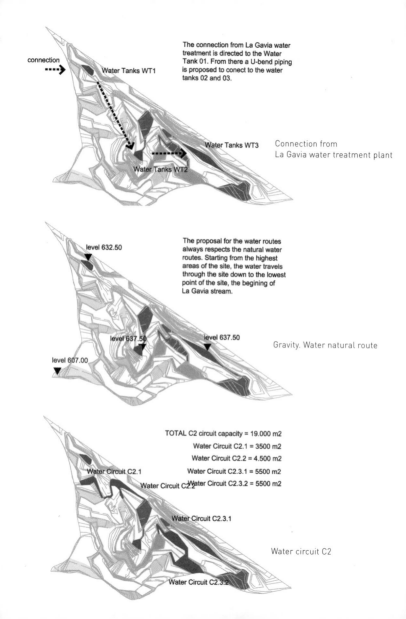

The connection from La Gavia water treatment is directed to the Water Tank 01. From there a U-bend piping is proposed to conect to the water tanks 02 and 03.

connection

Water Tanks WT1

Water Tanks WT3

Water Tanks WT2

Connection from
La Gavia water treatment plant

level 632.50

The proposal for the water routes always respects the natural water routes. Starting from the highest areas of the site, the water travels through the site down to the lowest point of the site, the begining of La Gavia stream.

level 637.50

level 637.50

level 607.00

Gravity. Water natural route

TOTAL C2 circuit capacity = 19.000 m2

Water Circuit C2.1 = 3500 m2

Water Circuit C2.2 = 4.500 m2

Water Circuit C2.3.1 = 5500 m2

Water Circuit C2.3.2 = 5500 m2

Water Circuit C2.1

Water Circuit C2.2

Water Circuit C2.3.1

Water circuit C2

Water Circuit C2.3.2

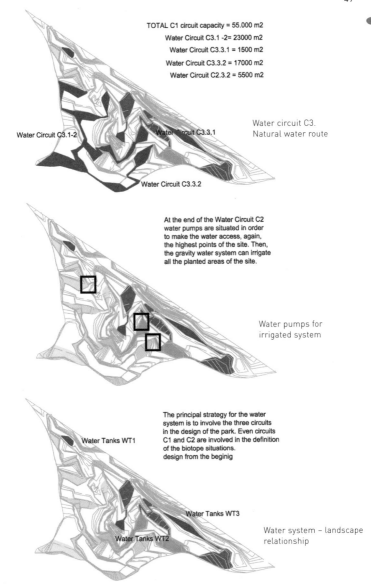

TOTAL C1 circuit capacity = 55.000 m2
Water Circuit C3.1 -2= 23000 m2
Water Circuit C3.3.1 = 1500 m2
Water Circuit C3.3.2 = 17000 m2
Water Circuit C2.3.2 = 5500 m2

Water Circuit C3.1-2

Water Circuit C3.3.1

Water Circuit C3.3.2

Water circuit C3.
Natural water route

At the end of the Water Circuit C2
water pumps are situated in order
to make the water access, again,
the highest points of the site. Then,
the gravity water system can irrigate
all the planted areas of the site.

Water pumps for
irrigated system

The principal strategy for the water
system is to involve the three circuits
in the design of the park. Even circuits
C1 and C2 are involved in the definition
of the biotope situations.
design from the beginig

Water Tanks WT1

Water Tanks WT3

Water Tanks WT2

Water system – landscape
relationship

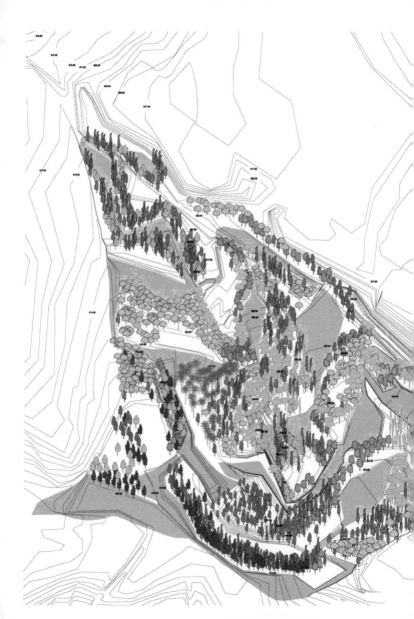

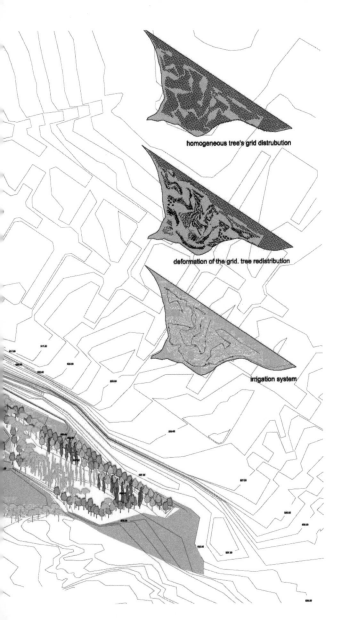

homogeneous tree's grid distrubution

deformation of the grid. tree redistribution

irrigation system

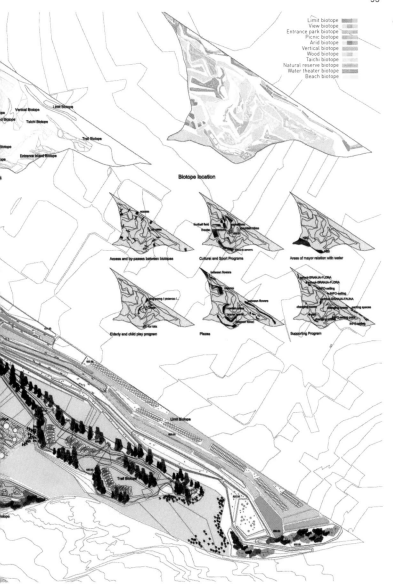

Limit biotope
View biotope
Entrance park biotope
Picnic biotope
Arid biotope
Vertical biotope
Wood biotope
Taichi biotope
Natural reserve biotope
Water theater biotope
Beach biotope

Biotope location

Access and by-passes between biotopes

Cultural and Sport Programs

Areas of mayor relation with water

Elderly and child play program

Plazas

Supporting Program

VR vertical biotope

Water circuit: water tank 02
Water-program relationship:
only visual contact
Base vegetation: populus nigra,
populus alba, pinus sylvestris,
celtis australis
Specific biotope vegetation:
laris decidus

KD kids biotope

Water circuit: C3
Water-program relationship: visual
and physical contact
Base vegetation:
populus nigra, populus alba, robinia
pseudoacacia, celtis australis
Specific biotope vegetation:
salix alba

AR arid biotope

Water circuit: C3
Water-program relationship:
visual and physical contact
Base vegetation: robinia
pseudoacacia, cercia siliquastrum,
celtis australis, populus nigra
Specific biotope vegetation:
oles europaea

WT water theater biotope

Water circuit: C3
Water-program relationship:
visual and physical contact
Base vegetation:
celtis australis
Specific biotope vegetation:
phylostachia aurea

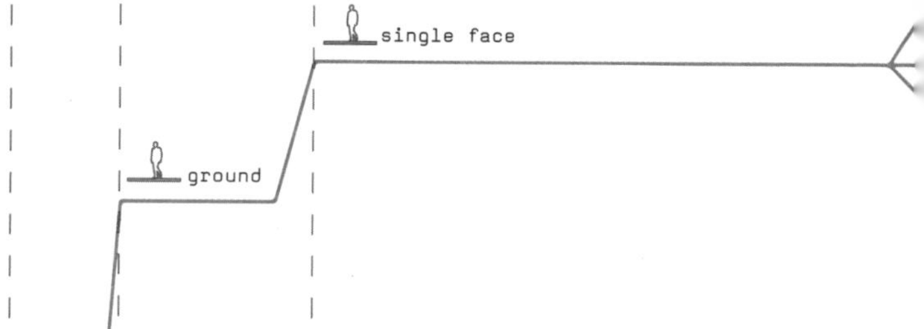

single face

ground

SE Coastal Park & Auditoriums
Barcelona | 2002-2004

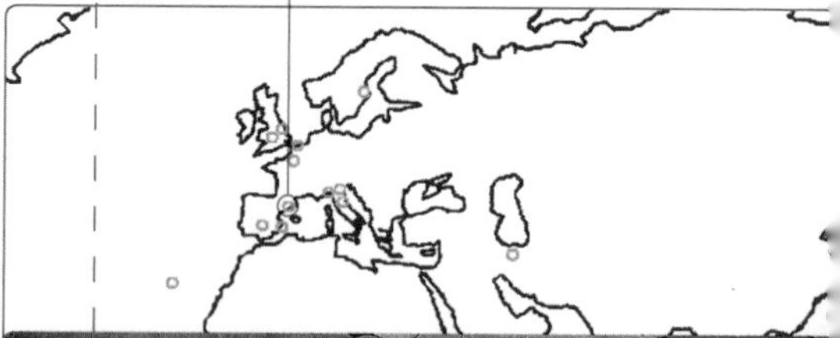

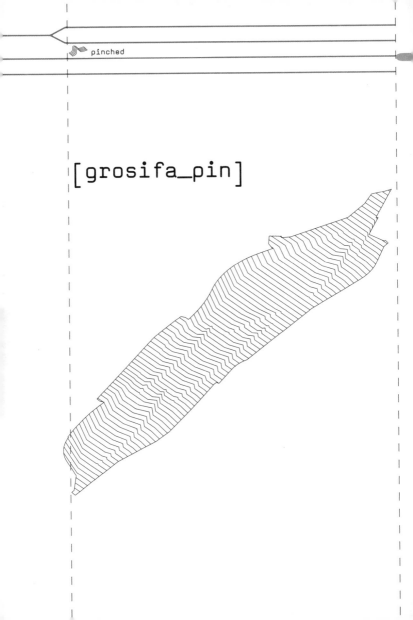

pinched

[grosifa_pin]

The southeast coastal park and auditoriums project is part of the infrastructures that the city of Barcelona has planned as the Host City for the International Forum of Cultures to be held in the year 2004.

Our proposal intends to constitute itself as an alternative to the rational geometry, artificial and linear, consistent or contradictory and organic geometry approximations that intend to reproduce the picturesque qualities of nature. Our proposal explores strategies that produce organizational complex landscapes to emerge through the production of topographies artificially generated by a mediated integration of rigorous modeled orders. The organizational prototype that we propose for the park is borrowed from a frequent model in coastal areas: the dunes.

They are a form of material organization with little internal structure, the sand, that is shaped by wind. The programmatic distribution structure is fundamentally based on the analysis of the different sport and leisure activities to take place on the platforms that allow the topographies to be generated.

Those activities are modeled as a network of diverse circuits. They will allow for a gradation of the different paths or activity zones, from walking to running, biking, skateboarding and a series of performance and relaxing areas.

Geometrical definition
of the topography

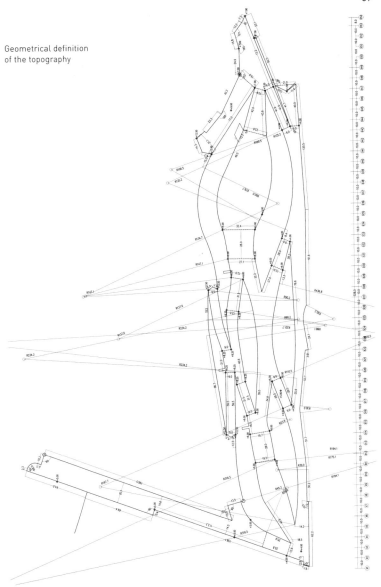

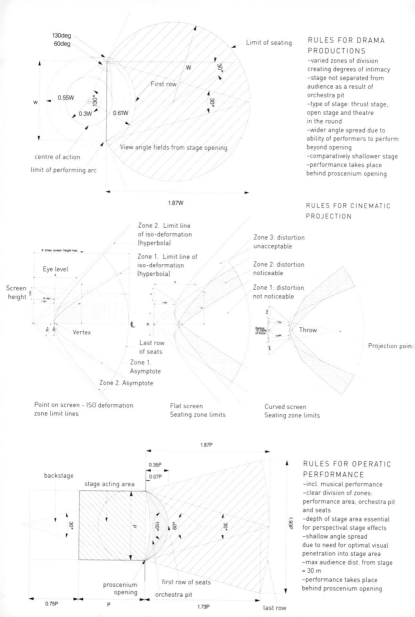

RULES FOR DRAMA
PRODUCTIONS

–varied zones of division
creating degrees of intimacy
–stage not separated from
audience as a result of
orchestra pit
–type of stage: thrust stage,
open stage and theatre
in the round
–wider angle spread due to
ability of performers to perform
beyond opening
–comparatively shallower stage
–performance takes place
behind proscenium opening

RULES FOR CINEMATIC
PROJECTION

Zone 3: distortion
unacceptable

Zone 2: distortion
noticeable

Zone 1: distortion
not noticeable

130deg
60deg

Limit of seating

W

30°

First row

30°

0.55W

130°

0.3W

0.61W

centre of action

limit of performing arc

View angle fields from stage opening

1.87W

Zone 2. Limit line
of iso-deformation
(hyperbola)

Zone 1. Limit line of
iso-deformation
(hyperbola)

8 times screen height max.

Eye level

Screen
height

Vertex

Last row
of seats

Zone 1.
Asymptote

Zone 2. Asymptote

Throw

Radius
of 100%
of throw

Projection poin

Point on screen – ISO deformation
zone limit lines

Flat screen
Seating zone limits

Curved screen
Seating zone limits

RULES FOR OPERATIC
PERFORMANCE

–incl. musical performance
–clear division of zones:
performance area, orchestra pit
and seats
–depth of stage area essential
for perspectival stage effects
–shallow angle spread
due to need for optimal visual
penetration into stage area
–max audience dist. from stage
= 30 m
–performance takes place
behind proscenium opening

1.87P

0.35P

0.07P

backstage

stage acting area

30°

P

110°

60°

30°

1.93P

proscenium
opening

orchestra pit

first row of seats

0.75P

P

1.73P

last row

61

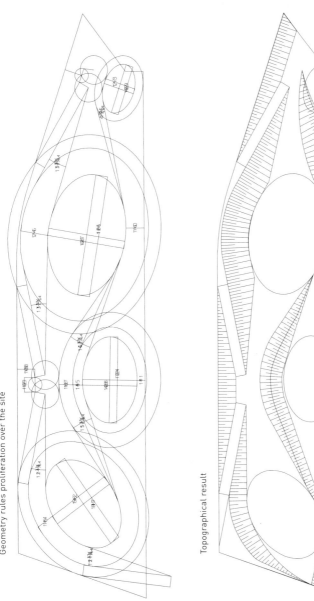

Geometry rules proliferation over the site

Topographical result

Slope geometries

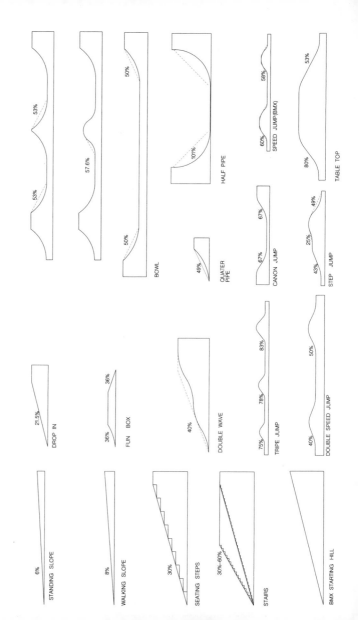

STANDING SLOPE — 6%

WALKING SLOPE — 8%

SEATING STEPS — 30%

STAIRS — 30%–60%

BMX STARTING HILL

DROP IN — 21.5%

FUN BOX — 36%, 36%

DOUBLE WAVE — 40%

TRIPE JUMP — 75%, 78%, 83%

DOUBLE SPEED JUMP — 40%, 50%

BOWL — 53%, 53%, 57.6%, 50%, 50%

QUATER PIPE — 49%

HALF PIPE — 101%

CANON JUMP — 67%, 67%

STEP JUMP — 43%, 25%, 49%

SPEED JUMP(BMX) — 60%, 58%

TABLE TOP — 80%, 53%

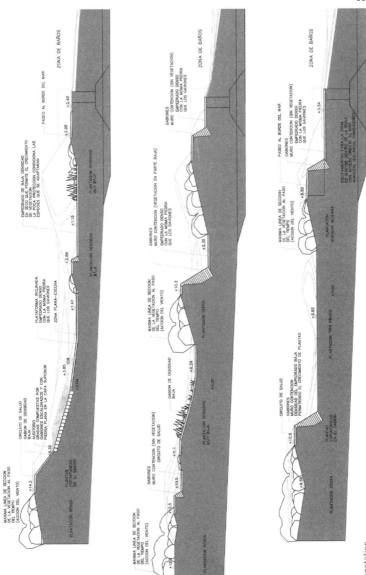

Vegetation

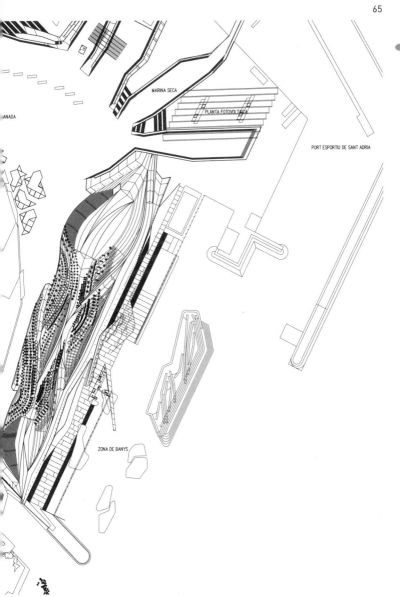

MARINA SECA

PLANTA FOTOVOLTAICA

ANADA

PORT ESPORTIU DE SANT ADRIA

ZONA DE BANYS

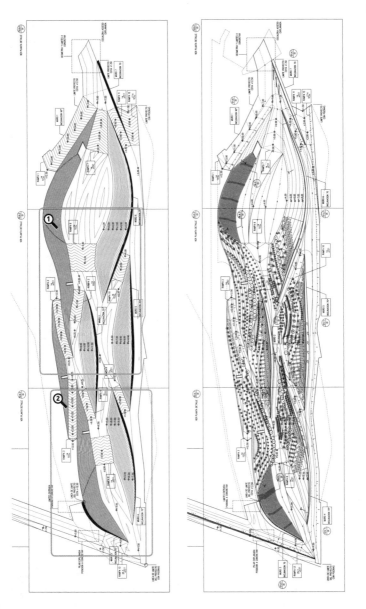

Topographic plan and vegetation plan

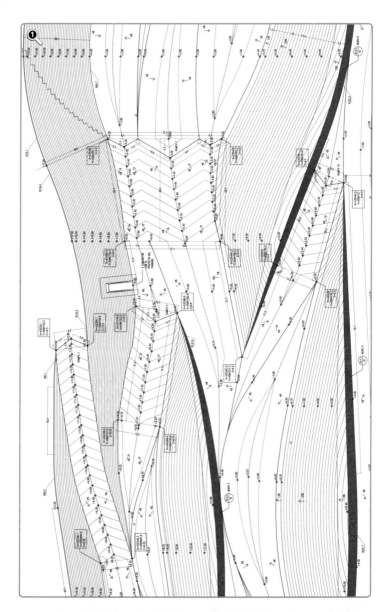

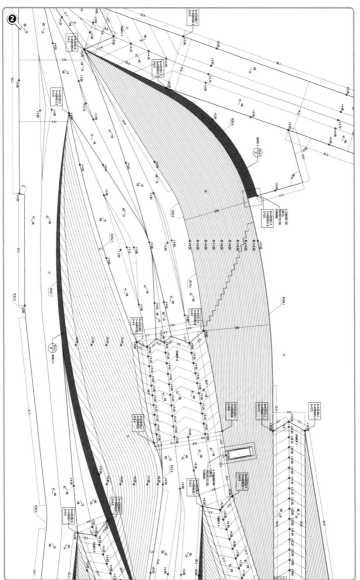

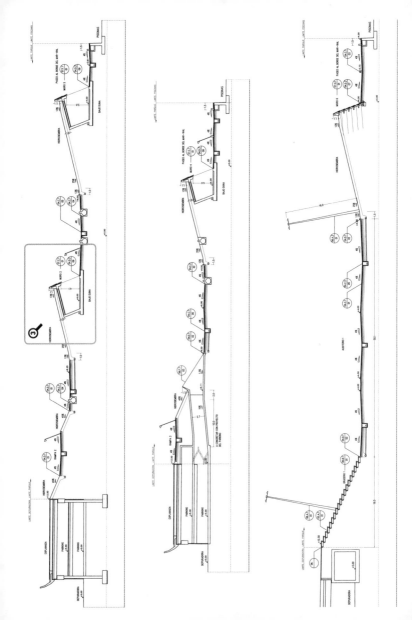

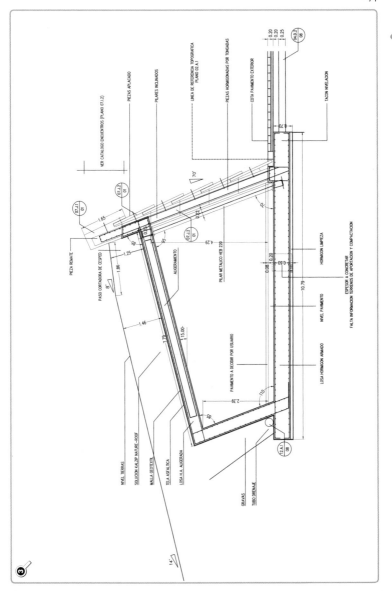

VER CATALOGO ENCUENTROS (PLANO 07.12)

PIEZAS APLACADO

PILARES INCLINADOS

LINEA DE REFERENCIA TOPOGRAFICA PLANO 02.A.1

PIEZAS HORMIGONADAS POR TONGADAS

COTA PAVIMENTO EXTERIOR

TACON NIVELACION

0.20
0.20
0.25

(04.0.2)
08

0.70

70°

0.21

(07.12)
01

(07.11)
01

1.65

(07.12)
01

PIEZA REMATE

PASO CORTADORA DE CESPED

1.25

40°

4.29

PILAR METALICO HEB 220

ALUDERAMIENTO

HORMIGON LIMPIEZA

0.20

0.08 0.60

10.79

NIVEL PAVIMENTO

ESPESOR A CONCRETAR
FALTA INFORMACION TERRENOS DE APORTACION Y COMPACTACION

1.86

8°

1.46

1.79

15.00

PAVIMENTO A DECORP POR USUARIO

LOSA HORMIGON ARMADO

2.59

70°

40°

NIVEL TIERRAS

SOLUCION ALKLZIP NATURE-ROOF

MALLA GEOTEXTIL

TELA ASFALTICA

LOSA H.A. ALIGERADA

GRAVAS

TUBO DRENAJE

(13.A.1)
08

14°

Paving system

BIFURCACION 01 PLANO 04.B.1 / 04.B.2

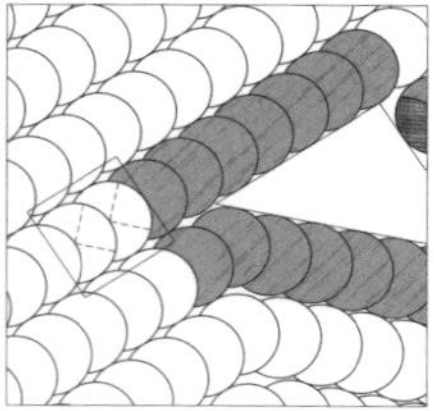

BIFURCACION 02 PLANO 04.B.1

BIFURCACION 03 PLANO 04.B.3

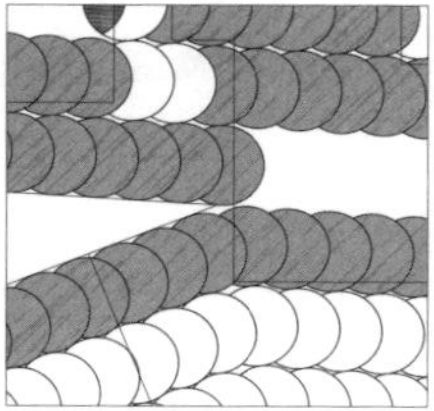

BIFURCACION 04 PLANO 04.B.3

BIFURCACION 05 PLANO 04.B.3 / 04.B.4

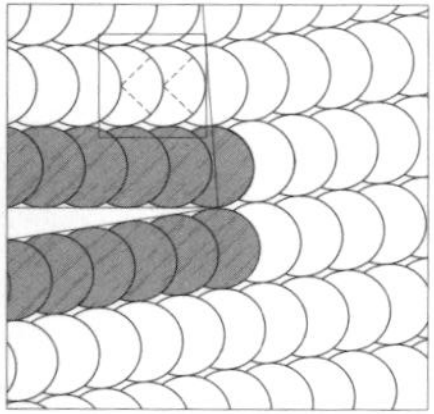

BIFURCACION 06 PLANO 04.B.4

BIFURCACION 07 PLANO 04.B.4

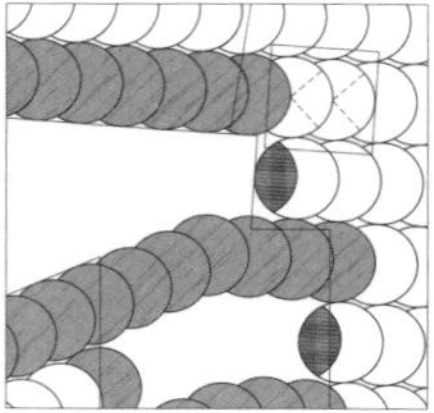

BIFURCACION 08 PLANO 04.B.4 / 04.B.5

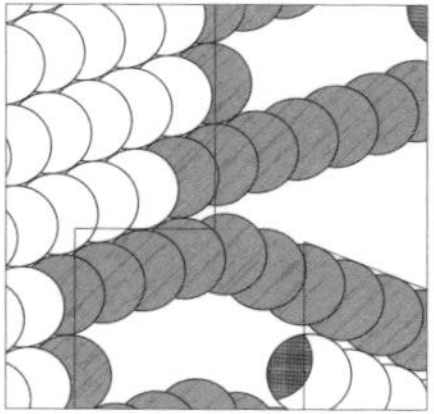

BIFURCACION 09 PLANO 04.B.5

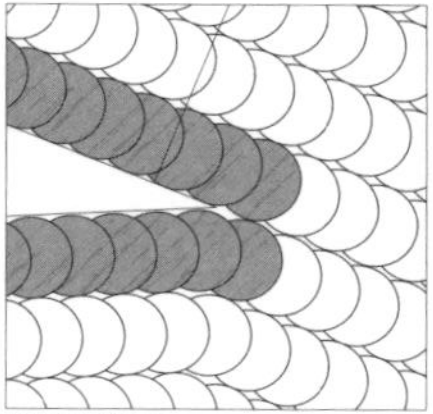

BIFURCACION 10 PLANO 04.B.5

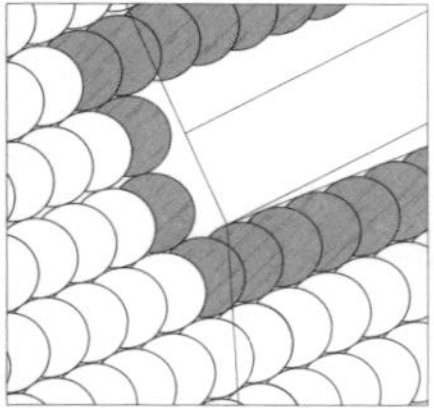

BIFURCACION 11 PLANO 04.B.7 / 04.B.8

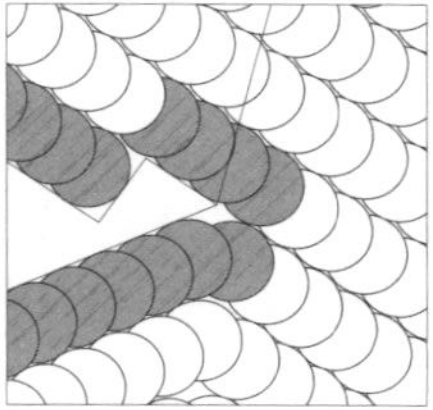

BIFURCACION 12 PLANO 04.B.8

BIFURCACION 13 PLANO 04.B.8

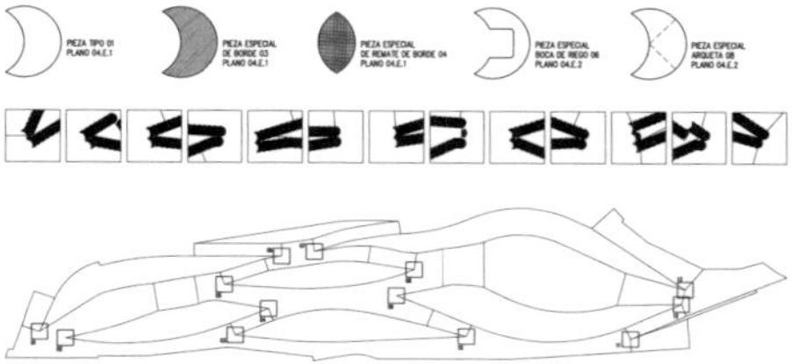

SITUACION DE LAS BIFURCACIONES

Paving elevations

SITUACION DE LA ZONA ESTUDIADA

NOTA

LAS RAMPAS DE LA ZONA ESTUDIADA HAN SIDO ABATIDAS
POR LO QUE ESTAN REPRESENTADAS EN VERDADERA MAGNITUD

SUPERFICIE: 3909.15 M2
NUMERO TOTAL DE PIEZAS: 25316

LEYENDA PIEZAS ESPECIALES

03 PIEZA ESPECIAL DE BORDE PLANO 04.E.1
04 PIEZA ESPECIAL DE REMATE DE BORDE PLANO 04.E.1
05 PIEZA ESPECIAL SUMIDERO PLANO 04.E.1
06 PIEZA ESPECIAL BOCA DE RIEGO PLANO 04.E.2
07 PIEZA ESPECIAL TABIQUETE PLANO 04.E.2
08 PIEZA ESPECIAL ARQUETA PLANO 04.E.2
09 PIEZA ESPECIAL LUMINARIA PLANO 04.E.2
10 PIEZA ESPECIAL PAPELERA PLANO 04.E.3
11 PIEZA ESPECIAL POZO PLANO 04.E.3

ACERA 6
ACERA 4
ACERA 7
ACERA 10
ACERA 15

→→ PENDIENTE DE EVACUACION DEL 4 % EN LOS LATERALES DE LA ACEQUIA

→ SENTIDO DE EVACUACION DE LA LIMAHOYA DE LA ACEQUIA

● IMBORNAL

DESCRIPCION DEL SISTEMA DE DRENAJE CONSTITUIDO POR ACEQUIAS
PLANTA GENERAL 12.A.1

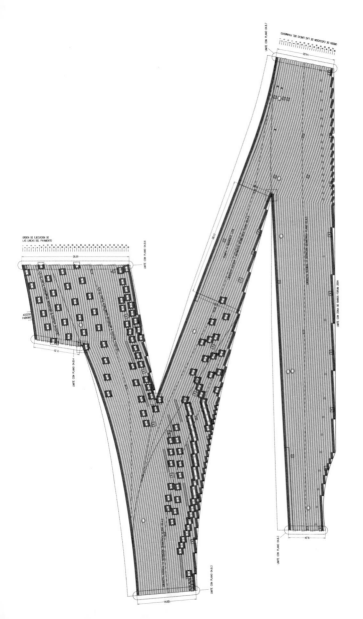

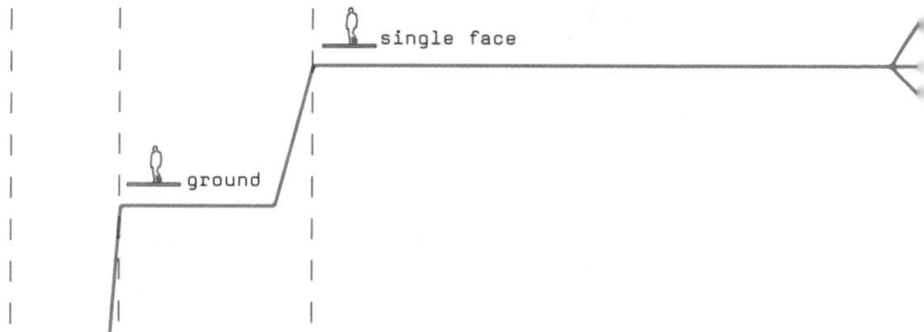

single face

ground

Rural High-Speed Terminal
Perafort | 2002

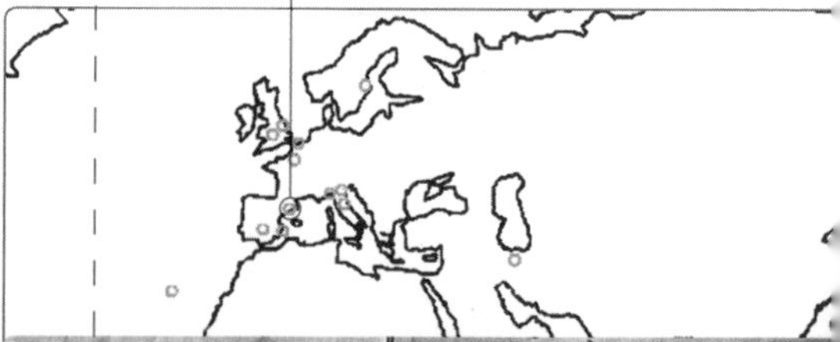

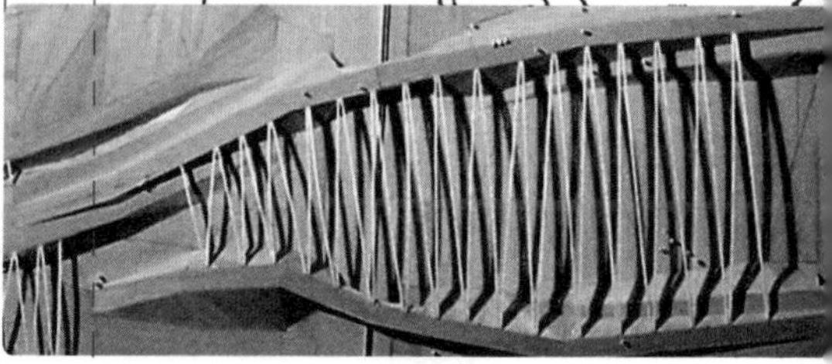

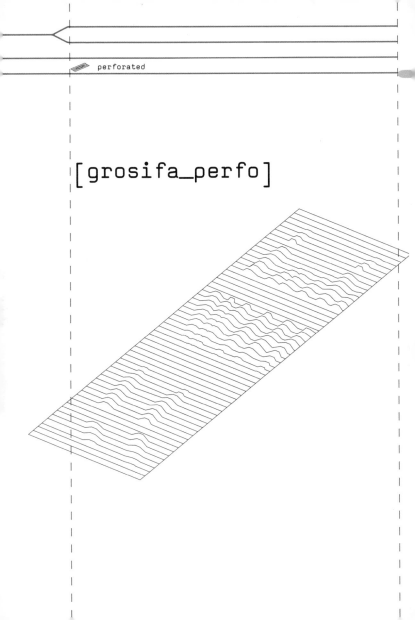

perforated

[grosifa_perfo]

The pervasive proliferation of the High Speed infrastructure in Europe has already produced some unexpected situations. As the network becomes increasingly extensive, it seems like a good moment to reflect on the kind of situations that are being produced by this sudden irruption of very large infrastructures in existing conditions of urban or territorial organization. Especially in Europe, where urban and territorial structures have been built over centuries and have acquired a particular kind of consistency, the High Speed Railway will produce some new situations whose urban and territorial potential has yet to be tapped.

Particularly in Spain, where the population is very concentrated in dense urban centers, and where the topography is rather rugged, the dynamics of the engineering of such railway networks will probably create some important nodes in locations that are likely to have a very low population density. The sudden deployment of a railway transportation node in a rural area is likely to happen in several locations, and the potential of such intersections should be anticipated and exploited.

This is the case of Perafort, a location that is chosen not because of its urban centrality one of the major roles of the High Speed lines is to connect urban nodes by high-speed ground transportation – but because of its proximity to a number of infrastructures and for reasons related to the engineering of this type of infrastructure. Perafort is close to Tarragona, Salou, Port Aventura, Reus Airport, and the Morell industrial area, but the local density is of relatively small importance. Similar cases will develop in relation to locations such as El Vallès, also in Catalonia, but probably everywhere, and it is worth thinking of this situation as a prototypical situation.

This is the object of this study: not just to try to give a form to this particular problem in this particular location, but also to develop a series of prototypical strategies for these types of situations.

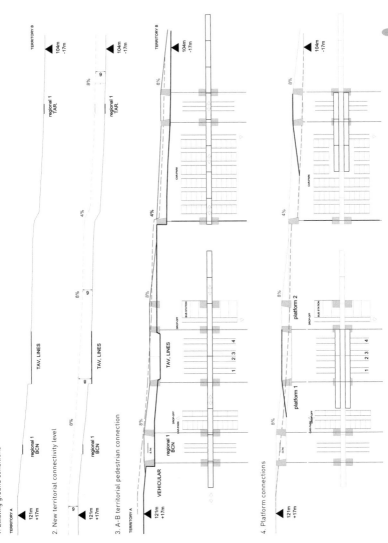

85

1. Existing ground conditions

2. New territorial connectivity level

3. A–B territorial pedestrian connection

4. Platform connections

Our objective in this analysis has been the development of generic strategies that will activate the relationship between the local topography and infrastructure, with the requirements of this kind of infrastructure as a generator of the project.

A series of observations guide our proposals:

When implementing these kinds of infrastructures, there is automatically a disconnection of the territories on both sides of the station that decreases the critical mass of the local development. Our proposal is an attempt to maximize the possibilities of crossing the tracks – maintaining the access across the tracks as much as it was before the placement of the station.

These links are of topological nature, but they also relate to rainwater management, continuity of ecosystems, underground water levels, and other existing systems that are usually interrupted by the introduction of heavy infrastructural elements.

Both the landscape and the ecological discontinuity generated by these kind of operations are things that we have tried to foresee by using particular types of structure in the project that literally continue the earth link through the infrastructure. These kinds of infrastructural operations tend to produce extensive operations of earth removal and ground reconfiguration that cause disruption in neighboring areas. Our strategy is to use this displaced local ground as the primary construction material in the project.

In order to meet these three basic criteria, we have devised a construction system fundamentally structured through a series of mounds, formed with ground taluses, nearly perpendicular to the railroad tracks, that will be shaped to produce a high threshold of physical continuity across the tracks, balancing with the topography on both sides. Ground stabilization technologies will be the primary technical device for the construction of the infrastructure,

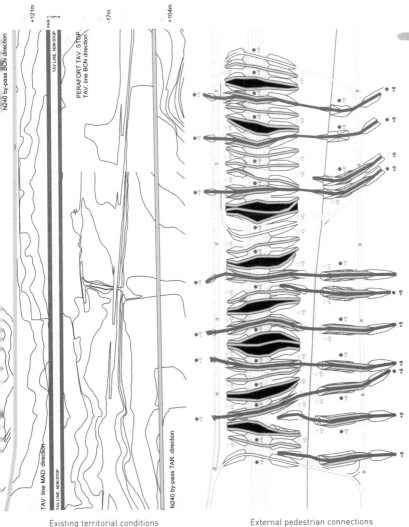

+121m

track 1
track 2&3&4

N240 by-pass BCN direction

TAV. line MAD. direction

TAV. LINE. NON STOP

TAV. LINE. NON STOP

PERAFORT TAV. STOP.
TAV. line BCN direction

-17m

N240 by-pass TAR. direction

+104m

Existing territorial conditions

External pedestrian connections

and its geometrical determination will be fixed by the economies defined by the following parameters:

1. Threshold of 250 meters for vehicular traffic and 70 meters for pedestrian traffic
2. Rainwater permeability: one main water pipe every 10 meters
3. Green continuity: trees planted along the pedestrian ways.
4. Structural roofs: free structural spans, from 5 meters to 40 meters maximum
5. Pedestrian ways: from 3 meters to 9 meters in width
6. Parks above tracks: 1 every 100 meters along the tracks

The basic system and set of associated facilities that make up the complex is:
1. Traffic access: two entrances and two exits
2. Drop-offs: located 40 meters from the station platforms densities: from series of 10 units to series of 30 units
3. Parking: located 100 meters from the train platforms densities: 600 parking spaces
4. Bus Terminal: located 60 meters from train platforms densities: 12 bus platforms
5. Complementary programs: 10,000m² of retail outlets, cafés, waiting areas
6. Pedestrian ways:
7 direct territorial connections
26 platform inter-connections
2 bus-train platform connections
11 car park/train platform connections
7 north/west territorial connections
11south/east territorial connections

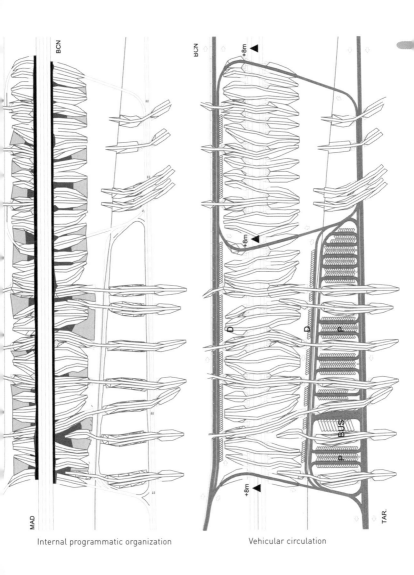

Internal programmatic organization

Vehicular circulation

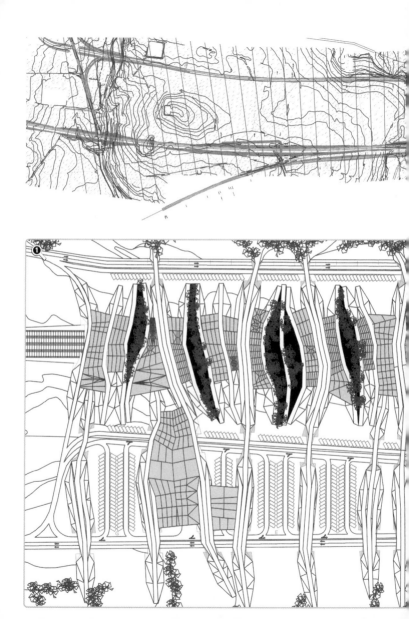

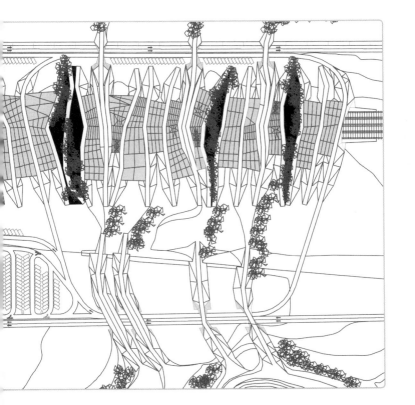

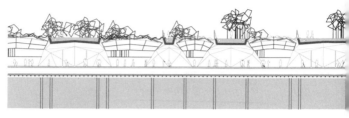

Longitudinal section

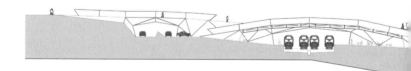

Transverse sections

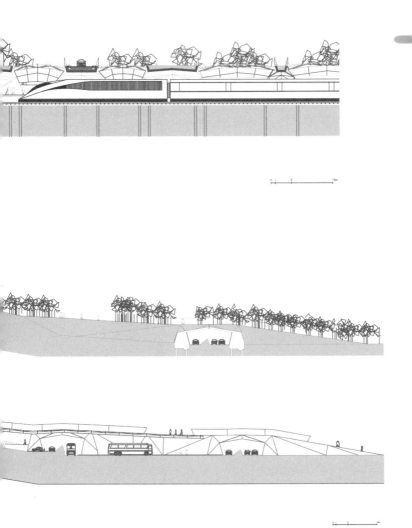

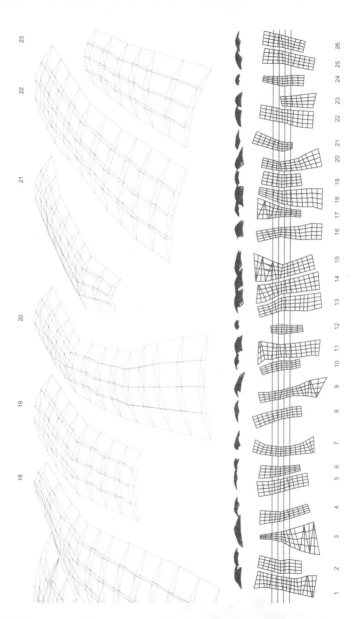

Who's Afraid of Formalism?
Sanford Kwinter

True formalism, we imagine, has been under seige for
nearly as long as it has occupied – and mostly merited – the
forefront of rigorous analysis in the arts and the inexact
sciences. But in truth, this has not been the case. For in fact,
it is only the poor or degenerate formalisms – the *merely*
"formalistic" – that have drawn cogent challenge from so-
called higher-minded, more ecumenical modes of analysis.
"Poor formalisms" I would claim, are really just *unextended*
formalisms: parodic analytical methods derived from the
great and genuine aesthetic and epistemological innovations
of modern, avant-gardist tradition, but which have simply
forgotten that that is what they are. For the poverty of what
is today collectively referred to by the misnomer "formalism,"
is more than anything else the result of a sloppy conflation
of the notion of "form" with that of "object." The form problem,
from the time of the pre-Socratics to the late twentieth century
is, in fact, an almost unbroken concern with the mechanisms
of *formation*, the processes by which discernable patterns
come to dissociate themselves from a less finely-ordered field.
Form, when seen from this perspective, is ordering *action*,
a logic deployed, while the object is merely the latter's
sectional image, a manifest variation on an always somewhat
distant theme. The form of the object (or the form of the
expression) and the form of the theme (form of the content)
are in truth in continual dynamic resonance, and, when
grasped together by formalist analysis, open up onto a field
of limitless communication and transmission.
What I call true formalism refers to any method that
diagrams the proliferation of fundamental resonances and

demonstrates how these accumulate into figures of order and shape. The very idea that the figure of a façade, the plan of a villa, or the marquetry of a given urban tissue might enfold within it a resonant, transmissible logic of internal control, one that can be at once dissociated from its material substrate *and* maintained in communicative tension with it, was once an assertion of great contentiousness. The moment of its rigorous demonstration became one of the watersheds, not only of modern aesthetics, but of modern science and philosophy as well.

Yet the configuration of the contemporary polemic is deeply misleading. It holds, among other things, that an enlightened science of "meaning," of ideology, or of commitment can, and ought to, be mustered as a palliative and corrective to a sterile, abstract academicism that seizes only the visible but lifeless schemata of things, one that weaves its pallid array of skeletal elements into a fraudulently brilliant, self-fulfilling but world-denying view. Such a position might be partly valid – it could be seen as attacking the poor formalisms of the object – that is, if this latter were not in fact but the concoction of the former's own flawed understanding. Indeed there is not, and never has been, any such thing as "meaning" or "ideology," not, in any case, one separate from the physics of history and power, a physics, not incidentally, which is always a physics of *forms*: be it the form of an idea, the form of an epoch, or the form of a tool. True formalism holds out for us the real possibility both for a pragmatic description of historical emergence (why this object, institution or configuration here, in this place, at this time, and not that?), and the superseding of the tired and wooly metaphysics that continues to dog thought today, the metaphysics of the signifier.

Formalism demonstrates first and foremost that form is resonance and expression of embedded forces. The best local formalisms (those of Henri Focillon, Arnold Schoenberg, Michel Foucault, etc.) show that these embedded forces are themselves organized and have a pre-concrete, logical form of their own. The dynamic relation between these two levels of form is the space where indeterminacy or historical becoming unfolds. Extended or true formalisms are different only in that they also describe relations of resonance and expression *between* local forms or form systems. This is why most anti-formalists are essentially but poor formalists themselves; they see only the shell of object-forms and sad enclaves of inert matter, never the resonating *field* of wild, directed formation. The great formalists, on the other hand, have always been able to peer *into* the object toward its rules of formation and to see these two strata *together* as a mobile, open and oscillating system subject to a greater or lesser number of external pressures. The manifest form – that which appears – is the result of a computational interaction between internal rules and external (morphogenetic) pressures that, themselves, originate in other adjacent forms. The (pre-concrete) internal rules comprise, *in their activity*, an embedded form, what is today clearly understood and described by the term *algorithm*. Algorithmic formalism (the most dynamic, extendable kind) was an invention of Goethe's and remains the basis of all robust, generative formalisms (including those being used today in computational biology). Among other things, Goethe posited the concept of a "type" as an abstract formative principle to be acted upon by other primary transformative processes. This may well be the source of a disturbing misunderstanding today regarding the role of generative or "deep structural" elements in designed systems and design processes. For the type concept is *never* a development of a supersensuous Platonic *eidos* (one intuits here the tendentious, reductive influence of Derrida), but is related rather to a dynamic inner intelligibility (the *eidos* of the Physicians, linked to *dynamis* or power), or to actualization as in the formal causes of Aristotle (*eidos* in its relation to the entelechies or to *energeia*). Type is at least partly active, and it is on this active aspect that we need to concentrate if we wish to give place to new extended formalisms.

Ernst Cassirer once said of Goethe that his work completed the transition from the *generic* view to the *genetic* view of organic nature. He was referring to the break from the tabular space of the *genera* of the Linnaean classifications with their emphasis on what is constant and fixed to a *generative* space where the processes of coming-to-be are given shape. Goethe's formalism, like all rigorous and interesting ones, actually marks a turning away from the simple structure of end-products and toward the active, ever-changing processes that bring them into being. With any luck, twenty years from now, one will be able to make the same claim for certain architects that Cassirer made for Goethe's science. And should this in fact not come to be, it will be far more the fault of the one-dimensional semioticians and ideologists who propagate the cliché of the "social construction of meaning" than of second-rate poor formalists who merely trivialize a powerful method and inadvertently lend credence to the airless arguments of the former group.

Local Knowledge
Mark Wigley

Architects are often asked to dream up schemes that completely change the face of a place that they barely know. Their models and drawings establish a dramatic contrast between the fabric of the existing city and a wide array of exotic implants. It's a kind of invasion by architecture. A foreign takeover. The outsiders arrogantly project their fantasies onto someone else's city. Do they really understand the local traditions, rhythms, pathology, and complications? What kind of feel do they have for the place? Can it be anything other than the superficial feel of the tourist, even if it is the earnest tourist who deliberately wanders away from the guided tour to take snaps of unadvertised local color? Tourists, like any other kind of invader, always leave their mark. Architects simply want to leave huge marks. As they travel through the world, they imagine it completely transformed behind them. They want to leave a trail of architecture, a shiny wake of memorable structures. Always on the move, the architect is a kind of industrial harvester, relentlessly churning up unsuspecting cities, mixing elements picked up from other places into the mulch of building parts and depositing tightly bundled assemblages behind them. Shell-shocked inhabitants cautiously come out from what is left of their town and see if they can do anything with what has landed.

Wouldn't any city be better off with a local architect? Wouldn't it be better to use someone who feels the local condition in his or her bones, someone who is actually part of that condition? Wouldn't the architecture be less invasive? Less brutal. More sensitive, responsive, responsible...

This nagging doubt is usually avoided by establishing a
working relationship between a foreign architect and
a local architect. This is most obvious in international
competitions where designers from very different countries
line up with their carefully chosen local collaborator.
The local is meant to act as a guide to the tourist, identifying
local customs and dealing with local politics, construction
practices, legal processes, and so on. The local eases the
arrival of foreign ideas by exporting a little local thinking.
A continuous relay of information is set up between the local
site and the foreign office. The respective principals may
only occasionally meet but the designated job architects at
each office will see a lot of each other and the spaces
between meetings are filled with a steady flow of memos,
faxes, phone calls, and emails. Local interacts with foreign
in a specially constructed transit lounge, a no-man's land
of international exchange that disappears the moment the
project is completed or abandoned.
Most traces of this relationship are effaced and it is never
discussed, even though the architecture of the twentieth
century was completely dependent on it. It was demanded
by the ever-accelerating mechanisms of transportation and
communication. A globe showing the daily movements of
all architects would increasingly be blackened out with a
dense network of overlapping lines. This physical mobility is
tied to the mobility of imagery. There is a strong correlation
between the international circulation of photographs of an
architect's work and the circulation of the architect.
The internationalism of modern architecture, for example,
the fantasy of the twenties and thirties that the same design
could be built in any city on earth, depended on both the
circulation of a relatively small set of generic images between

the magazines of countless countries and the international
readership of a select group of three or four elite magazines.
Architects travel because representations of their work
are already travelling. The higher the profile of the architect
in publications, the higher the architect's mobility, and
therefore the higher the number of local architects needed.
Each roving architect is aligned with more and more
stationary architects. The strategic importance of the local
architect grows exponentially with the increased mobility of
the global designer.

This generic organization establishes a strict hierarchy that
subordinates the local rather than responds to it. The local
architect is erased from the publicity of the project, almost
invisible in the symbolic moments of sketches, speeches,
and publications. It does not matter if the creative influence
on the project has actually been substantial. Indeed,
the erasure is likely to be even more extreme in such cases.
Yet the close supervision of construction is almost always
carried out by the local architect, allowing all the weaknesses
of the design to be credited to the local and all the strengths
to the foreigner. The name of the local figure only surfaces
if something goes wrong. The local is ritualistically sacrificed.
Yet this is usually a willing sacrifice. The local architect
typically runs an efficient office that does not mind operating
behind the scenes. It is rarely an office that wants to dominate
the local situation. To have such an ambition would precisely
be to aspire to he right to travel and build somewhere else
that is only granted to the biggest names. The most ambitious
architect does not want to be anyone's subordinate and
the foreign architect does not want a rival. The local architect
effectively chooses to be absorbed into the foreign office.
A different form of mobility then.

Quite literally, the local typically visits the foreign office more often than the foreigner visits the site. The local figure is transformed into a prosthetic extension of the outside. Turning a local into a foreigner would seem to be the first step in turning local buildings into something else.

The local architect, the figure called for by the hyper-mobility of the well-known architect, is actually the figure of an institutionalized insensitivity to the local.

The apparent exception is those architects that refuse to act as anyone's local agent and yet are reluctant to travel. Certain high profile architects advertise their own immobility, and a specialized type of critic has evolved to celebrate them by celebrating the local as a site of resistance to the foreign. Concepts of regional specificity are developed and books and special issues of magazines are dedicated to "local" architects. The same does not happen to the foreign. It is never celebrated as such. The foreign remains forever inauthentic. Despite being almost everywhere dominant, it is tacitly understood to be in some way illegitimate. Even the most dedicated internationalists secretly cling to a rhetoric of the local. Each hyper-mobile architect insists that they bind their trans-national or personally idiosyncratic style to the specific conditions of each site. Almost never will an architect declare an active disinterest in the local, even if such a disinterest is not only evident in their work but is its most striking characteristic. The standard collaboration between foreign and local architect is a key part of this dissimulating rhetoric of sensitivity.

Likewise, the self-declared elite locals are secretly mobile. They put their work on the road more often than advertised. The very impression that they are stationary is created by critics who have taken over the role of constant international

movement. The traditional relationship between local and
foreign architect gets reproduced in strategic alliances
between local and foreign critics. Local critics become the
guides to visiting travel writers. Tourism is dressed up as
scholarship. The real purpose of the writing is to facilitate
the mobility of imagery. Images of an architecture sensitively
embedded in the unique conditions of a certain place circulate
through every place and inevitably influence the work of
architects operating in entirely different contexts.

Take the most extreme cases, architects acting as their own
client. What could be more local than an architect's design for
his or her own house or studio? Or, even better, a conflation
between studio and house, a conflation, that is, of the identity
of a particular place, the identity of the architect, and the
identity of their work. The most celebrated example is Frank
Lloyd Wright's Taliesin, the home-base that was necessarily
redesigned when he moved from the mid-west to the desert.
Wright famously insists on site specific local architecture, an
architecture of the land, and uses his own homes to exemplify
the argument. But what happens when he exports the same
formal language to Japan? And what happens when the 1911
publication of images of his work in Europe, accompanied
by a text on the glory of "indigenous structures" carrying
national traits and a dismissal of "imported folly," in fact acts
as the primary inspiration for the placeless geometry of the
De Stijl movement, which in turn would turn out to be a key
ingredient in the evolution of the formal vocabulary of the
"International Style." Local idiosyncrasies and trans-national
generic forms turn out to be intimately bound together.
Which raises the basic question: what exactly is it that
foreigners miss that only the locals can see? After all, to be
your own client presupposes understanding yourself which,

in the century since Freud's discovery of the unconscious, seems less and less possible. Perhaps no one is more foreign to us than ourselves. The tradition of architects as their own client may not be the most promising paradigm of architectural design. Surely the foreigner can see things the local cannot, local forms of blindness even. Tourists often see more than their guides.

Anyway, what is a local exactly? Do you have to be born there? Do your parents have to be from there? Can you just have been living there for a long time? If so, how long? Is someone from a town nearby a local or a foreigner? Perhaps the best local architect is the one who remains slightly foreign, sitting on the edges looking in, taking advantage of both being local and a little foreign. Any town is itself an endless mix of local and foreign. The population is always changing. People keep arriving and leaving. The town is always on the move, which doesn't mean that its identify changes.

Flux is a key part of identity. Multiple forms of foreigness combine in a local mix, a unique form of heterogenity. The local is nothing more than a way of defining the outside and negotiating with it. The local is not to be found in a particular place. Rather it's a way of finding things, a way of seeing the world. Places are never isolated, they never simply exist on a certain spot. The local can never be pointed to. It is always embedded in complex ever-shifting array of networks that ultimately envelope the globe. Local conditions involve complex interactions between local and foreign. If the local knows the local better than anyone, the knowledge is of a certain way of interacting with the foreign. The local architect is one who knows how the foreign is routinely engaged. Indeed, the local architect is a already a kind of foreigner. Architects are foreigners. They see local conditions from a special kind of outside. They infect the local with foreign elements. They have always been travelers. Homer tells us that Daedalus, the founder of Greek architecture, imported his key design ideas from Egypt. Even the foreign/local partnership was already established in ancient Greece with the figure of the mobile and highly paid state architect who controlled the key commissions. The most celebrated medieval master masons constantly moved throughout Europe while the masonic guilds established local control in association with the visitors. The academic figure of the architect established in the Renaissance is precisely that of the traveler. The whole point of the theory of architecture produced by endlessly rewriting Vitruvius is that it could be applied in any place. It was the mobility of architecture in the form of drawings (only made possible by the recent industrialization of paper production) that facilitated such a roving application. Architects were able to detach themselves from the actual construction on particular sites and move freely in an abstract intellectual realm.

At the beginning of the nineteenth century, this mobility was enhanced by the emergence of architectural journals and in the second half of the century, photographs accelerated the process by taking over from etchings. Architecture could move more quickly. Something built in one place would appear in countless other places. The computer has of course taken things to a new extreme. It is no longer a fixed image that circulates. The image has itself become mobile. There is no fixed original. The process of design never stops. Drawings are just print-outs of ever changing computer models. Click on a drawing on the web and it starts to wriggle and grow. People working in different places work simultaneously on the same model. The design studio is no longer to be found in one place. It is partly on the plane, the train, the hotel and the holiday house. The relationship between local and foreign architect is established electronically. Indeed, the local architect has become an even more integral part of the mechanism of design.

At once the representative of the local and the foreign, the local architect simply disappears into the unending process. In fact, the very idea of the local architect is a contradiction in terms. Architecture is only architecture (as distinct from building) by virtue of exceeding the local. Books on local architecture carefully reconfigure the situation to make the local seem like a singular unified identity visible to the outside. But any design that would exactly conform to this image would be unfaithful to the local. Everyday life is filled with gaps, interruptions, shocks, and frustrations that are glossed over by any seamless image. Furthermore, architecture is itself an interruption of the everyday, a displacement of routine, even if its producers have nominated the everyday as their inspiration.

The essential foreignness of the architect is already evident in their unique way of seeing buildings. To see a building as architecture is already to step outside of everyday conditions. Precisely because people are immersed in buildings, they don't see them directly. The structures are usually experienced obliquely, in a state of distraction. The architect's direct look at a building transforms it. Simply to see architecture is to begin to turn the world into a foreign place, to make the local strange. The architect goes further, mentally slicing what is seen into sections and subjecting them to diverse analyses (aesthetic, programmatic, technical, phenomenological, and so on). If anything, the architect's eye is like that of an insect–countless little openings simultaneously recording different details which are then synthesized into an idiosyncratic collage that even other architects don't necessarily recognize. The architect's gaze turns a structure or environment into something else. To commission an architect, even a sensitive architect dedicated to the everyday specifics of a particular place, is to already to reach outside the local, to go beyond those specifics. Architecture will always be invasive in the end. It's a clumsy art. Architects inevitably import ideas from afar. Think of the metaphysical discourse that underwrites architectural theory and without which there would not be a discipline. Generic formal ideas are seen to be embedded into specific material situations. The very idea of form is the idea of the material world reaching outside itself to be touched by an abstract order. Architects are agents of the outside. It is no surprise that they are always wandering, always reaching outside the limits of building for inspiration and legitimation from other fields. The architect is a full-time tourist. This is why the local designer can so smoothly conspire with outside forces. The local architect is already a foreign agent. The resulting brutality of architecture is inevitable, unending, desirable.

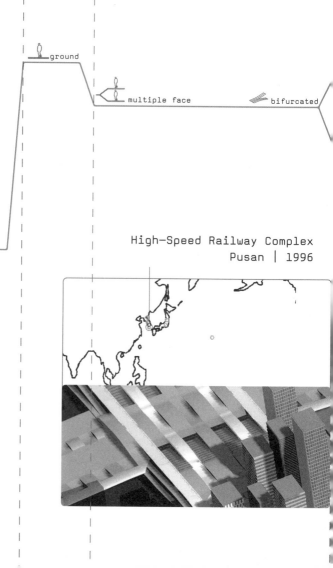

ground

multiple face

bifurcated

High—Speed Railway Complex
Pusan | 1996

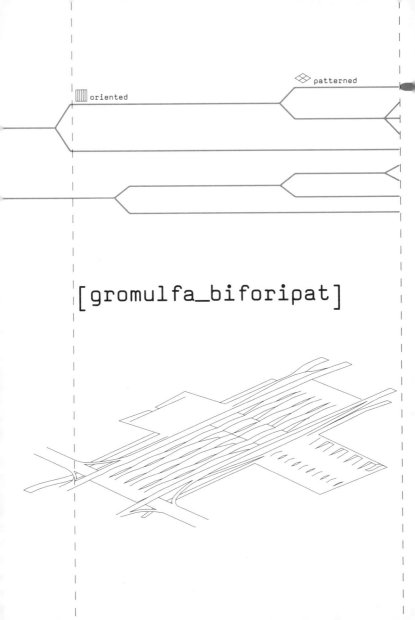

oriented

patterned

[gromulfa_biforipat]

Travel is no longer an event, but a routine. This proposal for a new high-speed railway for the City of Pusan aims at incorporating the transportation infrastructure into the urban structure. The eastern waterfront of Pusan used to be the location of the industrial harbour, and the entire infrastructure associated with it. The railway lines and the main traffic artery of Chungjang Road have severed the links between Pusan and that waterfront. Our proposal for the Highspeed railway Complex is to turn the roof of the terminal into a waterfront deck, that, placed at level +15.70m, will give the citizens the possibility of regaining visual control over the bay area, and to produce a public space where the civic life is strongly related to the waterfront. The scale of construction and the public nature of the complex provide an ideal opportunity to light the urban ground over the tracks and over Chungjang Road, to connect the urban centre with the seashore.

The brief asked for the station to be designed to provide service to both the highspeed link and to the local rail lines, integrated into one structure. The volume of the passengers and the frequency of the trains in the station, –one highspeed train every four minutes– encourages us to see the station more as a terminal for a "national subway," having Pusan, Seoul and Tejeon as sectors of the same metropolitan structure.

The need for a more efficient traffic system to handle this amount of passengers suggested an airport-like system, with differentiated arrivals and departures.

Our proposal for the Concourse is to provide a very large, structure-free, non-orientated space, interweaved with the Ocean-Plaza in order to provide easy exit to the outside. On each side of the Concourse, four "bays" will provide access to the four groups

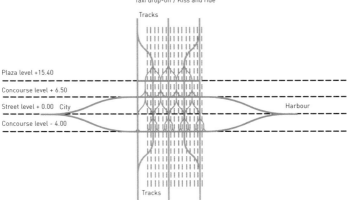

Taxi drop-off / Kiss and ride

Tracks

Plaza level +15.40

Concourse level + 6.50

Street level + 0.00   City   Harbour

Concourse level - 4.00

Tracks

Taxi drop-off / Kiss and ride

City

Complex   Complex

Complex

Harbour

Harbour

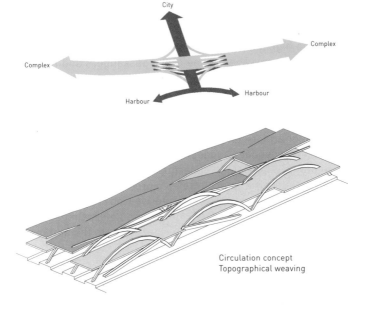

Circulation concept
Topographical weaving

of two specialised platforms, Arrivals and Departures, of both regular and highspeed trains. From the concourse on its western side we will be able to reach Pusan Subway Station, the Metropolitan Bus bays, a short-term car park, and a taxi drop-off/pick-up area.

The concourse spans the rail tracks at level +8.50m, the lowest possible level given the required headroom for the trains, and bifurcates either towards the docks/ waiting rooms to access the platforms, or to the plaza-level/ drop-off zone at +15.70m. By locating platform access control in the docks, the aim is to turn the concourse into a conditioned urban bridge over the tracks, suitable for the entertainment and commercial activities that serve not only the station complex, but also the city as a whole. As the existing station should remain operative throughout construction, the structural system is governed by the platform lines. A system of arches running parallel to the platforms supports undulating decks in the form of a shredded surface, striated in the direction of the tracks. The arches allow the introduction of a large-span structure that reduces the interference of the structural system and maximises the presence of the structure of the building.

In order to provide the cuts in the surface that will allow ventilation and light to enter the station area, the roof deck is supported on eye-shaped trusses with 4.0m structural depth, and spanning the crowns of the consecutive arches. The deck will alternate between being supported by the lower member of the truss and the upper one, behaving sometimes more like a low arch, and sometimes more like a catenary.

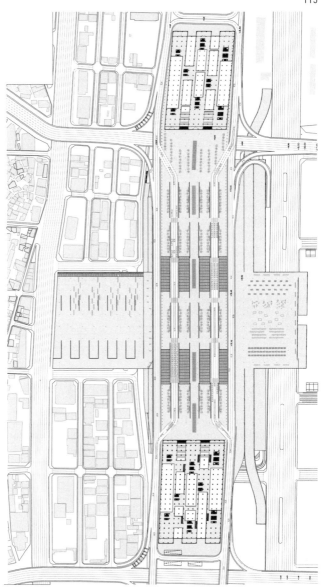

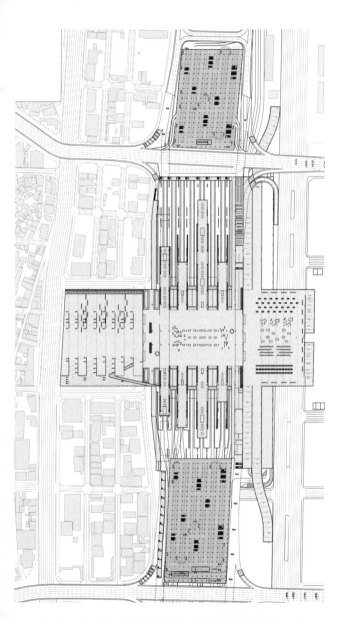

Plan level -1

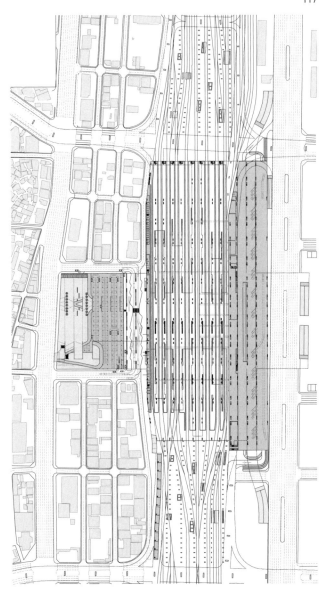

Plan level -2

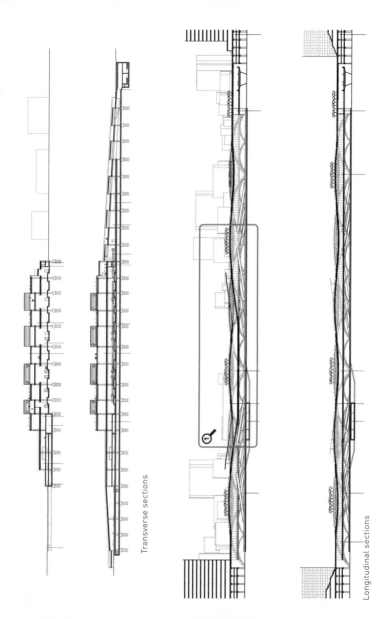

Transverse sections

Longitudinal sections

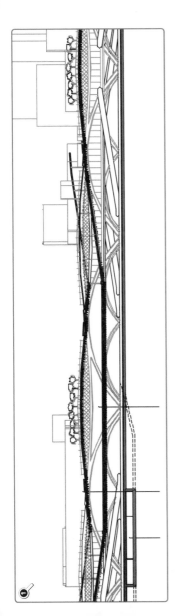

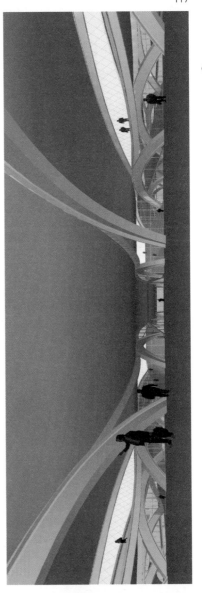

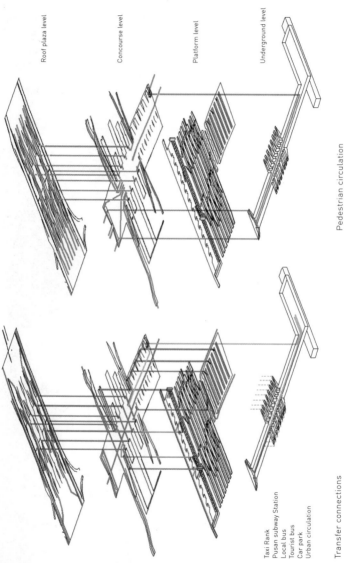

Roof plaza level

Concourse level

Platform level

Underground level

Pedestrian circulation

Taxi Rank
Pusan subway Station
Local bus
Tourist bus
Car park
Urban circulation

Transfer connections

Citizens —— Parking —— Tourist buses —— Local buses —— Tube —— Taxi

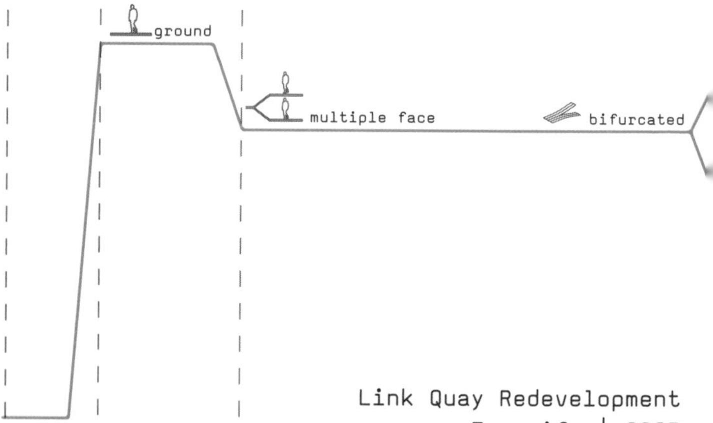

122

ground

multiple face

bifurcated

Link Quay Redevelopment
Tenerife | 2003

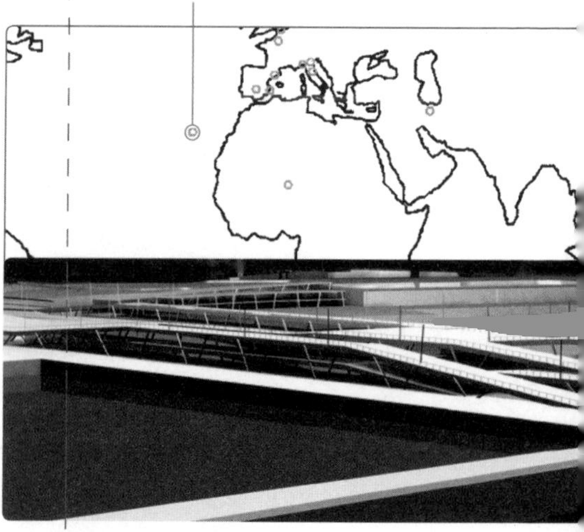

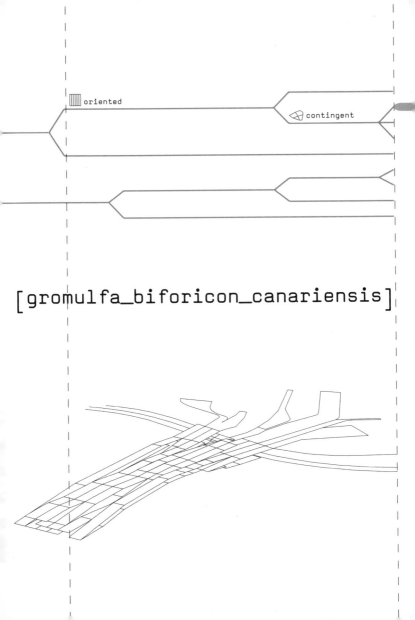

Based on the careful analysis of different aspects of the site, our proposal takes advantage of the opportunity to develop the centre of Santa Cruz and to make maximum use of the infrastructure of the existing port while bearing in mind the future expansion of the port zone. Our master plan project for the Enlace Pier is formulated with an infrastructural approach more than a problem of urban design. The scale of the project and its potential effect on the entire port frontage suggested the need for a synthetic attitude. This has been fundamentally based on the manipulation of topographic conditions and infrastructural systems, rather than making a proposal of urban design interventions. Our strategy is structured by a roadway, a tectonic and topographic system capable of lending coherence to the entire port frontage. It tacility reacts with the specificities of each zone of the project site. This system reuses the existing transport infrastructure of the port and connects it directly to the adjacent urban grid, developing like an organic growth differentiated from the urban fabric.

Our proposal is based on the construction of a topographic order capable of unifying the future installations of the maritime façade. This order emerged following two fundamental considerations:
1. The need to connect the port precinct with the urban structure, which involved resolution of the differences in alignment between the city at the lowest level and the pier platforms.
2. The need to solve the conflict between pedestrian traffic and the roadway infrastructure that passes along the length of the port required the prolongation of the urban fabric onto the port precinct.

Existing

City

Avenue/Circulation
Service road

Port

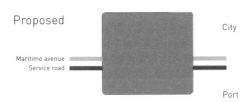

Proposed

City

Maritime avenue
Service road

Port

The topographic structure that we propose consists of prolonging the principle venues of the city over the port precinct at the lower level of the urban façade, except for the intersection at the level of the port service route, now converted into a ring road that frees the maritime avenue of non-local traffic. As urban piers, this prolongation will occupy various diverse functions, activating the port terrain with new urban activities and leaving the determination of other eventual uses to the future needs of the city. These 'urban piers' involve a growth similar to the port structure. The linear prolongation of the city react to local conditions— the depth of the platform or the difference in levels— to produce singularities within the general system. By using a linear structure similar to that used on the piers, maximum advantage can be made of the surface contact between the water and the ground, with as little construction as possible. To get the most out of the operation, our strategy of urban penetration into the port precinct would be produced with linear structures, easily arranged into series, with a good relationship between the perimeter and surface areas. Like building systems common to any infrastructure, the construction of the whole ensemble will be made possible with a minimum number of structural solutions. Minimal variations in the structure will make multiple conditions possible. The sectional variations in the height of these bands allow for the ventilation and sentinel illumination of spaces situated below the structure, as well as permanent physical and visual connections between the new urban spaces and the programs set below the surface.

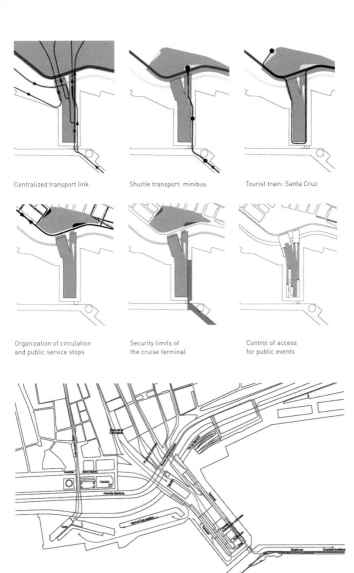

Centralized transport link

Shuttle transport: minibus

Tourist train: Santa Cruz

Organization of circulation
and public service stops

Security limits of
the cruise terminal

Control of access
for public events

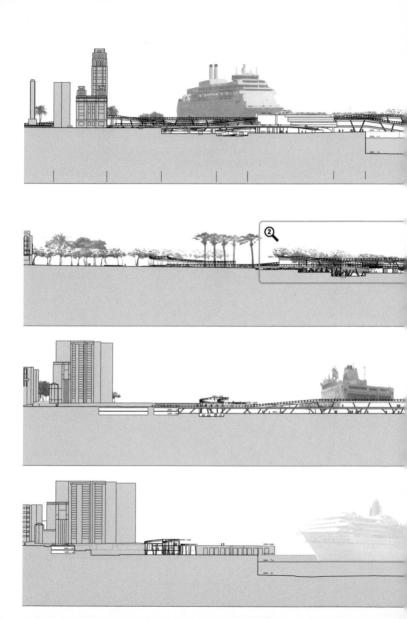

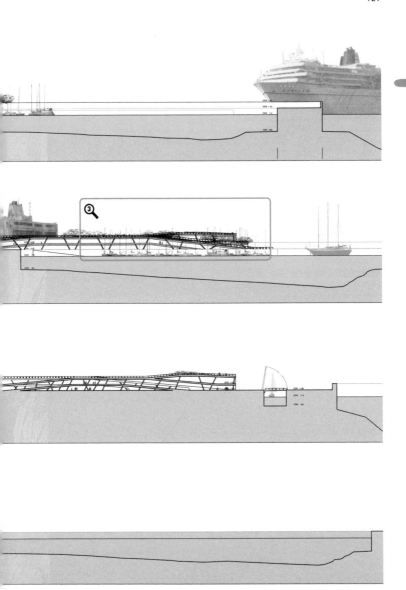

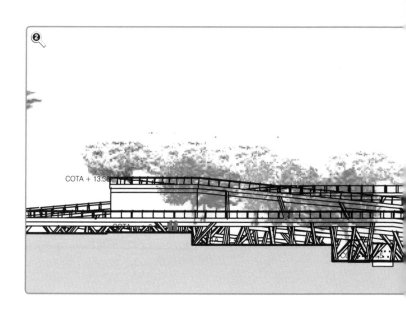

COTA + 13.36

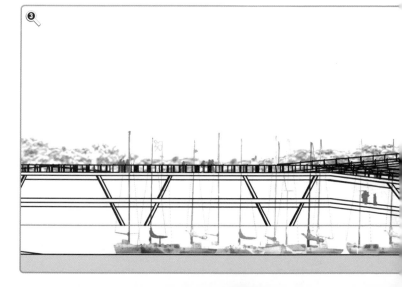

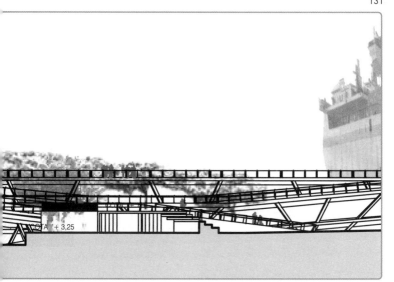

COTA + 3,25

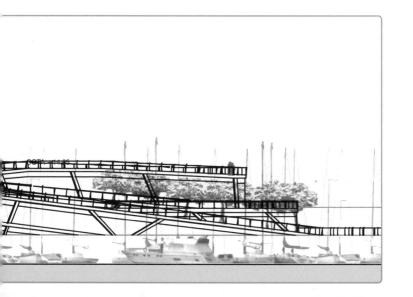

COTA + 1,25

Maritime Plaza circulation diagram

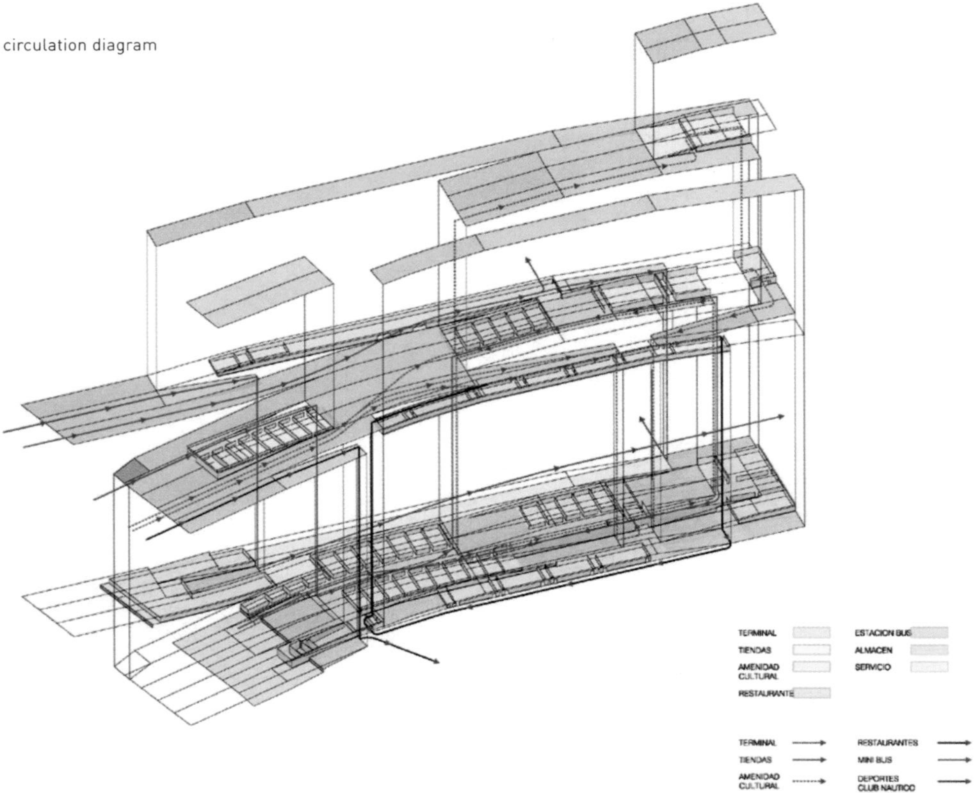

TERMINAL
TIENDAS
AMENIDAD CULTURAL
RESTAURANTE

ESTACIÓN BUS
ALMACÉN
SERVICIO

TERMINAL
TIENDAS
AMENIDAD CULTURAL

RESTAURANTES
MINI BUS
DEPORTES CLUB NÁUTICO

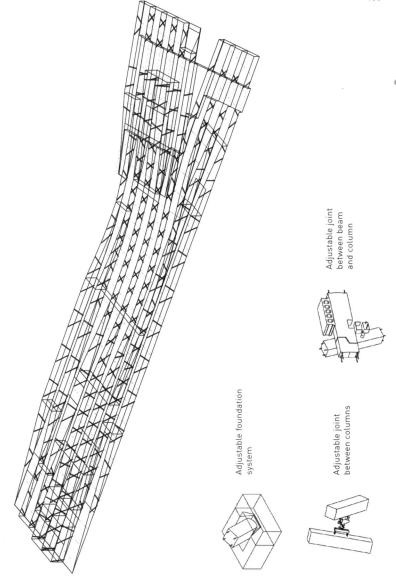

Adjustable joint
between beam
and column

Adjustable foundation
system

Adjustable joint
between columns

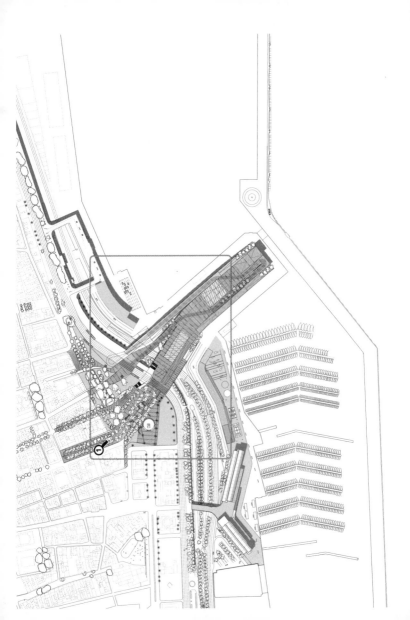

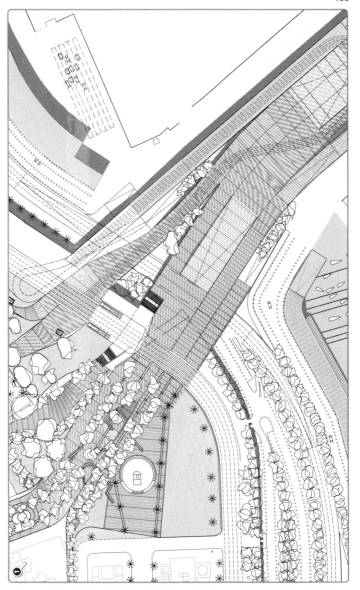

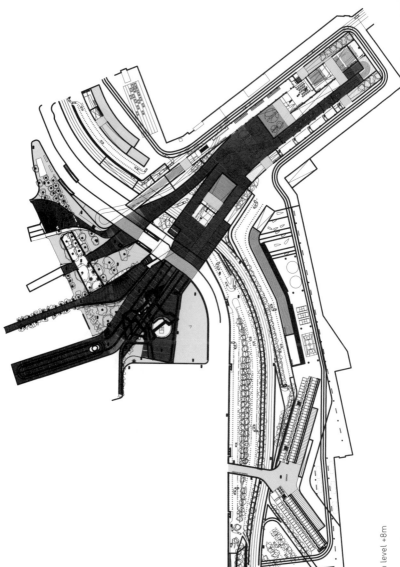

Plan level +8m

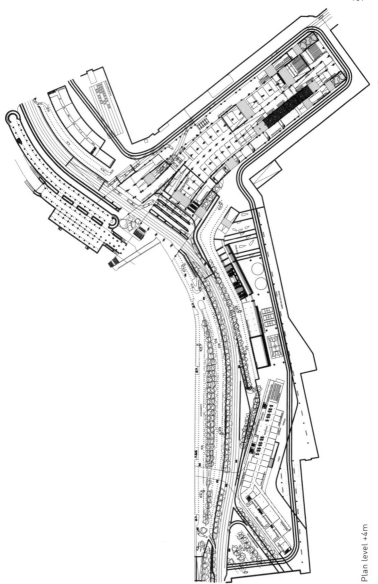

Plan level +4m

ground

multiple face

bifurcated

Ponte Parodi
Genoa | 2000-2001

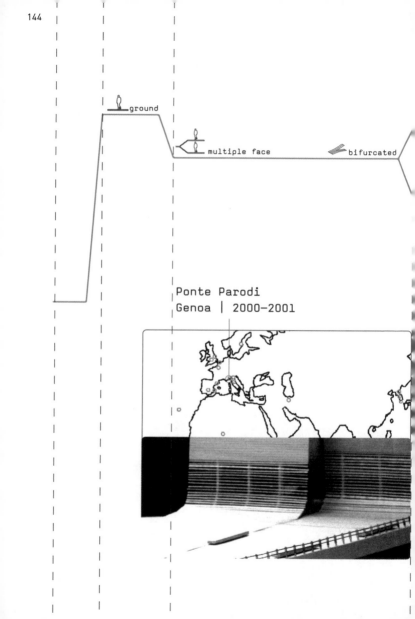

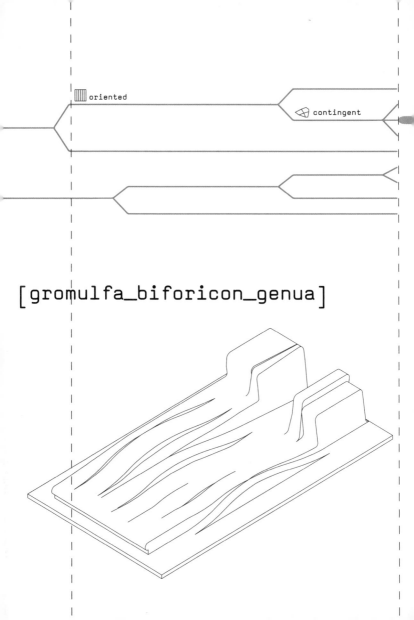

oriented

contingent

[gromulfa_biforicon_genua]

Our proposal for Ponte Parodi aims to recover the relationship between the city of Genoa and the waterfront lost after the industrial harbor took over the Basin and the infrastructure over the waterfront. This recovery should also provide new uses and possibilities for the redevelopment of the old harbor and the waterfront as a powerful magnet of tourist and urban activity. We have developed the project with an infrastructural approach to public space, very much in the spirit of docks but with a different function: the provision of an infrastructure that enables multiple arrangements of public urban life. The fantastic possibilities of Ponte Parodi as an urban enclave arise from its topographical nature and its location. In a city characterized by extreme topography and by a resulting dense fabric, the possibility of exploiting such an extension of open ground is critical. The topography of Ponte Parodi could become a bold and unprecedented synthesis between urbanity and sea life. The fundamental topographical traits of this project arise from those considerations. In an attempt to construct a topography that preserves the horizontal nature of the building mass, while allowing for a sustainable amount of volume to be built on the pier, we have made topography of extremes. Part of the built mass is concentrated in a tower to be located on the Northwest side of the complex; the other part of the project will develop as a low and extensive mass, well connected to the ground level.

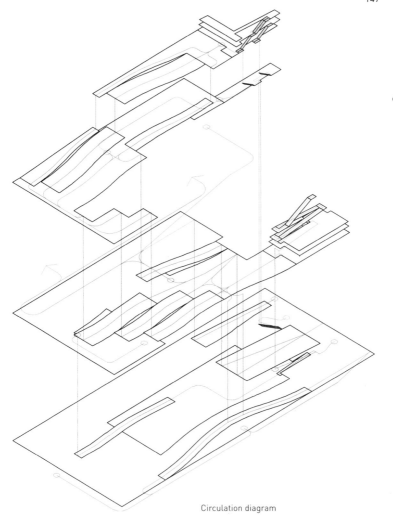

Circulation diagram

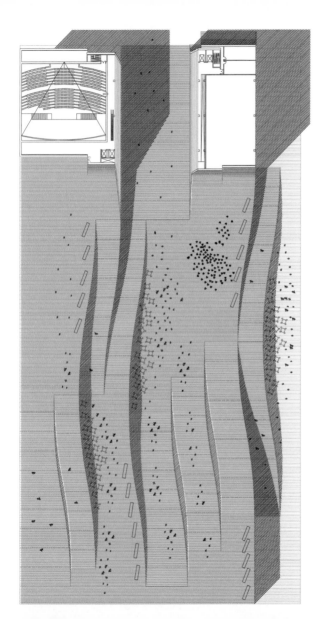

Plan level 0

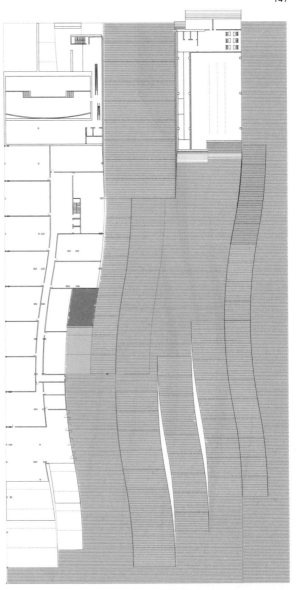

Plan level -1

Plan level - 2

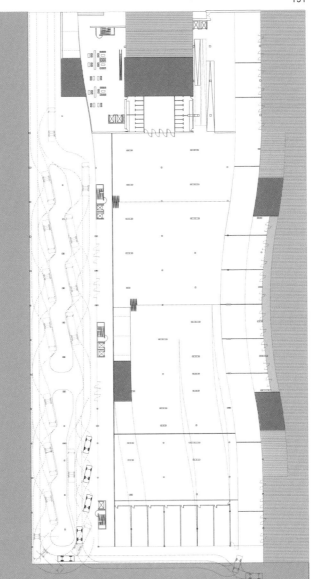

Plan level –3

Tower structure and facade system

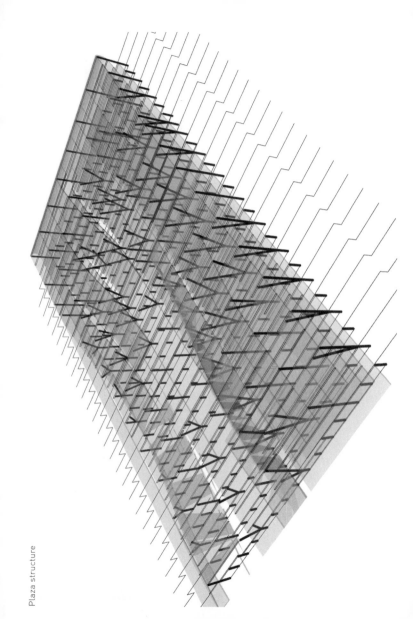

Plaza structure

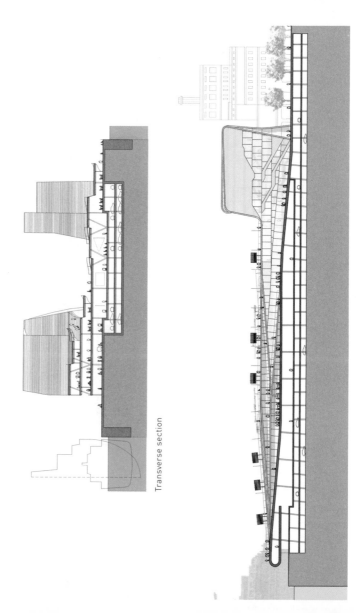

Transverse section

Longitudinal sections

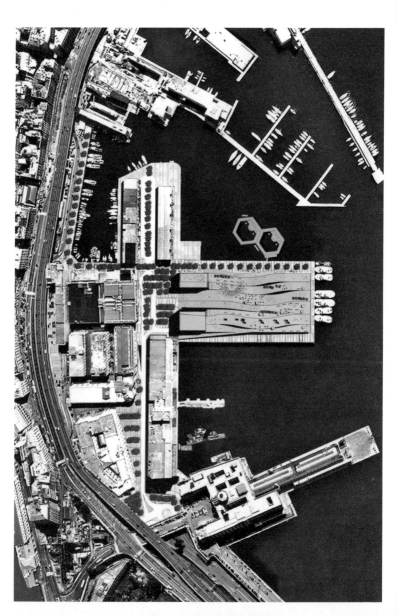

ground

multiple face

bifurcated

South Bank Centre
London | 2001

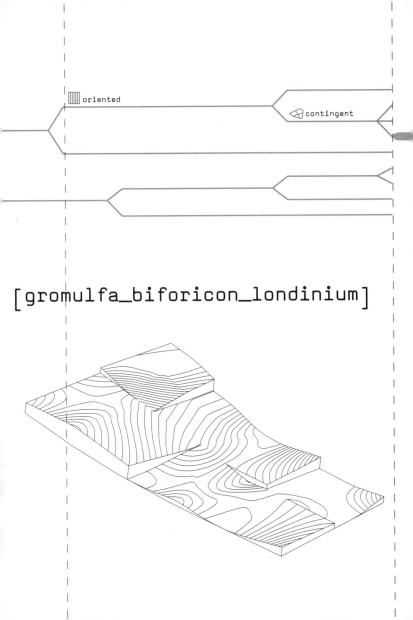

oriented

contingent

[gromulfa_biforicon_londinium]

Our approach to the SBC site develops the two items of the proposed masterplan that we judged most important:
To break with the conventional opposition between built structures and open public space as one of the most interesting developments in the realm of architecture and urban design today.
To break with the conventional opposition between the realm of the arts and the commercial activity as complementary types of the contemporary public space.
To overcome these two traditional oppositions is, in our opinion, the most critical aspect of the project as a piece of urban topography, and what will make this complex a unique topography world-wide.
Our proposal builds on the masterplan scheme, proposing a shredded surface that will constitute the surface of the public open space as the roof over the function rooms, mainly "black boxes" containing auditoriums and projection rooms, but also the Museum of the Moving Image, retail spaces and offices.
The cuts in the surface not only provide access to the arcade spaces that serve as a collective foyer to the different functions, but also provide light and ventilation to the otherwise subterranean spaces, establishing continuities between the park and the functions. They also provide access to the different levels of the complex, rising from ground level at Queen's walk to the level of the future Shell development, to connect through the Shell complex to the level of the Waterloo Station walkways.
This shredded surface, which acts as an infrastructure to the complex, continues ramping up and down inside the volume to produce the access systems in the arcade space that will join under an east west covered promenade all the public spaces in the complex. This promenade will link the more popular stretch in front of the GLC building and the London Eye with the more classical artistic environment of the Royal Festival Hall, the Hayward, etc., integrating the different forms of artistic performance, between the more exclusive to the more popular.

INTERNAL ANCHORS

The programmatic mass may be classified into three identifiable anchors, i.e. concert hall, film centre and multiplex. Individually they attract users that enter at various points around the site. The overlap of their connections creates the possibility of an internal circulation thereby achieving a more even distribution of circulation between site and its surrounding.

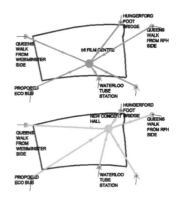

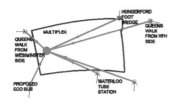

EXTERNAL ANCHORS

Cultural facilities external to site acts as anchor attractions fed by various circulatory sources. The possibility of making connections to these anchors accross and around the site creates opportunities to blur the interface between the interior and exterior of the building.

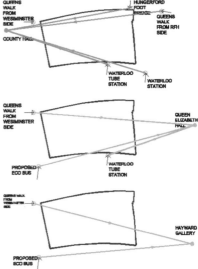

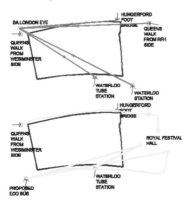

The commercial element of the brief will generally be arranged at existing ground level, acting as connective tissue between the different arts venues of the complex. These commercial activities will not detract from the quality of the arts environment that the complex must have, but, on the contrary, help to penetrate the complex with the everyday life of the surrounding urban environment, and increase the penetrability of the large mass that the area requirement of the brief generates.

In respect to the office space volume that the masterplan proposes, we believe that it can contribute to the integration of the arts and the everyday urban life, avoiding the monofunctional arts culture that predominated in the original South Bank project, maximising the use of the area as a public space.

The challenge is to ensure that it does not have an excessively dominant appearance or compete inappropriately with the building that represents the best of the existing South Bank complex, the RFH. Our proposal includes a series of alternative re-distribution of the office space to minimise its appearance, to be considered within the context of the masterplan.

Above all, our proposal is a physical organisation able to give consistency to the complexities of the brief, and to react to the complexities of the development into a process that will fine tune the balance between the four fundamental oppositions that the project aims to reconcile:

The opposition between a building complex and a metropolitan open land denomination. (that is, the opposition between landscape and buildings)

The opposition between an arts facility and the commercial uses that need to be integrated in the complex.

The opposition between an autonomous arts complex of global significance, and its operation as a local complex of amenities and public space with an intense relationship with its hinterland.

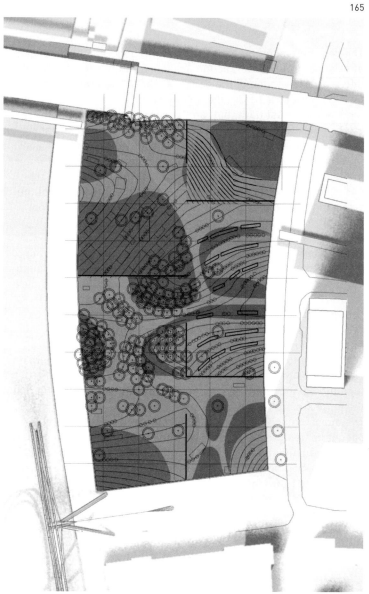

PHASE 1

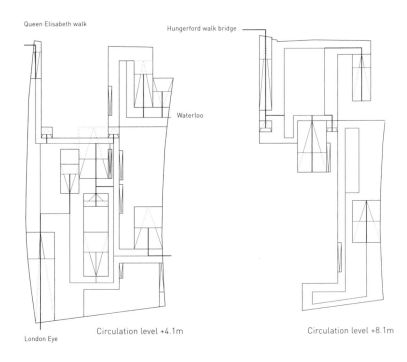

Queen Elisabeth walk

Hungerford walk bridge

Waterloo

London Eye

Circulation level +4.1m

Circulation level +8.1m

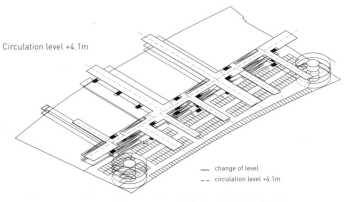

Circulation level +4.1m

—— change of level
-- circulation level +4.1m

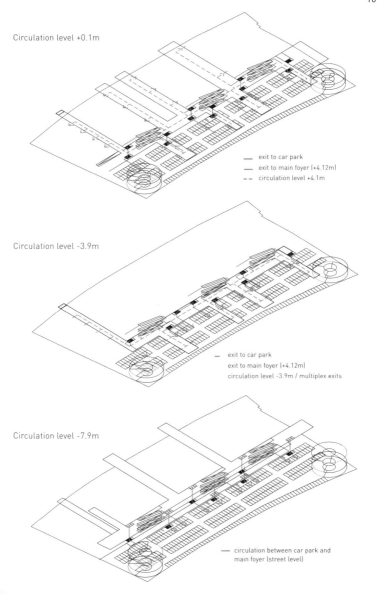

Circulation level +0.1m

— exit to car park
— exit to main foyer (+4.12m)
-- circulation level +4.1m

Circulation level -3.9m

— exit to car park
exit to main foyer (+4.12m)
circulation level -3.9m / multiplex exits

Circulation level -7.9m

— circulation between car park and
main foyer (street level)

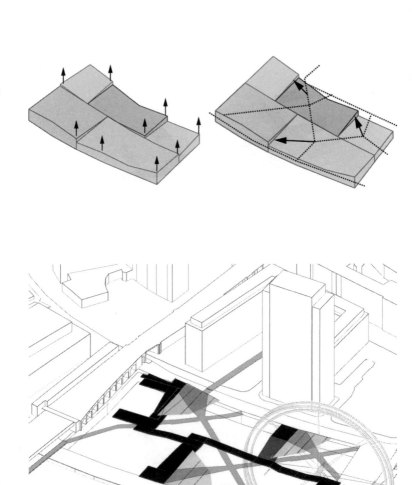

Foyer - landscape folds

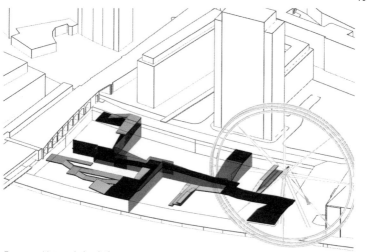

Foyers and internal circulation

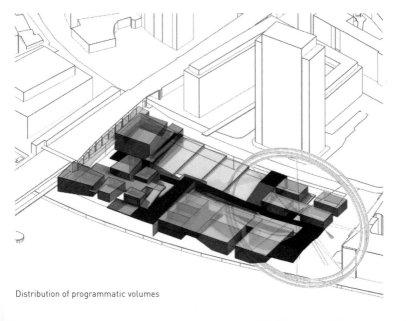

Distribution of programmatic volumes

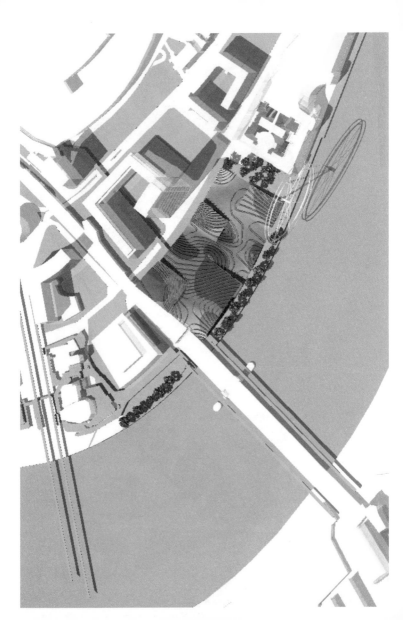

ground

multiple face

bifurcated

Technology Transfer Centre
La Rioja | 2003

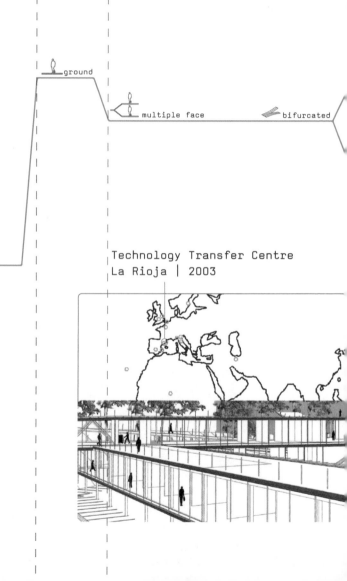

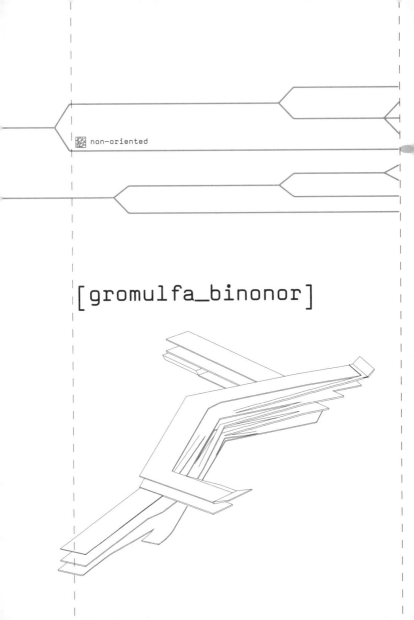

non-oriented

[gromulfa_binonor]

The complex is located in the outskirts of Logroño, the capital of La Rioja Region and is due to host three different institutions dedicated to the education, research and nurturing of individuals and companies in the sector of world-wide-web services and technology. The centers to be hosted in the complex are:

1. A National Educational Center dedicated to training people in the world-wide-web related sector.

2. A Center for Technology Transfer where researchers and special courses on world-wide-web related services and technologies.

3. An Incubator for Companies offering services on world-wide-web related sector.

The site is a beautiful stretch of low-land by the Iregua River, currently used as a tree farm, and animal hospital for local endangered species by the Government of La Rioja. The land is almost entirely on a level slightly higher than the Iregua River, at approximately +371m above sea level, and is planned to become part of the Metropolitan Park System running along the Iregua River. The land is bordering with the River on the East, with a plateau at level +380m above sea level where major commercial centre and housing development is being built, with a water purifying plant on the north and to the south with the Zaragoza Avenue, one of the major traffic arteries on the northern outskirts of Logroño, which is running basically at the same level +380m of the urban developments to the west of the site.

The main accesses to the site are from the Zaragoza Avenue, where the bus public transport is concentrated and from where the vehicular access to the site is located, and from the west, where a high density urban fabric will be operational in two years. The site will also become accessible by pedestrians from the river side, once the Iregua River Park becomes operative.

The access road is placed along the west edge of the site, that is formed as a very steep drop, formed with retaining walls and is a narrow and sloped road linking the +380m level at Zaragoza Avenue with the + 371m of the site. This pathway, named Camino de los Lirios, is bordered by very large and leafy Elm trees, which constitute one of the most valuable elements of the site.

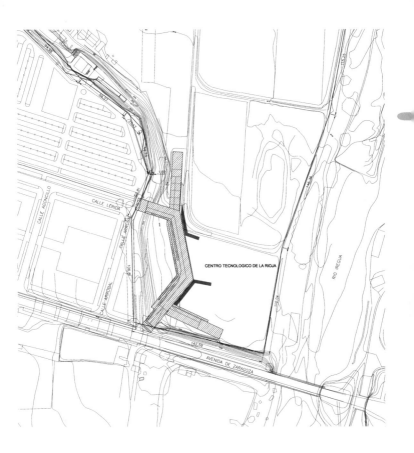

Our project emerges as an attempt to make the building an integral part of the landscape, both as a topographical event and as an experience, trying to produce an environment where nature and technology become intrinsically connected.

The building is organized in such a way that the three institutions become part of a single organization, allowing the collective facilities to be shared between the three institutions, and to minimize the security, cleaning and maintenance costs.

The organization of the building aims at maximizing the integration of the landscape into the building's spaces, and adopts a linear structure that maximizes the surface of contact with the outside. The classrooms and offices that constitute the majority of the functional spaces in the building are organized along a corridor space that threads through all the dependencies. The corridor space will contain the public spaces of the building, opened to the outside gardens and the rooms will be opened on the other side of the building towards the river landscape and the tree farms. This linear structure has been placed roughly on a north-south orientation, parallel to the topographical cornice that forms the western edge to the site. Such location allows the building to surround the Elms along the Camino de Los Lirios, claiming the slope as an internal garden featuring the trees. The building has been organized into a two storey bundled structure that encloses part of the site as a more internalized outside space, branching out on different levels to connect both with the surrounding urban levels and with the future River Park. On a smaller scale, the western face of the building provides with terraces looking towards the Elm garden, and shredding into open-air ramps establishing topographical continuities between the building and the garden. The sectional dislocation between the two floors of the building generates automatically these terraces and a cantilever on the East façade that will protect the fully glazed façade from the sun. The roof of the building becomes a kind of public belvedere over the river park, being connected to the city level on two ends through lifting bridges. A green pergola extends from this level to protect the glazed façade from direct sun exposure.

179

Transverse section

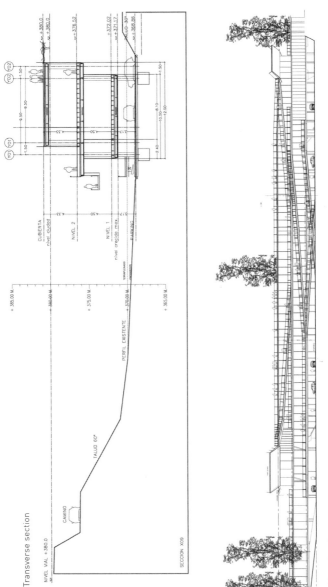

NIVEL VIAL +380.0

+395.00 M.
+390.00 M.
+375.00 M.
+370.00 M.
+365.00 M.

CUBIERTA
nivel ciudad

NIVEL 2

NIVEL 1

nivel crecida máx.

PARKING

CAMINO

PERFIL EXISTENTE

TALUD 60°

SECCION X09

+380.0
+376.52
+372.02
+371.17
+368.86

West elevation

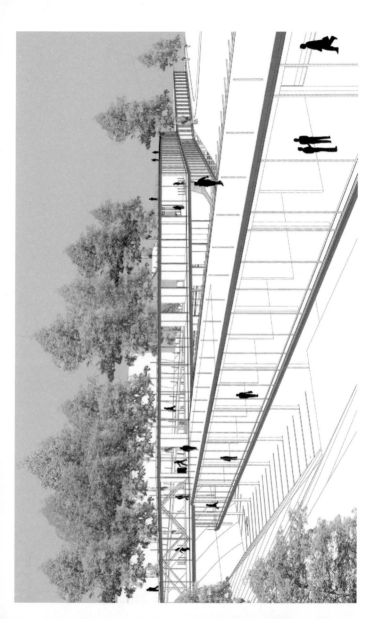

Parking level

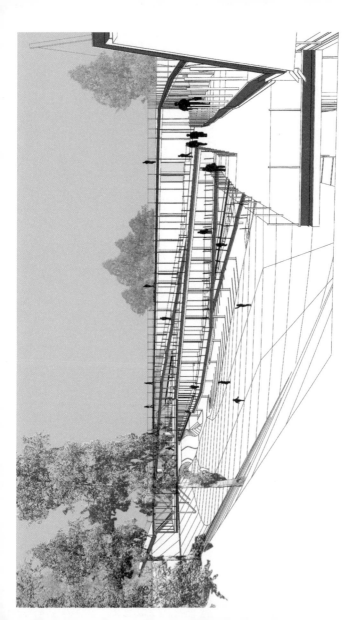

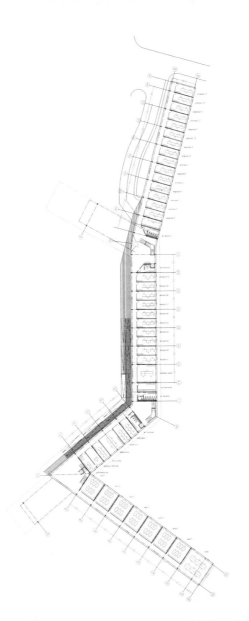

1st floor level

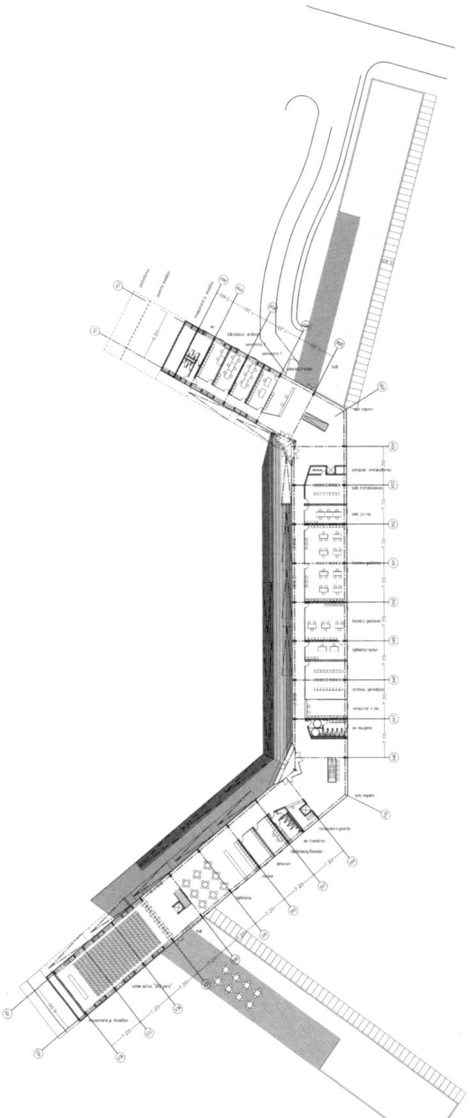

2nd floor level

ground

multiple face

perforated

High-Speed Railway Complex
Florence | 2002

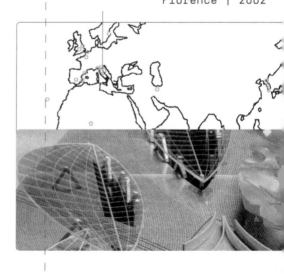

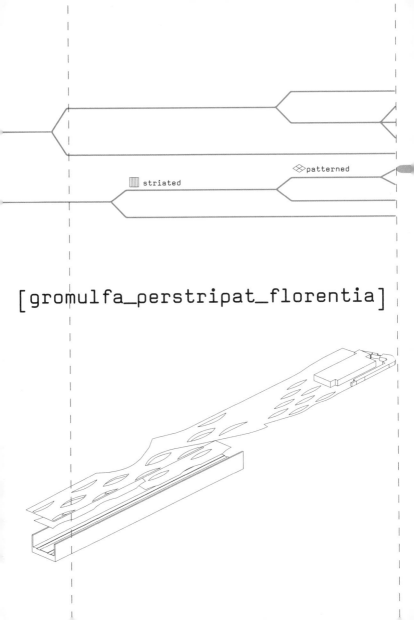

striated

patterned

[gromulfa_perstripat_florentia]

The latent potential of the new Florence high speed railway project arises from the physical coincidence of the multimodal transportation complex infrastructure, built around the high-speed railway terminal station, and a system of open public spaces that will constitute the geometrical centre of a new international urban complex dedicated to leisure, trade, tourism and the arts: the redevelopment of the Macelli area as a new cultural metropolitan centre, the future plan to convert the Mercato del Bestiame into an international centre for restauration, the new exhibition centre to be developed in the Fortezza da Basso and the existing convention centre area, the Santa Maria Novella station and the surrounding areas. These new facilities will be located between Florence's historical centre and the emerging development pole in the Novoli district. This convergence of systems of public space and multimodal transportation systems is what lays down the possibility to synthesize a paradigmatic new type of contemporary metropolitan structure. The municipal plan coordinated by Zevi sets an axis of public infrastructures and public spaces, exactly coincident with the location of the new station, that we have taken as the main feature of our scheme. The technical fact that the new high-speed tracks will be running 25 m below ground, precisely to avoid interference with the existing urban fabric is the new technical reality that is giving raise to a consistent and complementary relationship between public urban space and transport infrastructure that will produce an entirely different urban phenomenology.

The convergence of systems of public space and multimodal transportation system sets the possibility to synthesize a paradigmatic new type of contemporary metropolitan type. Our strategy is the erasure of the station volume as an identifiable object

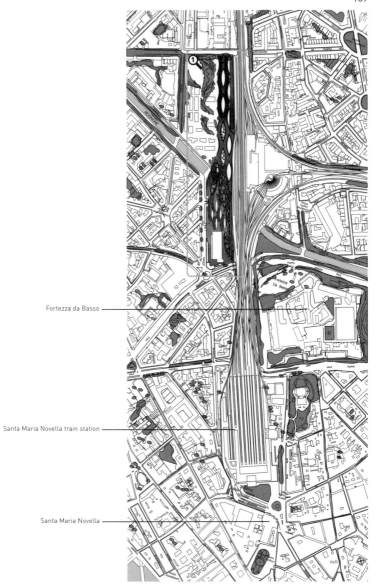

Fortezza da Basso

Santa Maria Novella train station

Santa Maria Novella

from the surrounding urban landscape, by blending it into the park that the Municipal Plan determines in the site of the future station. Rather than making a gesture to signify the gate to the city, we will get the visitors to magically appear in the middle of it; the citizens will also be transported from the park into another city, almost imperceptibly, without noticing it: a camouflaged station that will receive visitors in the most welcoming environment: a Central Park in the new centre of Florence.

If European cities were once regional centres of accumulation of capitalist wealth, now they have become global nodes of 'flexible accumulation' compressing and expanding time and space to allow for a virtual manipulation of post-colonial capitalist extensions. Where static, enclosure and gates determined in the past the qualitites of building in cities, dynamics, flow, connections and bifurcations have become the core of the contemporary urban phenomenology.

In this new order, travel does no longer require a significant rite of passage, the city does no longer need a wall and a gate. The hybridisation of the public space with the transportation infrastructure is one of the most distinctive features of the contemporary city. Rather than monumentalise, objectualise travel, making a gate or a wall, the emerging prototypes of transportation infrastructure need to establish a seamless continuity, spatially and formally, between the urban space and the transportation systems. Transportation interfaces should not try to replace the gates nor the palaces, like in the Novecento, but rather become the contemporary equivalent of the plazas, the public spaces.

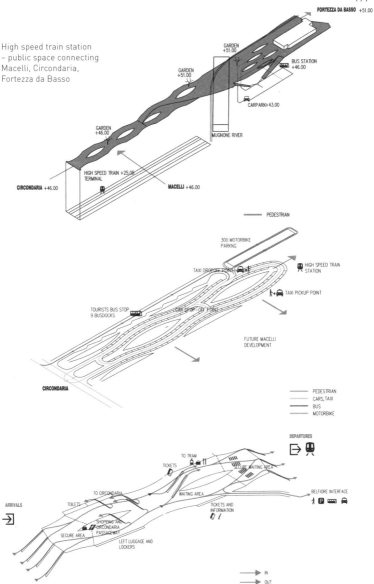

High speed train station
– public space connecting
Macelli, Circondaria,
Fortezza da Basso

Structural concepts
Due to the strict technical, financial and schedule constraints
of the project, the formal organisation is largely the output
of the structural system and the construction process. Like in
Santa Maria dei Fiori, the formal organisation of the project
is determined by the economies of the supply route, the order
of construction, and the structural system. Four fundamental
factors determine the choice of the structural system:
1. The functional organisation of placing a garden over a station,
while maintaining visual connections across the different levels of
the project: the garden, the concourse and the platform levels.
2. The underground structure should be designed to resist
lateral soil pressure. The structural requirement for the horizontal surfaces to butress the retaining walls in the middle and
top of the section with a frequency no lower than 50 m, to avoid
buckling of the walls, while allowing for frequent penetrations
of the slabs. The structure should have enough resistance
against earthquake and sufficient strength to withstand fire or
collision damage in case of accident.
3. The necessity of using the tracks on the embankment as a
main supply route through the construction process, and
the stringent schedule constraints that sets preference for a
prefabricated construction system.
4. The economic constraints suggest also the use of prefabricated systems with a high degree of repetition and easiness
of assembly. Quality control on such complex site will be
difficult and the system should be designed to simplify and
rationalise the construction procedure, without compromising
the design. The system should try to reduce the construction
period as much as possible.

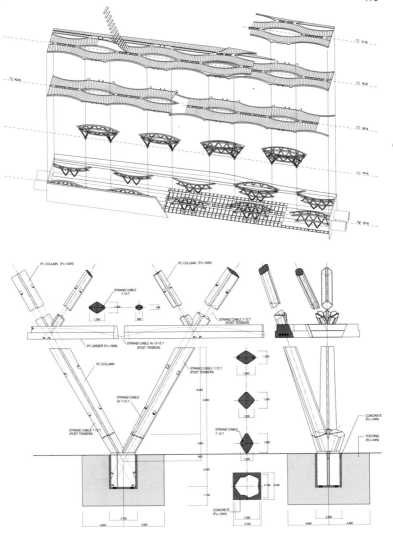

Structural system

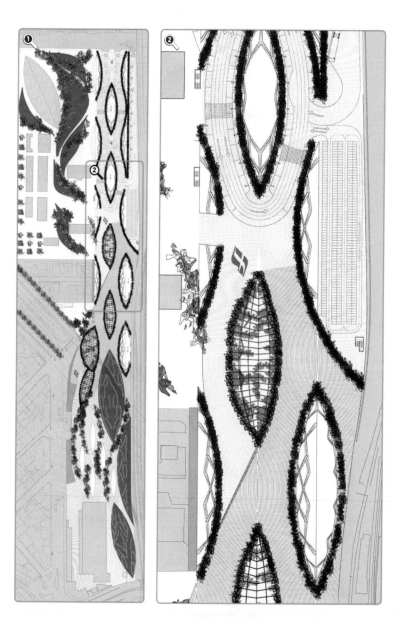

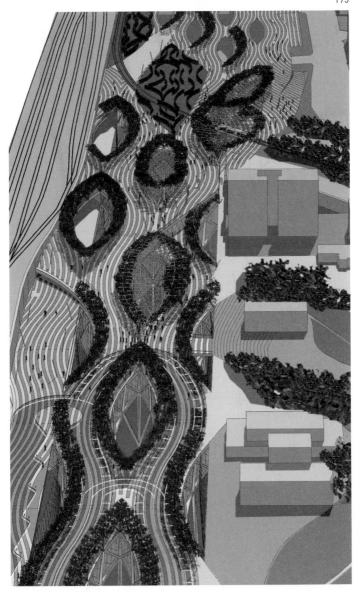

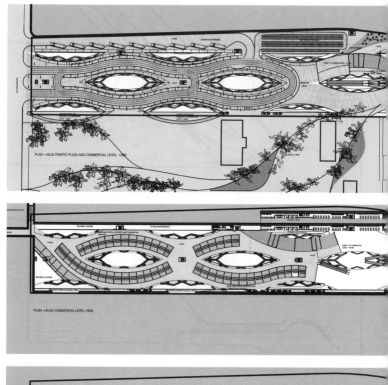

PLAN +46.00 TRAFFIC PLAZA AND COMMERCIAL LEVEL 1/500

PLAN +40.00 COMMERCIAL LEVEL 1/500

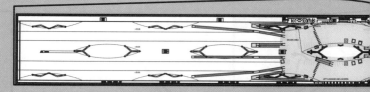

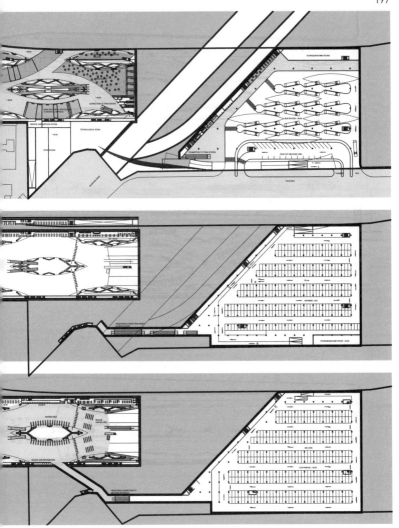

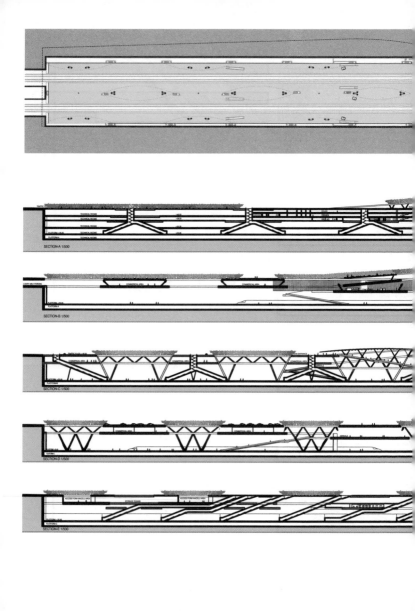

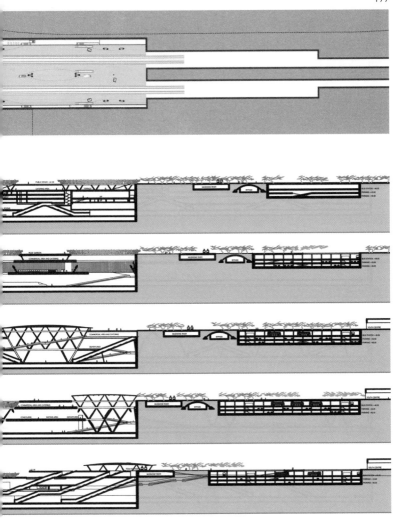

We propose that all energy (power, heating and cooling) be produced centrally for the whole station. The economy of scale ensures high operating efficiencies and enables environmentally friendly energy sources to be incorporated within the budget. The associated equipment and other central plant is housed in the main technical rooms. From here, energy will be distributed to local plant rooms serving each separate function. The main route for horizontal and vertical services distribution is through the large double walled construction running parallel to the platforms. The double wall also houses all local technical rooms an equipment. Because energy will be produced centrally, individual supplies to each function will be metered to facilitate charging/billing for energy used. For comfort and energy efficiency, local environmental control systems are tuned to the needs of each space.

Transverse section

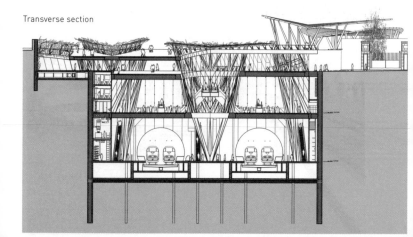

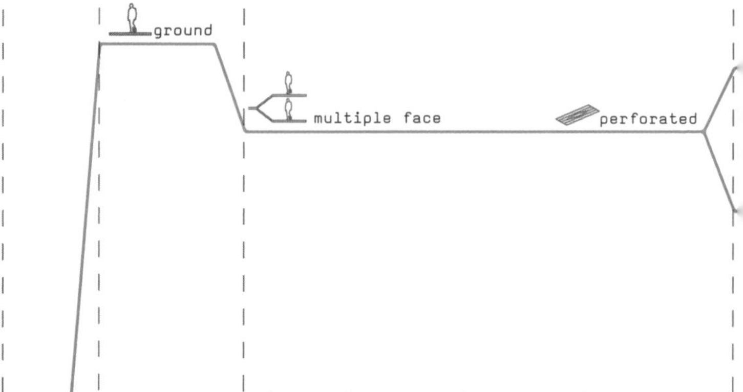

ground

multiple face

perforated

Novartis Underground Car Park & Gate
Basel | 2003

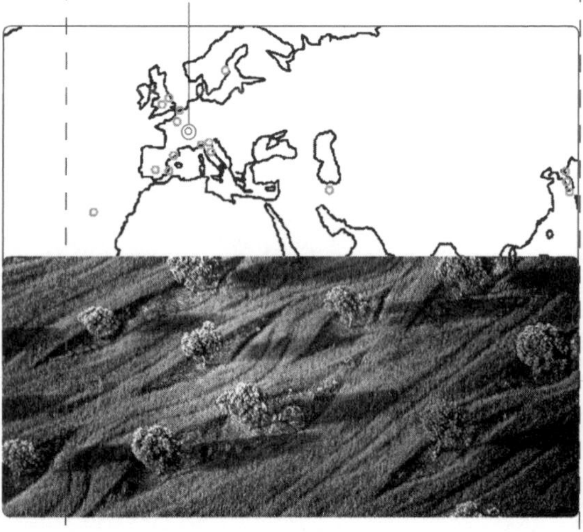

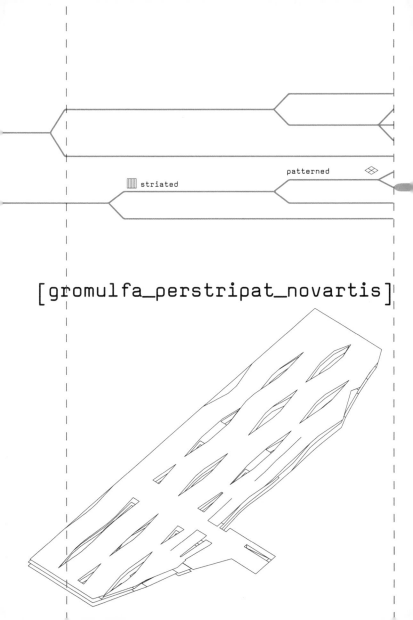

striated

patterned

[gromulfa_perstripat_novartis]

Novartis is a company dedicated to life sciences, to the investigation and manipulation of nature. Our proposal for the Novartis Campus Main Gate and Traffic Interface arises from a reflection on the current status of biotechnology in the context of contemporary culture as an increasingly important domain of knowledge between the Natural and the Artificial. In this proposal we have attempted to produce an assemblage between the two components of the project –the park and the parking– as a speculation on how the artificial and natural processes may be able to generate new forms of mutual enhancement.

More than ever before, the natural and the artificial are literally merging into each other. GM food, animal cloning, organic prosthetics, biological computers, the human genome... are the indexes of an era when the distinction between nature and artifice have become obsolete both to describe and to produce the environment of the 21st Century. Novartis is an organisation that thrives on these developments, and the Southern Interface to the Campus is an ideal occasion to explore, exploit and capture the potential of these emerging artificial ecologies in the design of the company's future environment, and its representation.

Rather than simply placing a picturesque park on top of a conventional car-park, our ambition is to produce a new composite, what we call Thick Park, where features of each organisation are used to enhance the other organisation.

The intention is to establish a continuity of landscapes between the Novartis Garden and the public green spaces that will surround it in the future.

The parameters of relationship between both organisations are of performative and geometrical nature:

- Both entities produce a cycle of mutual feedback that feed each other with their respective waste: The cars of the parking dispose

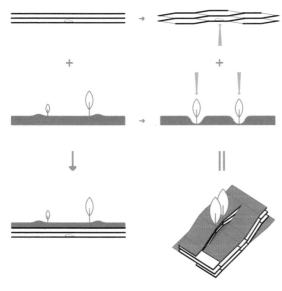

whole = sum of the parts

whole = <u>more</u> than the sum of the parts

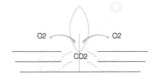

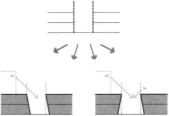

| Fire escapes | Not seing cars | Not seing anything | Trees |

of CO_2 that is consumed by the vegetation of the park, that in turn disposed of O_2, that is consumed in the combustion engines. That is the reason to propose the plantation of vegetation at regular intervals through the parking, so that the CO_2 is processed by the plants before being released onto the open air. Openings through the parking act as "lungs" of the scheme.

- The geology of the park is purely artificial, but rather than being an arbitrary replica of nature it will be directly produced by the undulations of the parking slabs that make the connections between the park surface and the two levels of parking below.

- The ventilation, escape and daylighting of the car-park is produced by the regular penetration of the park inside the parking, producing a regular pattern of deformation of the parking bands and the park spaces:

1. The parking can operate without any mechanical air extract, as it has openings to the outside with more frequency than the 20x20m grid required by the Swiss regulation.

2. Almost all parking spaces are adjacent to a courtyard where vegetation grows, which means there is daylight all through the parking, with substantial saving also in lighting maintenance.

3. Fire escape distances are viable through the pattern of openings and the perimeter of the parking.

4. Most of the exits into the Campus can be done directly into the park, making it a very pleasant route in and out of the parking. The resulting structure is an alveolar structure occurring simultaneously in plan and section, and regulated fundamentally by the geometric characteristic of a parking structure: bands deflecting in plan to allow for the penetration of the park into the structure, but also deflecting in section 1,5m up or down in order to produce continuity between the park and the two levels of the slab.

The space of the thick park is like a three-dimensional honeycomb.

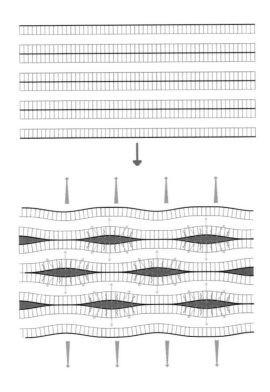

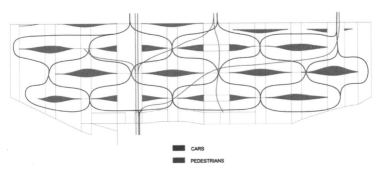

CARS

PEDESTRIANS

Our proposal is to recover here a medieval tradition linked to the University rather than to a corporate headquarters: In the first instance our proposal is aimed at producing a true Campus Garden, as an adequate complement to the ambitions of the Novartis Campus as the environment of an organisation fundamentally aimed towards research and knowledge. The Novartis Campus Medical Garden will not only provide the opportunities for relaxation and embellishment of the Campus, but it will represent Novartis commitment towards pharmacological research, and hopefully become a source of knowledge.

Rather than assembling plants according to Phylogenetic origin, family and genus, of most use to a biologist and to a more generic chemical enterprise, our Novartis Hortus Medicus returns to the roots of the first university gardens of Europe in search of a more efficient representation of the Pharmacological ambitions of the company. We envision our landscape as a curatorial enterprise, very much like those Hortus Medicus addressed the emerging medical faculties of plants described in classical writings on materia medica.

In this context, we propose a Hortus Medicus structured not by botanical but medical nomenclatura, an accessible and inspiring garden as it would befit an ambitious medical faculty. Well aware that medical sciences have moved beyond herbariums for their main subject of study, we envisage the various spaces of the garden not as medical production facilities, but as a space of retreat, recreation and inspiration, a bewildering labyrinth of smells, colours and shapes, the historic foundation of medical research.

For the Novartis Medical Garden we propose an additional secondary reading of medical uses through a remapping of substances onto the human body. Rather than a pure catalogue, a modern herbarium, this garden will facilitate a reading of botany through its historic relevance in the medical treatment of patients.

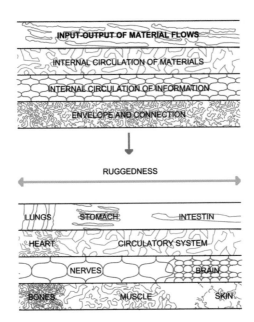

INPUT-OUTPUT OF MATERIAL FLOWS

INTERNAL CIRCULATION OF MATERIALS

INTERNAL CIRCULATION OF INFORMATION

ENVELOPE AND CONNECTION

RUGGEDNESS

LUNGS   STOMACH   INTESTIN

HEART   CIRCULATORY SYSTEM

NERVES   BRAIN

BONES   MUSCLE   SKIN

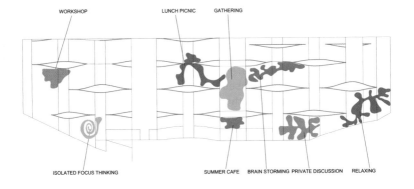

WORKSHOP

LUNCH PICNIC   GATHERING

ISOLATED FOCUS THINKING

SUMMER CAFE   BRAIN STORMING   PRIVATE DISCUSSION   RELAXING

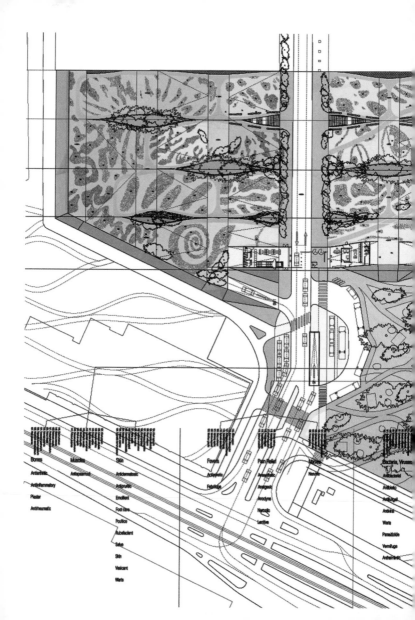

Bones
Antiarthritic
Antiinflammatory
Plaster
Antirheumatic

Muscles
Antispasmodic

Skin
Antidermatosic
Antipruritic
Emollient
Foot care
Poultice
Rubefacient
Salve
Skin
Vesicant
Warts

Fevers
Antiseptic
Febrifuge

Pain Relief
Analgesic
Anesthetic
Anodyne
Narcotic
Sedative

Vectors

Bacteria, Viruses
Antibacterial
Antibiotic
Antifungal
Antiviral
Warts
Parasiticide
Vermifuge
Antihelmintic

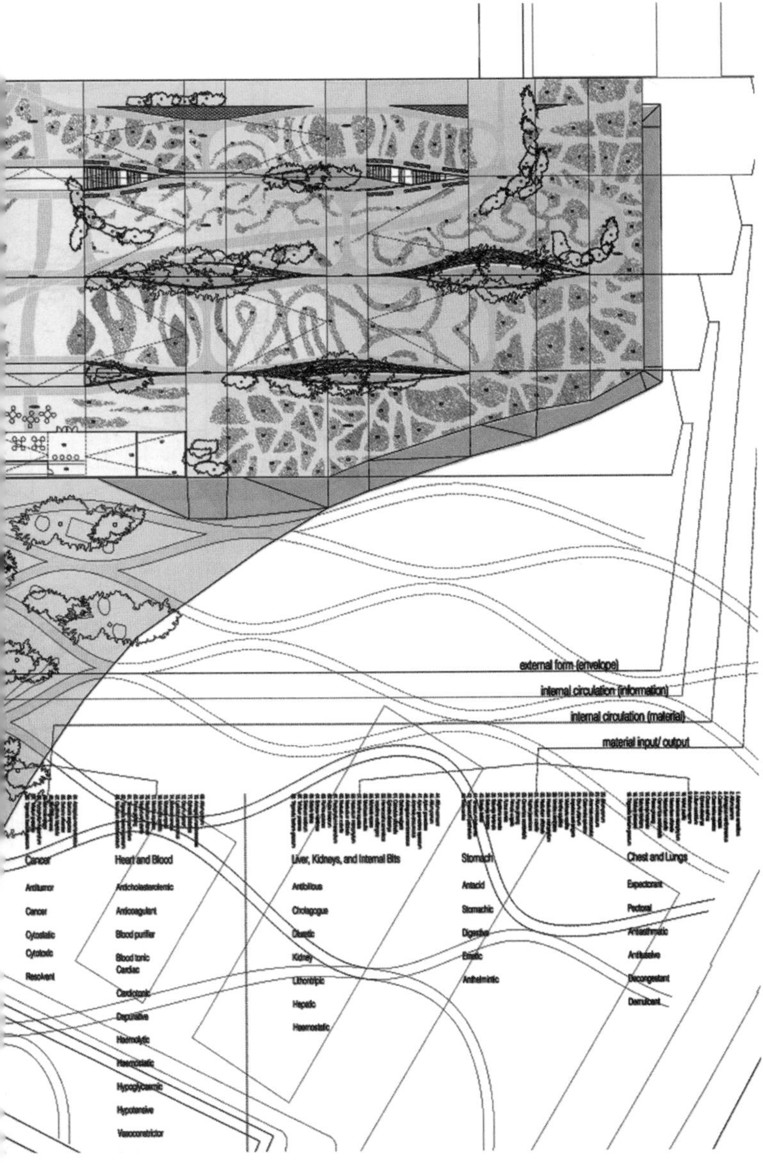

external form (envelope)

internal circulation (information)

internal circulation (material)

material input/ output

Cancer	Heart and Blood	Liver, Kidneys, and Internal Bits	Stomach	Chest and Lungs
Antitumor	Anticholesterolemic	Antibilious	Antacid	Expectorant
Cancer	Anticoagulant	Cholagogue	Stomachic	Pectoral
Cytostatic	Blood purifier	Diuretic	Digestive	Antiasthmatic
Cytotoxic	Blood tonic	Kidney	Emetic	Antitussive
Resolvent	Cardiac	Lithontriptic	Anthelmintic	Decongestant
	Cardiotonic	Hepatic		Demulcent
	Depurative	Haemostatic		
	Haemolytic			
	Haemostatic			
	Hypoglycaemic			
	Hypotensive			
	Vasoconstrictor			

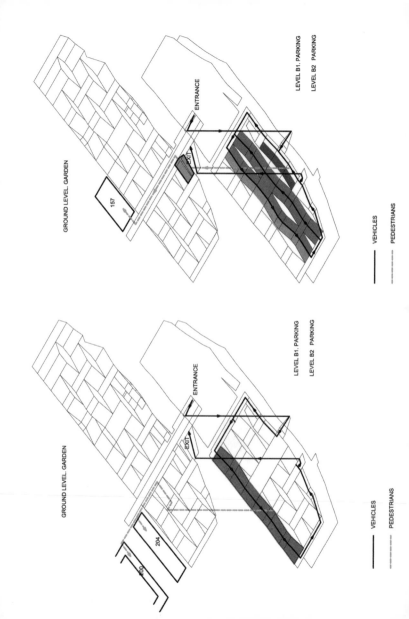

GROUND LEVEL. GARDEN

ENTRANCE

EXIT

LEVEL B1. PARKING
LEVEL B2. PARKING

157

——— VEHICLES
········· PEDESTRIANS

GROUND LEVEL. GARDEN

ENTRANCE

EXIT

LEVEL B1. PARKING
LEVEL B2. PARKING

204

——— VEHICLES
········· PEDESTRIANS

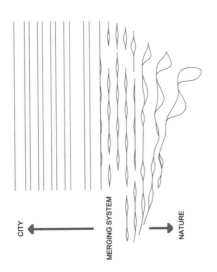

CITY ← MERGING SYSTEM → NATURE

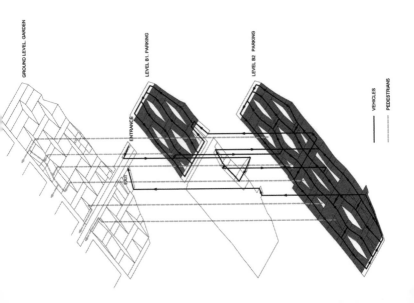

GROUND LEVEL GARDEN

LEVEL B1. PARKING

LEVEL B2. PARKING

ENTRANCE

EXIT

VEHICLES

PEDESTRIANS

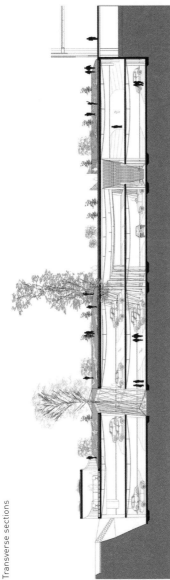
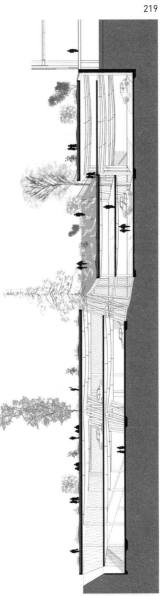

Transverse sections

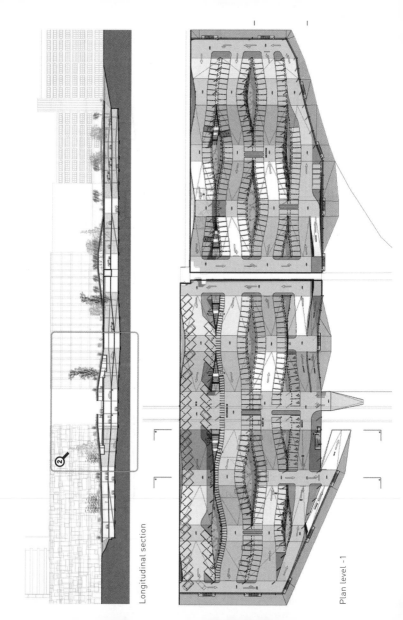

Longitudinal section

Plan level - 1

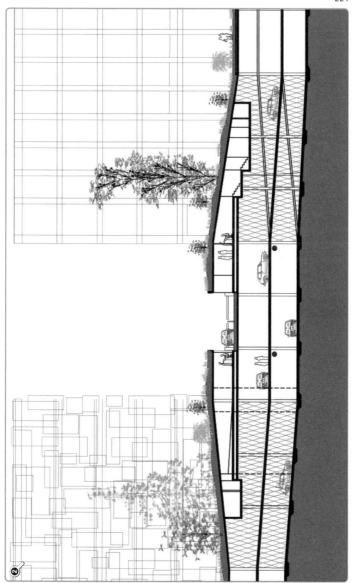

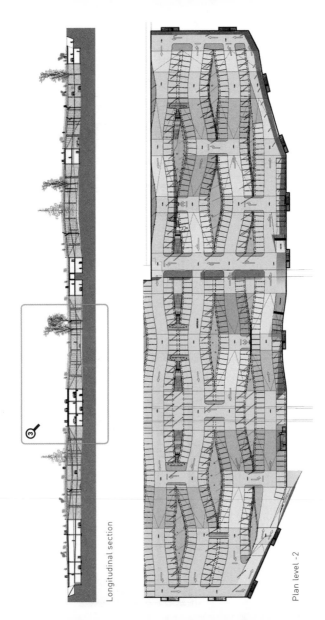

Longitudinal section

Plan level - 2

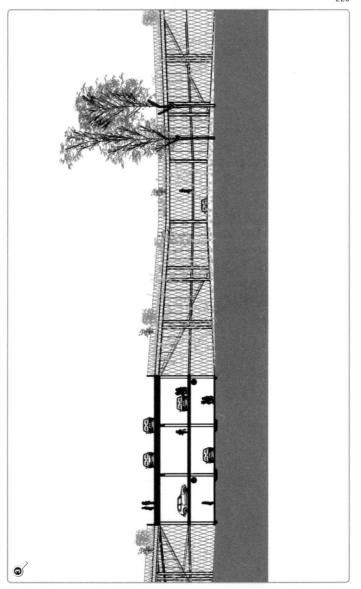

ground

multiple face

perforated

International Port Terminal
Yokohama | 1996–2002

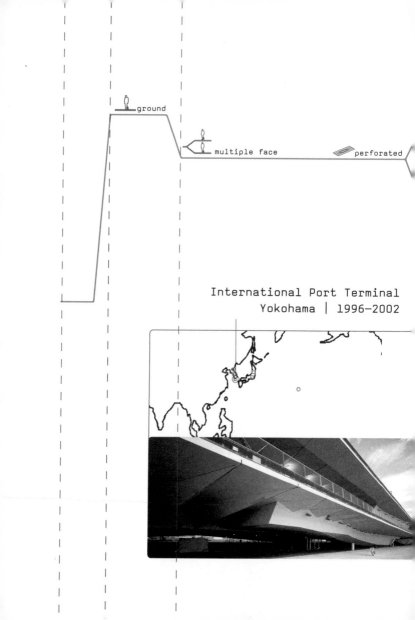

striated

contingent

[gromulfa_perstricon]

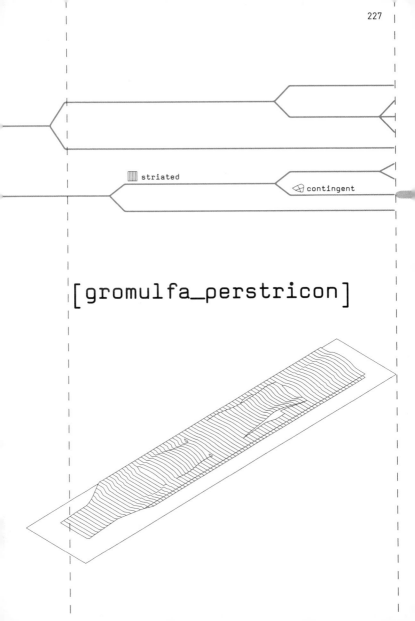

The Yokohama project started from the possibility of generating organisation from a circulation pattern, as a development of the idea of a hybridisation between a shed – a more or less undetermined container – and a ground. Our interest in the circulation pattern was an attempt to move forward from similar approaches already developed during the 70's, where circulation was organised and then "architecture" deployed on the circulation diagram, but in a more consistent manner in which circulation can literally shape space. We had been involved in the past in designing transportation buildings and we were very interested in them precisely because of the brutal limitations they have, and the many determinations the program automatically imposes on space.

Usually, a transportation building works as an input-output device, with very clear orientation: departures and arrivals. We were more interested in exploring the possibility of a transportation infrastructure that could operate less as a gate, as a limit, and more as a field of movements with no structural orientation. We also looked specifically to pier structures, to discover the characteristic linearity of these structures: you enter from the root, walk to the end, and you either leave in a ship, or you have to return on your own steps. This imposes a strong orientation on the space that we were interested to challenge.

Our first move was to set the circulation diagram as a structure of interlaced loops that allow for multiple return paths. The connection between the circulation paths was always set as a bifurcation, so that rather than setting the program as a series of adjacent spaces with more or less determined limits, we articulated them in the continuity of a branched sequence along the circulatory system. What we then called "the no-return diagram" was basically the first attempt to provide the building with a particular spatial performance.

The second decision in the process was that the building should not appear in the skyline, to be consistent with the idea of not making

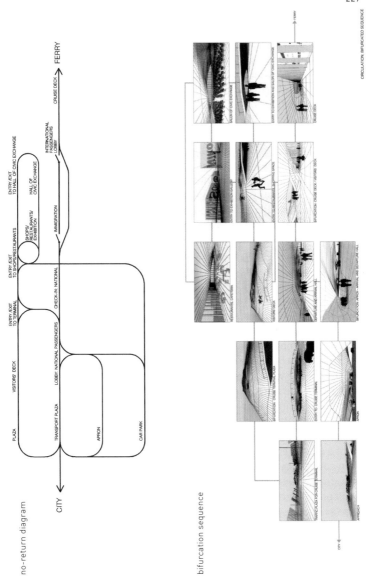

no-return diagram

CITY ← → FERRY

PLAZA · VISITORS DECK · LOBBY NATIONAL PASSENGERS · CHECK-IN NATIONAL · IMMIGRATION · HALL OF CIVIC EXCHANGE · INTERNATIONAL PASSENGERS · CRUISE DECK

ENTRY /EXIT TO TERMINAL · ENTRY /EXIT TO SHOPS/RESTAURANTS · ENTRY /EXIT TO HALL OF CIVIC EXCHANGE

TRANSPORT PLAZA · APRON · CAR PARK

SHOPS/ RESTAURANTS/ EXHIBITION

bifurcation sequence

CIRCULATION. BIFURCATED SEQUENCE

a gate on a semantic level as well, by avoiding the building becoming a sign. This immediately led to the idea of making a very flat building, and from there we moved into turning the building into a ground. Once we decided that the building would be a warped surface, we sought to produce an argument of consistency between the no-return diagram and the surface as a geometrical argument by associating a surface to every segment of the no-return diagram, and a surface bifurcation to every bifurcation of the line. To spread the building mass as thin as possible, we occupied the maximum area possible within the site. This, and the requirement of placing straight boarding decks 15m from the pier's edge along both sides of the building to connect to moving bridges, is what determined the rectangular footprint of the building. The association between segments of the diagram and surfaces gave us a basic metrics of the main chapters of the program: every segment of the no-return diagram had an associated size in square meters, which divided by the width of the pier provided the length of every surface between bifurcations. By proceeding in this manner we managed to produce the first approximation of the final form of the project, a three-dimensional version of the no-return diagram that resembled a kind of lasagne of warped surfaces.

The next decision was how to make the form structural. The obvious solution of supporting the surfaces with columns was not consistent with the aim to produce space and organisation literally out of the circulatory diagram, and a more interesting possibility was to try to develop a structural system out of a warped surface.

Some photographs we had of corrugated steel retaining walls suggested that we could use bent surfaces as a structural device, and we decided that our warped surface would be built as a corrugated sheet, using an undulated surface between two plates to provide sufficient structural strength; eventually the lower plate of this structure would be removed to simplify construction, turning

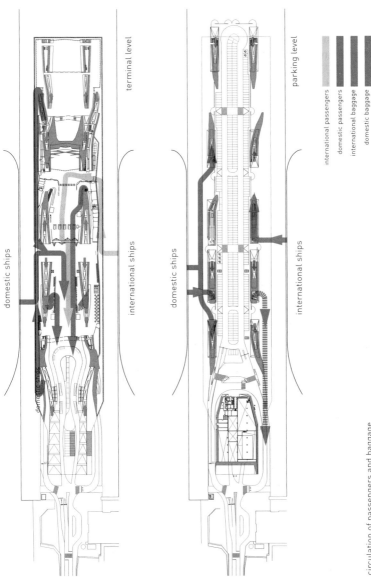

231

terminal level

parking level

domestic ships

international ships

domestic ships

international ships

international passengers
domestic passengers
international baggage
domestic baggage

circulation of passengers and baggage

the folded metal plates into a crucial expressive trait of the project. Higher strength zones would be produced by folding that surface at a larger scale, and this immediately became associated, as a matter of economy, with the ramp system linking the different levels of the building. The ramps became associated to the main longitudinal structural lines, running in two parallel lines along the pier, taking advantage of the depth of their bent to produce the largest structural elements. This association is extraordinarily important for the project, as it brings the structure and the circulation system together into the form in a complex whole, effectively achieving our primary goal of making the circulation affect directly the spatial definition.

As opposed to the assemblage between structure and circulation, which blended in a metamorphic manner, the program was to become integrated in a more sedimentary form. The programmatic strategies used in the project can be related to an interest in exploring what we could roughly denominate as intensive space: that is, the kind of spatiality where the capacity of space is not directly related to its size, and where the quality of space varies differentially, rather than as a discontinuity. A continuous and homogeneous space has been traditionally the instrument for flexibility, but intensive space is differentially flexible, which means that it offers multiple conditions in a continuum, in a similar way in which temperature, luminance, pressure or humidity tend to vary across a large room. Conventional programmatic distribution is fundamentally related to an extensive use of space and time: programs are allocated in particular extensions of space and time with well-defined limits. The traditional alternative to this traditional assignment is to avoid any determination of time and space, providing the maximum possible scale and openness. The potential of intensive space is to set up a degree of specificity without delimiting extensions. Very early on we decided to pursue an extremely reductive palette

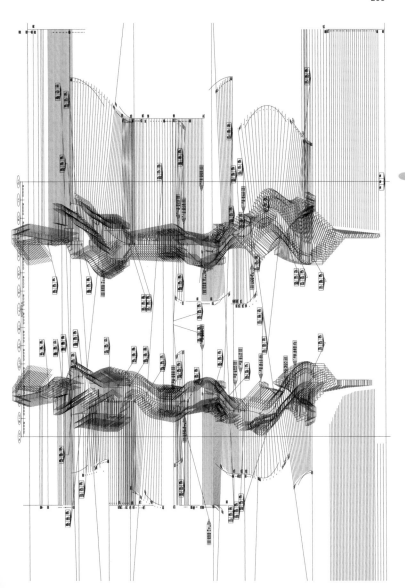

of materials in the project, in order to preserve what we judged as the main features of the spatial and geometrical determination of the project: the continuity across levels and between outside and inside spaces. Another important quality that we tried to preserve in the detailing of the project was the prevalence of horizontal surfaces as spatial enclosure, versus the vertical enclosure which was ideally non-existent. This automatically split the materials into two: steel and wood for each face of the horizontal surfaces, which would be very intensively crafted in geometry and texture, and glass and railings, which were part of the vertical surfaces and that should tend to vanish.

The most important determinations for the wood floor system were primarily in relation to the vaulted structural geometry, then to the need to comply with local handicap-access regulations for tilted surfaces. This programmatic condition is what produces the strange bumpiness of the surface, a new form of pleating at a different scale. The panelisation of the curved geometry of the roof is designed to minimize as much as possible the amount of irregular cuts of the wood slats, which produces the characteristic variation in the orientation of the slats by connecting the singularities in the topography with singularities of the panelisation.

For the glazing that provides lateral enclosure of the halls, our target from the beginning was clear: we did not want to have any mullions or other details to fix the glass, as if it were held magically. There are two fundamental cases in the glazing of the building: the longitudinal walls that separate the main halls from the boarding decks and surrounding terraces, and the transverse glazing that separates the halls from the roof plaza and forms the end walls. The first type has to endure the maximum deflection, as it is systematically located on and under the cantilevers, but is also the shortest in height (under 4 m). Here the glass is 19 mm thick, clamped to the floor and held with a neoprene sliding clamp

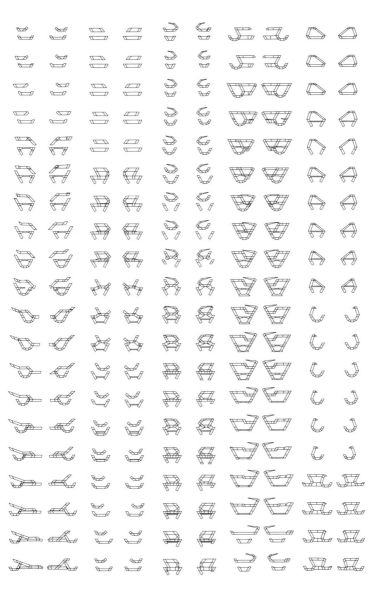

Girder templates

on the upper sash, where the deflection of the structure could be absorbed. The lower sash is hidden under the wood deck and the upper sash is embedded in the structure, so the fixing completely disappears; the glass is also tilted towards the outside to avoid frontal reflections in the glass and achieve maximum transparency. The transverse glazing does not have to sustain the same level of deflection, but reaches heights of 9m at some points and therefore requires perpendicular reinforcement to withstand wind forces. The solution to this problem is to fold the glass plane to provide strength to perpendicular wind loads.

The handrail system is also one of the main packages in the build-ing, given its extension and visual presence. Like glazing, hand-rails are elements that do not belong to the spatial model of the continuous surface; on the contrary, they establish limits, physical discontinuities, into a potentially seamless space. Like the warped wood deck, we were less interested in achieving effects at any cost than in setting out a productive relationship between effect and construction. Our model of transparency became, as for the rest of the elements on the roof deck, the fishermen's tools, the nets, the sails, the windsocks and the ropes... all those elements that vibrate with the wind and constantly change their form, floating in space yet delimiting spaces. We eventually chose a chain-link mesh, with the structural supports moved out of the vertical in order to enforce the floating, anti-gravitational effect that we had already found during the competition period as a latent potential of the overall organisation. Starting the design with a kind of tripod and – again – applying the idea of a system that differentiates to accommodate particular needs, the handrail system evolved into a series of V-shaped bars that support the handrail, which have the advantage of minimizing the number of points of fixation to the structure while allowing for an easier setting out of the elements on site.

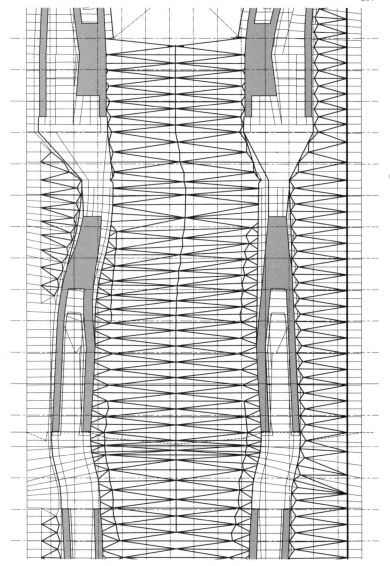

Reflected ceiling plan showing folds

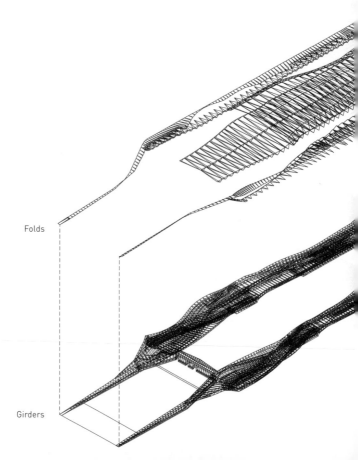

Folds

Girders

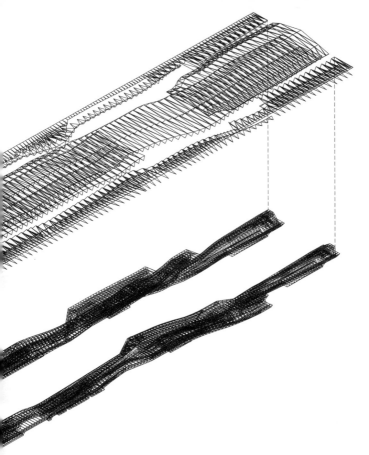

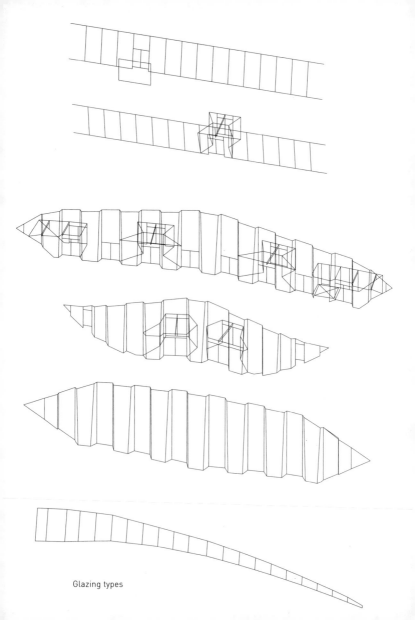

Glazing types

241

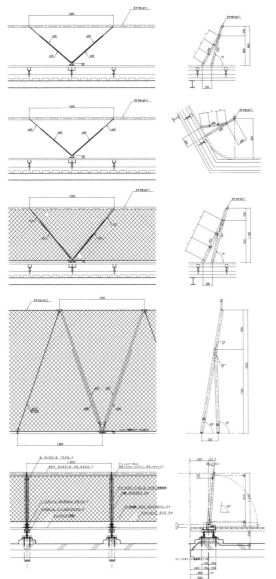

Handrail types

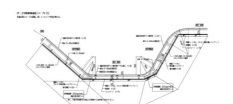

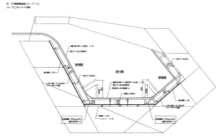

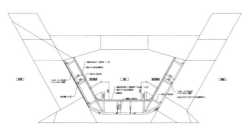

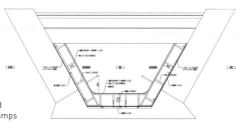

Variations of the wood
deck surface of the ramps

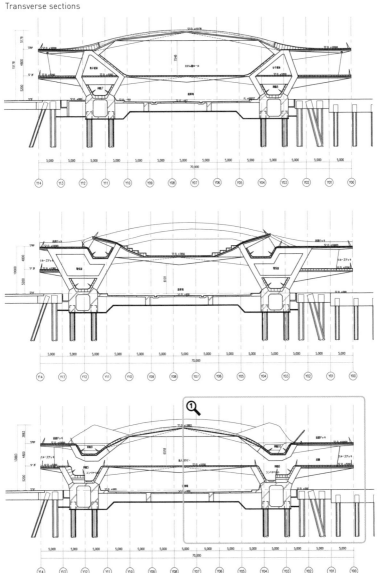

Transverse sections

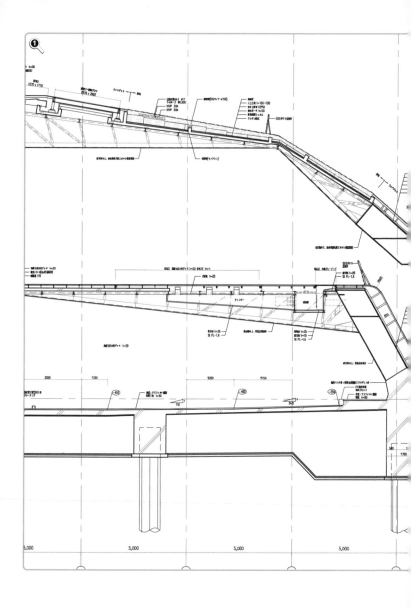

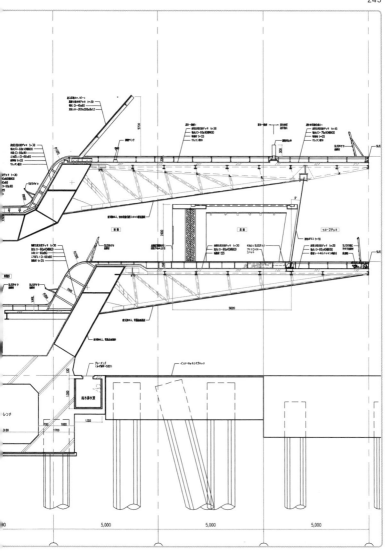

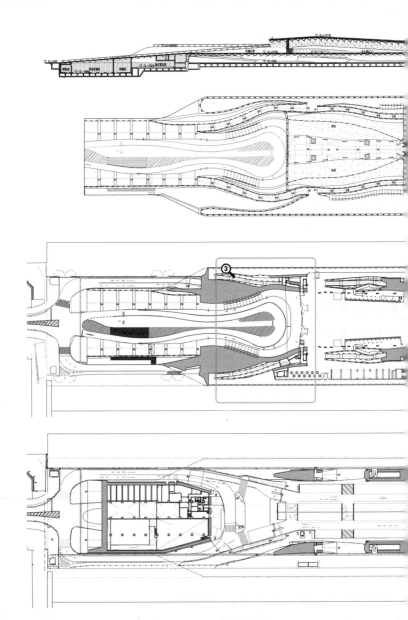

247

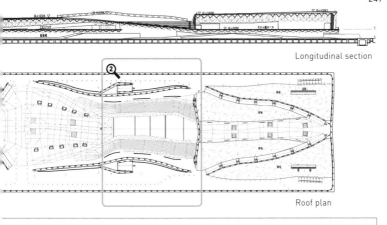

Longitudinal section

Roof plan

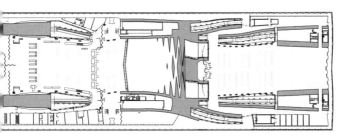

Terminal level plan

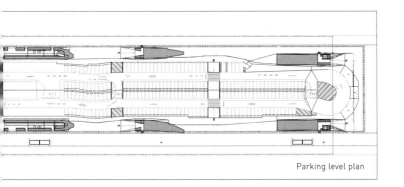

Parking level plan

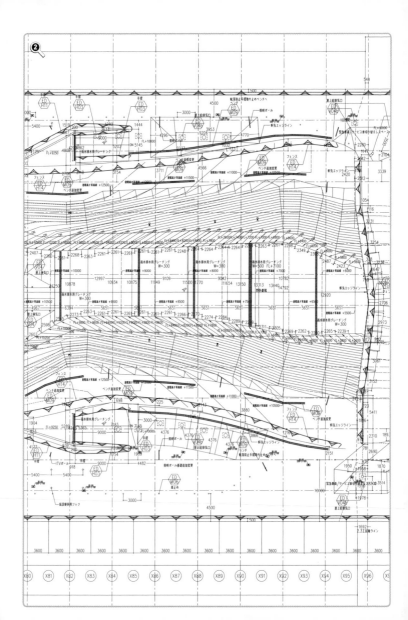

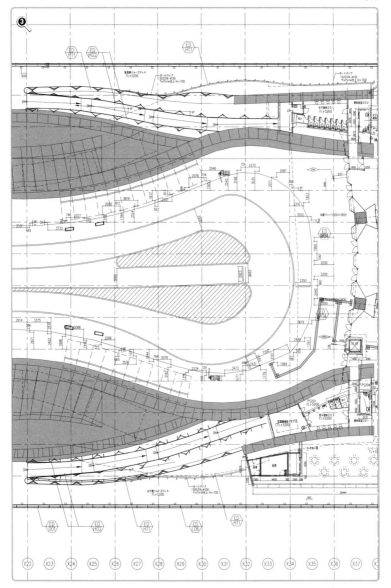

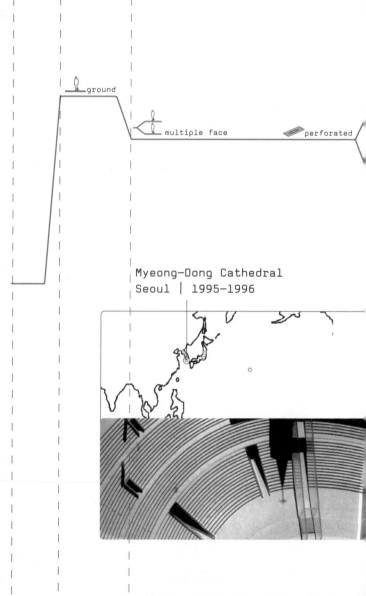

ground

multiple face

perforated

Myeong-Dong Cathedral
Seoul | 1995-1996

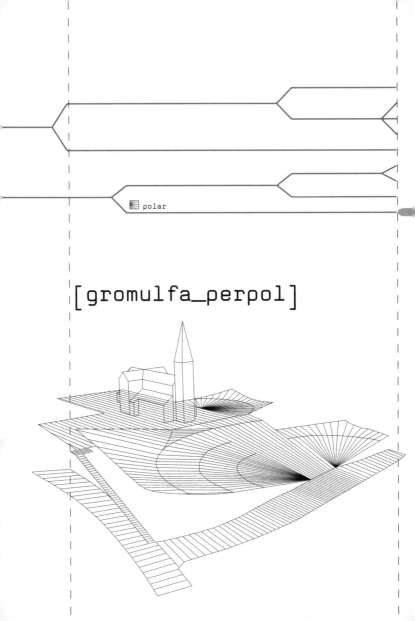

polar

[gromulfa_perpol]

The Myeong-Dong cathedral area in Seoul is the emblem of the Catholic Church and a symbol of democracy for Korea, being the site of students riots against dictatorship. The area surrounding the cathedral is the densest commercial area of Seoul, and the geographical centre of the city. The brief of the project required the design of a 35,000m² area to include an urban public space, surrounding the Myeong-Dong Cathedral, as well as a large religious convention and cultural center, to be constructed in two phases. The cathedral site borders very different conditions of an environmental, topographic and programmatic kind: the southern edge of the cathedral site is 11m higher than the northern edge, bordering the commercial street of Myeong-Dong; the eastern edge borders an elevated highway that is a major source of noise for the site; while the western edge borders a very incoherent urban fabric. Our approach was to focus on the coincidence of multiple, often contradictory, qualities within one site: secular/ religious, ephemeral/ permanent, commercial/ ritual, dynamic/ static...
The urban public space was proposed as a smooth topography, a slanted and deformed ground plane adjusting to the different environmental, topographical and programmatic conditions within and around the site: bridging the 11m difference in level between the commercial street and the plateau where the cathedral sits as a north-south transition; sloping up towards the west to protect the public space from acoustic intrusion from highway traffic; rising to the south and the east with a similar gradient, producing a conic surface, a shell-like plaza, where the different flows would tend to overlap, rather than be confined to restricted zones.
The same concept of integration is applied to the space of the convention hall below, where the different cultural and religious programs are grouped in such a way as to form a stadium, a differential space that, with the provision of retractable seating and folding vertical planes, could expand or shrink from being the largest auditorium in Seoul (11,000 spectators) to being small-scale meeting places.

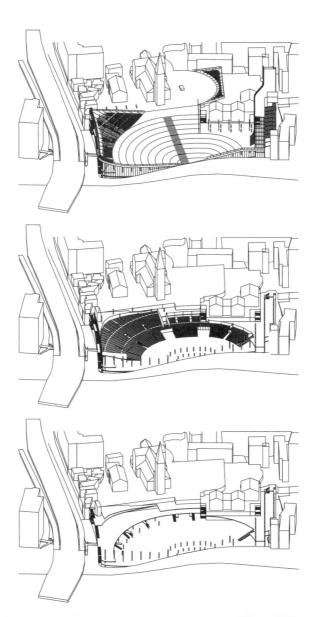

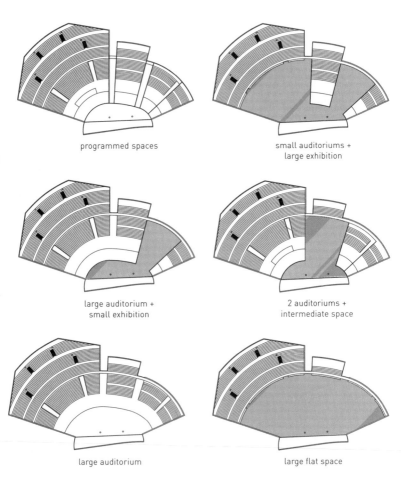

programmed spaces

small auditoriums +
large exhibition

large auditorium +
small exhibition

2 auditoriums +
intermediate space

large auditorium

large flat space

Auditorium scenarios

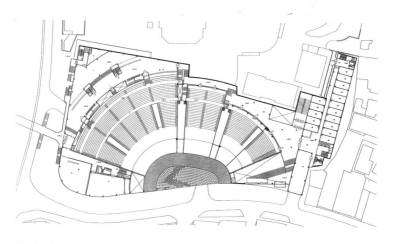

Plan level +38m

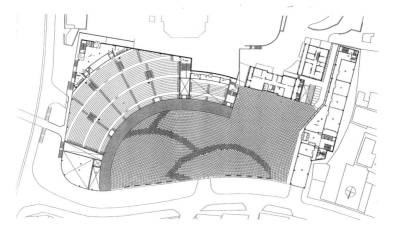

Plan level +43.4m

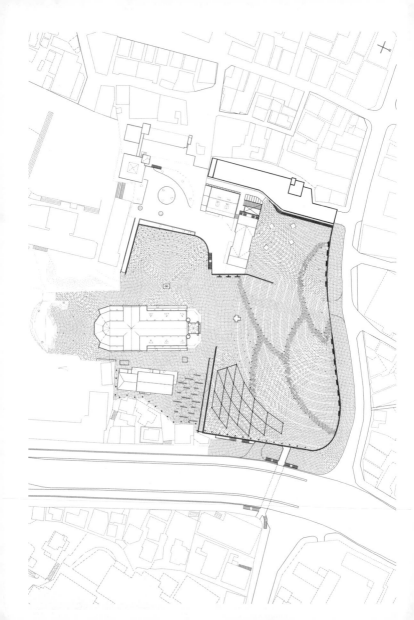

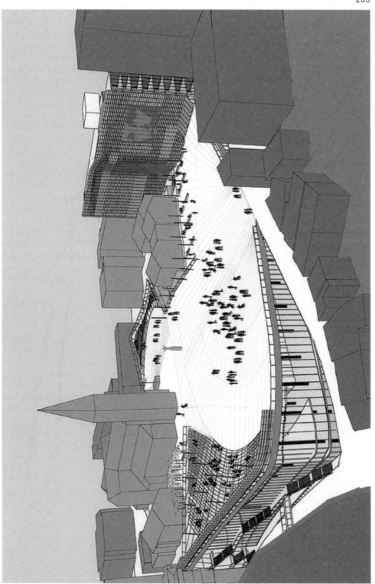

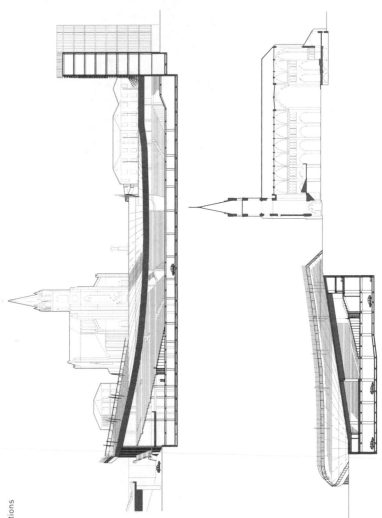

Cross sections

Same Difference
Detlef Mertins

During the early 1980s, in the heyday of the post-modern reaction against late modernism, the critic Demitri Porphyrios portrayed Crown Hall (1950-56), Mies van der Rohe's school of architecture at the Illinois Institute of Technology, as an architecture of total control and discipline. He called it "homotopic," requiring everything and everybody to conform to the grid of universal rationality, to the geometry that organized the building into a unified totality. "It was as if, by gridding space," he wrote, "one safeguarded against all accidents or indiscreet intrusions, and established instead an idealized field of likeness."[1] Instead of Mies's "immaculate homogeneity," Porphyrios promoted Alvar Aalto's work for what he called its "heterotopic" ordering sensibility. The individual parts of Aalto's Wolfsburg Cultural Centre (1958), for instance, were each given their own differentiated form in relation to their function, and were arranged into assemblages whose unity was seen to be open and inclusive. Porphyrios' interpretation was inspired by Michel Foucault's critique of the universalizing claims of humanism and his call instead for "heterotopias," such as the incongruous taxonomy of animals that Borges recounts from a 'Chinese encyclopedia.'[2] Foucault explained that where utopias offer the dream of a common locus or structure beneath all things, the heteroclite disturbs by secretly undermining language, destroying the syntax that causes words and things to hold together. However, where Foucault emphasized the capacity of heterotopias to corrode sameness and promote difference, Porphyrios focused on the forms of Aalto's heterogeneous

[1] Demetri Porphyrios, *Sources of Modern Eclecticism: Studies on Alvar Aalto* (London: Academy Editions/St. Martin's Press, 1982), p. 1.
[2] See Michel Foucault, *The Order of Things. An Archaeology of the Human Sciences* (New York: Vintage Books, 1973), p. xviii.

collage. In retrospect, Aalto's ordering sensibility appears to have produced representations of difference rather than deterritorializations that enable difference to emerge. Fixed and inflexible, Aalto's forms crystallized activities that were scripted in advance; an auditorium is an auditorium and an office is an office. In contrast, Foucault did not specify the form of heterotopia, but rather described its effects.

In this respect, it is worth recalling Mies's critique of Hugo Häring's organ-like functionalism in the 1920s. Where Häring wanted each part of his building to serve its intended function so precisely that a hallway would become narrower as it reached its end where fewer people would use it, Mies suggested that this limited the range of possible uses. Instead, he sought to achieve durability over time by making generous spaces that could serve a range of functions, even ones unforeseen. "The purposes for which a building is used," he contended, "are constantly changing and we cannot afford to tear down the building each time. That is why we have revised Sullivan's formula 'form follows function' and construct a practical and economical space into which we fit the functions."[3] Mies's pursuit of universal space implies, not a narrow conception of function, but a generous and open-ended approach to living, albeit within the structuring logics of industrial production and mass society that he accepted as givens to be worked through.

If we look not only at Mies's forms but also at the ways of life that they engendered, his pursuit of the universal within the historical conditions of the modern epoch takes on the character of a relentlessly destabilizing strategy within the practice of architecture and even within his own work as well. Throughout his career,

[3] "Christian Norberg-Schultz: A Talk with Mies van der Rohe," published in *Baukunst und Werkform* no. 11 (1958), pp. 615-618, trans. Mark Jarzombek and republished in Fritz Neumeyer, *The Artless Word. Mies van der Rohe and the Building Art* (Cambridge, Mass.: MIT Press, 1991), pp. 338-339.

Mies set his architecture against the perpetuation of old habits and in the service of emergent and experimental ways of doing things. In working on the Weissenhofsiedlung in 1926, he hoped to "open a new land" in which house and garden were merged into a fluid architectonic continuum that supported the *Lebensreform* ideal of living as much outdoors as in. On another occasion, he spoke of providing "a ground for the unfolding of life," suggesting that the architect be a catalyst for the process of becoming. Later in America, Mies's empty glass boxes – the "neutral frames" that were not entirely neutral after all – provided an infrastructure for the production of difference. This is what Alison and Peter Smithson sensed in their appreciation of the "recessive" and "loving neutrality" of Mies's late work, which they linked to a "new kind of light-touch inhabitation."[4] Mies wanted every person, like every building, to be free to realize their own immanent identity; for him, the aim of order was to bring together self-generated individualities without impinging on that freedom.

With its long-span structural system set on a ten-foot bay, Crown Hall was the only building at IIT that deviated from the twenty-four foot campus grid, which was based on the optimal size for a classroom. Perhaps the absence of classrooms in the architecture school suggested the deviation, but there were also no lecture halls or faculty offices. Instead, there was a single large room – 120 feet by 220 feet by 18 feet high, raised above the ground, and enclosed entirely by glass walls, translucent below and transparent above. It is in this space that the life of the school continues to unfold, subdivided only minimally by a multi-purpose space in the center. The open studio maximizes flexibility and the opportunity of shared experiences, enabling students to be aware of everything and participate fully. Focused inward yet extending out to the sky, the building is a catalyst for community within and connectivity beyond. It provides a lightly structured field for quo-

[4] Alison and Peter Smithson, *Without Rhetoric*, p. 19 and *Mies's Pieces*, pp. 16, 33.

tidian life and special events, calm yet alive, its rhythm changing over the course of the day and over the year, unified yet open. The central space has served for formal lectures, exhibitions, and events, including the memorial service for Mies and, recently, a wedding. It is also used for informal gatherings, pinups of student work, mock ups of floor plans, construction of large models, and simply hanging out. With rows of individual desks, the orderly regime of the studios is offset by an ad hoc manner of teaching and collaborative work. Professors gather students informally around someone's desk to talk about their work or wheel in chalkboards as needed with students sitting randomly on their boards or stools. Large models appear as needed and conversations erupt wherever drawings are pinned up or students work together. For the annual open house, as well as special occasions, the entire space is reconfigured into an exhibition hall. A few years ago, the central area was even carpeted with Kentucky blue grass. In 1958, a major concert by Duke Ellington turned Crown Hall – "the fish bowl of Tech" – into a ballroom with colored spotlights for nine hundred "smiling faces."[5] Recently, the experimental musical ensemble, MASS, transformed the building into a giant stringed instrument, with 24,000 feet of high-polish brass wire transferring vibrations directly into the steel structure. What makes Mies's universal space universal is not the grid, after all, which is simply one of several ordering devices and only appears strongly in the rendered plan, but the singularity of the large and largely unstructured room – an architecture that Mies described as "almost nothing," a void sandwiched between two uninterrupted horizontal planes in which anything, everything, and nothing can happen. Its relative emptiness transforms the iron cage of industrial rationality into an enabling device for emergent social formations and unforeseen events. Operating within but against the regime of the mass, Mies's universal

[5] The event is recorded in the yearbook *Integral*, 1958 (Chicago: The Students of the Illinois Institute of Technology, 1958), pp. 106-107.

space staged the uprootedness so central to the experience of modernity, as both a crisis and an opportunity for self-fashioning. Like Walter Benjamin's image of glass architecture as a milieu for a mode of dwelling that leaves no traces, Mies's glass boxes provoke an existential approach to life, drawing the occupant back to the blankness and potentiality of new beginnings, over and over again, promoting self-determination within yet against the world while safeguarding alterity.[6]

But what of the uniformity and repetition of Mies's work, building after building? To begin, Mies distinguished himself among the architectural avant-gardes precisely by *not* projecting a total vision for a new utopian society or city. Nevertheless, his work – especially in America – shares in the dream of a common locus or structure beneath all things that Porphyrios associated with utopia. It is this dream that gives Mies's work its consistency and rigor, a dream fuelled by the scientific literature that he read, beginning with the physics of Pierre-Simon Laplace (1749-1827), who sought to account for all phenomena across the terrestrial, molecular, and celestial scales in terms of one principle, the forces of attraction and repulsion between particles. The idea of a universal principle governing all of creation had become a central theme in the seventeenth century when a secular theology emerged, transforming the principle of God's homogeneous presence in the universe into a scientific postulate linked to a belief in humanity's capacity to hasten redemption through self-discipline and reform. The desire to reunite humanity with the Godhead was transformed into a program of reintegration in nature, seeking to align humanity with the governing principles of creation as revealed by science.

The goal of reintegration was powerfully re-articulated around 1900 by the zoologist Ernst Haeckel, who invented the science

[6] See Detlef Mertins, "The Enticing and Threatening Face of Prehistory: Walter Benjamin and the Utopia of Glass," in *Assemblage* 29 (1996), p. 6-23.

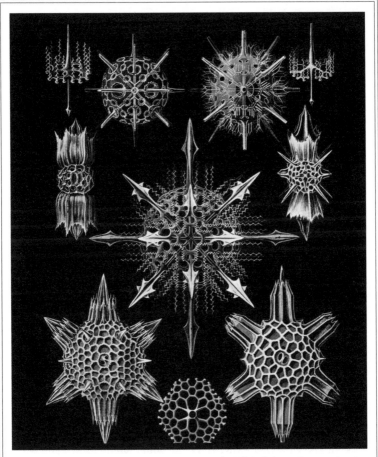

Fig. 1 Plate from Ernst Haeckel, *Art Forms in Nature* (1901), depicting various species of Radiolaria (a type of marine Protozoa). Courtesy of Prestel (E. Haeckel, *Kunstformen der Natur*. Munich & New York: Prestel, 1998, plate 41).

of ecology and popularized a monistic worldview in which society, politics, and the arts were to be modeled after nature. Haeckel discovered tiny microscopic sea creatures that he presented as exemplars for art and design, especially the radiolarians that were composed of the most primitive of elements (*Fig. 1*). The simplicity of the radiolarians was understood to be key to their multiplicity and universality, for they could assume an infinite variety of beautiful forms and adapt to different environments all over the world. Ever more powerful microscopes and telescopes confirmed the principle of structural homogeneity from the microscopic to the macroscopic while demonstrating the capacity of nature to produce an infinite variety of wondrous forms. This combination of homogeneity of structure with heterogeneity of individuation was reiterated throughout the twentieth century by scientists and by artists, architects and engineers eager of use science to fuel new invention. More recently, the sciences of complexity have updated this quest, once again providing new models that, in concert with new technologies, have inspired architects such as FOA. Over the past decade, the work of FOA has consistently explored the possibility of a new architectural paradigm – at once mathematical, spatial, and technological – one that corresponds to the order of nature (as best we know it) and, like nature, sponsors the proliferation of difference. Notwithstanding his expressed desire to establish a new language that could be broadly shared by others, Mies developed a corpus of work characterized by restless striving, experimentation, variation, and refinement. A drawing from the 1960s compares the elevations of seven clear-span buildings at the same scale, revealing just how diverse these buildings really are (*Fig. 2*). Different in size, from the tiny Farnsworth House and 50 x 50 House to the gargantuan Convention Hall (720 feet square), they are also different in structure, employing both one-way and two-way spanning systems, expressed alternatively above or

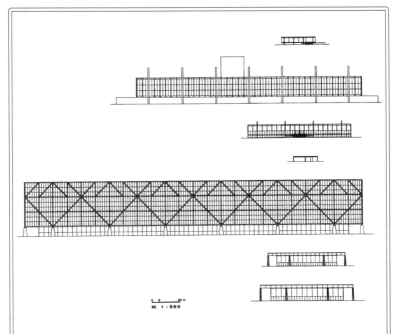

M. 1 : 500

Fig. 2 Office of Mies van der Rohe, Elevations for seven clear-span buildings drawn to uniform scale: Farnsworth House, Plano; National Theater, Mannheim; S.R. Crown Hall, IIT; 50 x 50 House; Convention Hall, Chicago; Ron Bacardi Administration Building, Santiago, Cuba; New National Gallery, Berlin [1969]. Courtesy Canadian Centre for Architecture. From Phyllis Lambert, "Mies Immersion," in *Mies in America* (Montreal: CCA, 2001), p. 422.

below the roof, with overhangs or without. They all use a modular grid, yet its dimension varies, as does that of the structure. Similar yet different from one another, these buildings cannot be reduced to the static model of industrial standardization or to a schema. If the specificity of programs, clients, sites, and local conditions accounts for much of their diversity, what is it then that unites them? While the idea of type might be helpful, it would have to be a dynamic conception of type, such as Goethe developed in his morphology of plants.

Consider a selection of leaves from the field buttercup (*Ranunculus acris*), arranged from the bottom of the stem to the top (*Fig. 3*). Despite its extensive range, the series nevertheless gives the impression of an overall unity. No one leaf, however, suffices as a measure or model for all the others.[7] Rather, their unity remains implied, contingent on the progression and transformation of the series, on what Goethe called the metamorphosis of the plant – "the process by which one and the same organ presents itself to us in manifold forms."[8] This unity remains open to the possibility that a new form will take its place among the others and inflect the series. So too, the form of Mies's long-span pavilions presents itself to the mind only through the progression of examples, as a generative field of movement or a form-making movement that leads to and from the resultant object. Because the unity of this movement-form includes other members of the series, it is constantly becoming other in order to remain itself. Its identity is founded precisely on the potency to be otherwise, demanding that the visible form be superseded again and again in an endless production of sameness and difference.

[7] See Johann Wolfgang von Goethe, *The Metamorphosis of Plants*, trans. Agnes Arber, in *Chronica Botanica* 10, no. 2 (Summer, 1946).

[8] Johann Wolfgang von Goethe, *The Metamorphosis of Plants*. Trans. Anne E. Marshall and Heinz Grotzke (Wyoming, Rhode Island: Bio-Dynamic Literature, 1978), p. 20.

Fig. 3 Leaves from the field buttercup (*Ranunculus acris*). Arranged as a graded sequence from the bottom of the stem (lowest left) to the top (bottom right), the leaves appear as a continuous transformation of a form that is never fixed but is always in motion, the movement-form of metamorphosis. Courtesy Ronald H. Brady, "The Idea in Nature: Rereading Goethe's Organics," in *Goethe's Way of Science: A Phenomology of Nature*, ed. David Seamon and Arthur Zajonc (Albany: State University of New York, 1998), p. 94.

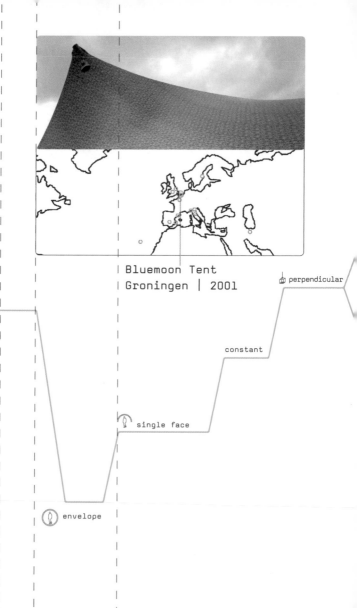

Bluemoon Tent
Groningen | 2001

perpendicular

constant

single face

envelope

[ensifacoper_placon]

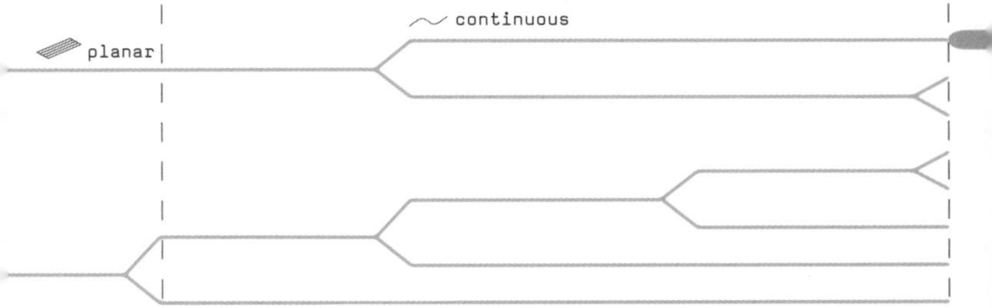

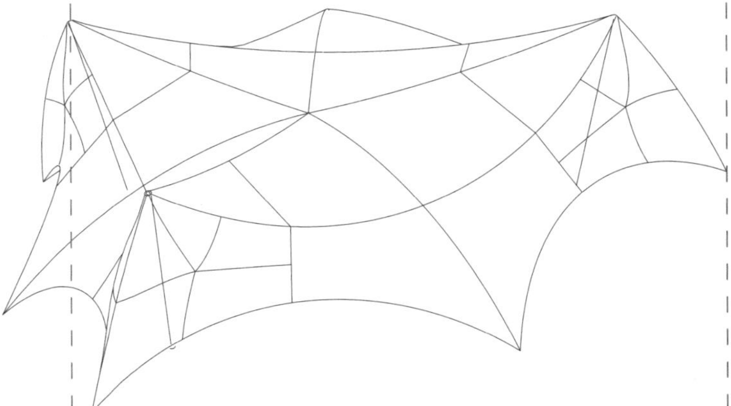

planar

~ continuous

After commissioning Wiel Arets with a masterplan extension as big as itself, the City of Groningen decided to commission Toyo Ito with a super-masterplan aimed at turning both halves into one again. Toyo Ito proposed Bluemoon, an operation where one project in the inner city and another in the future extension will be commissioned to four different architects to trigger virtual links between both extensions to stitch them back together. We were given two sites: one in the Schuitenwerksquartier, an area historically characterised by boat traffic, sluices, docks, and pensions and facilities for the travellers and the merchandises arriving to the city, to be used for residential use. The other lays in the future extension, located in the former location of the power plants that used to feed Groningen with electricity. Next to the railroad tracks, at the entrance to the new area to be developed, the site is to be used for a temporary train station, and a marketplace.

The links were not difficult to identify. Programmatically, our proposal was to create facilities for the travellers, the temporary inhabitants of Groningen, traders, tourists or drifters. Tectonically, we will use the paradigmatic nomadic material: fabrics. For the site in Europapark, the future extension of Groningen, we proposed a kind of large tent printed with a camouflage pattern that mimics the colours of the local vegetation, as an artificial green canopy to cover markets, passengers, events and beer gardens on the edge of the former cooling pool of the power plants.

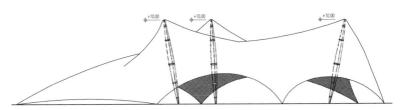

Side view showing structure

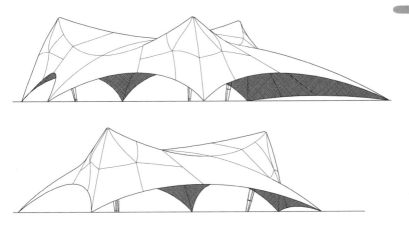

Elevations

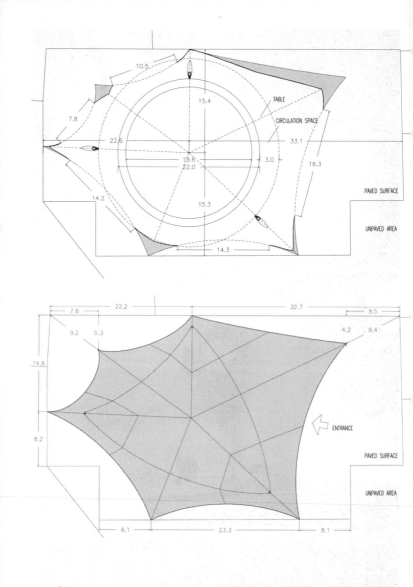

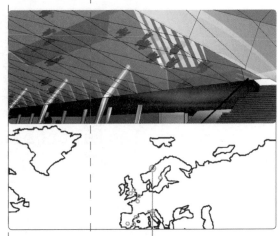

Ferry Terminal & Hotel
Tromsø | 2003

perpendicular

constant

single face

envelope

[ensifacoper_pladis_tromso]

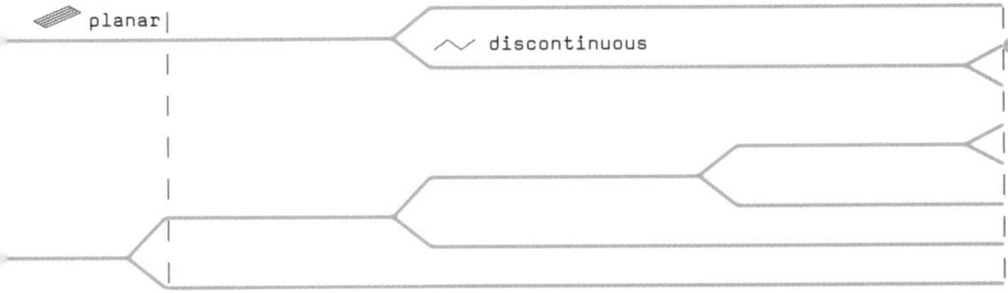

planar

discontinuous

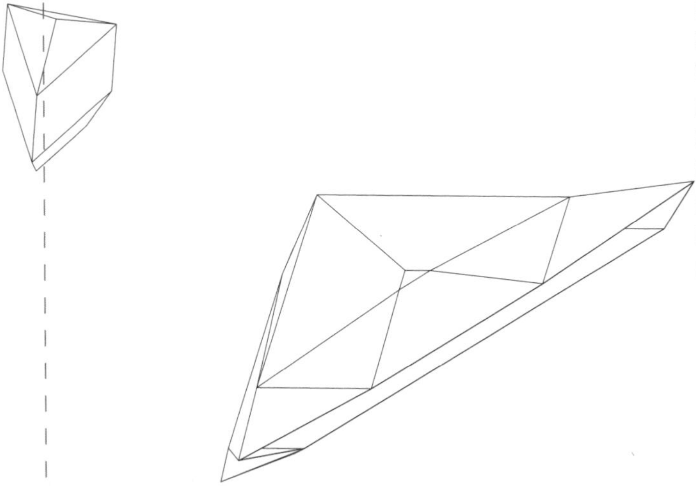

It is just over 100 years ago that Richard With founded the Hurtigruta services as a first scheduled means of travel between Tromsø and the more southerly world below. The location chosen for the newly constructed landing pier was the public church hill, meant to be as close to the heart of the settlement as possible. When the council decided to locate it in the Prost-neset, which it had acquired in 1842 to protect it as open ground of the city, it made a powerful statement on the role a pier or terminal should play within the city: not just as an object, a monumentalised gate, but rather as a program intertwined with public space.

Today, the emerging water walk that has been established at separate points along the city's shoreline is already forming the elements of a sequence of public spaces that open and connect the city to its coast. We propose to fill the remaining parts of the chain to form a continuous band of public places. Rather than just being a walkway, a thin line, we understand the inter-face between land and sea as an expandable, alternating zone. Through squares opening into the urban fabric and structures extending into the sea we propose a row of irregular shaped dia-monds-like crystalline surfaces, arranged as a necklace.

In an attempt to construct a topography that generates a maximum of public surfaces while allowing for a sustainable amount of volume to be built on the waterfront, we have created a topography of extremes. The terminal and conference is con-centrated as a low and extensive mass, well connected to the ground surface level while the hotel that forms the other part of the project will develop as a tower to be located on the North side of Skarven.

The basic geometry of the project consists of two adjoining triangles, one exterior but enclosed, the other warm but trans-parent and exposed. As large containers of space,

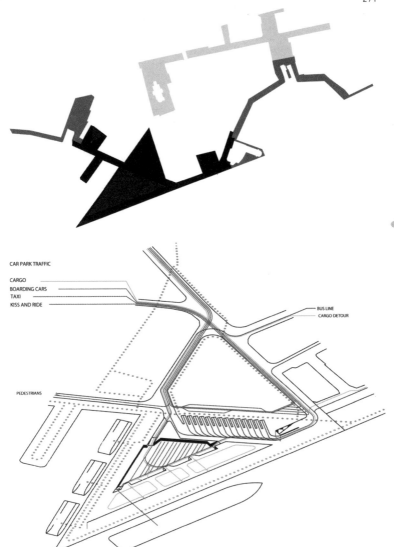

CAR PARK TRAFFIC

CARGO
BOARDING CARS
TAXI
KISS AND RIDE

BUS LINE
CARGO DETOUR

PEDESTRIANS

they minimize the surface to perimeter ratio. Their geometry is based on transformations of rigid orders, like an ice crystal grown under controlled temperatures to achieve a specific crystal pattern. The two triangles are transformed grounds, mediating regularity and irregularity of the public surface and ground condition. Climatically optimized, the terminal structure avoids articulate forms for a concentrated single volume, articulated only locally to solve connections with bridges and a canopy to shelter the drop-off zone.

Its two floors are clearly separated fields of activity, organised each according to their nature: the pier level dedicated to traffic infrastructure, the upper level as urban ground. By dividing the programs according to their respective overlaps and exclusions, the structure creates two transparent fields of complementary uses, each consistently inhabited by flows and events.

The mass of the building is cut and formed very similar to the processes of diamond cutting, in which geometries are derived from strict material orders of optical refraction. The edges fo the enclosure are triangulated to rise towards the sea, differentiating the spatial height and reflection pattern. Each plane of glass is equiped with internal coiling to allow for specific snow melting patterns in winter. Some areas would be completely liberated of snow to create specific views, others switched to produce patterns of covered and uncovered areas. The internal plass could become a warm public snow crystal, magically illuminated through sunlight, filtered through layers of snow. The conference centre would be covered most of the winter and spring months to reduce heat losses and produce a filtered ambient light, while the outer areas would be changing in snow patterns depending on use of the special galleries and their requirements.

Scenario 01
Auroris Borealis
February/October

Scenario 02
Tromsø Internasjonale Filmfestival
14-19 January 2005

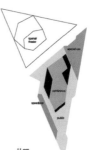

Scenario 03
35th Annual Arctic Workshop
3-5 April 2005

Scenario 04
Tromsø Fashion Week

Scenario 09
Nordnorsk Kunstmuseum

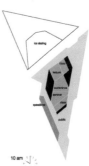

Scenario 08
Norsk Antropologisk Års Konferanse
2003

Scenario 07
Nord Lys Festivalen
23 January 2005

Scenario 08
International PEN Congress
6-12 December 2004

Scenario 10
Tromsø Realfagskonferansen
2003

The basic strategy of flow organisation aims to allow for the highest possible separation of conflicting types of traffic. Lifting all public functions except the speedboat arrival to the upper floor allows the integration of all traffic flows in one compact, sheltered but open space on pier level. Spatially, the terminal functions and the conference centre become the cover of the transport level below. It enables a circulatory diagram of optimum paths, allowing short interconnections between different modes of transport for all types of passengers and the highly efficient handling of cargo.

The massing creates three directions, facing the Hurtigruta, the speedboats and the new Roald Amundsens Plass. The program is oriented accordingly, as three linear spatial entities, two of which climatically enclosed and one open but sheltered. The ground floor program facing the speedboat landings consists of the Offices for the Tromsø Harbour Authority, Storage and Luggage handling spaces for the speedboats and the arrival hall for its passengers. The facade facing the new Plass and the city incorporates the bus terminal and connects the Plass to the upper level of the building. Lastly, the area orientated towards the Hurtigruta incorporates all the supply and cargo requirements. The upper floor is organised around a solid, crystal-like hexagon, which contains all congress facilities and associated services including most elements necessary for the terminal functions. All other programmatic elements are proposed as islands, floating on the vast extent of the continuous floor, giving temporal definition to its use. The fixed crystal of conference facilities is permeable from three sides, allowing the conference space to grow and shrink over time, truly integrating it into the surrounding public surfaces of the floorplate. Flows would

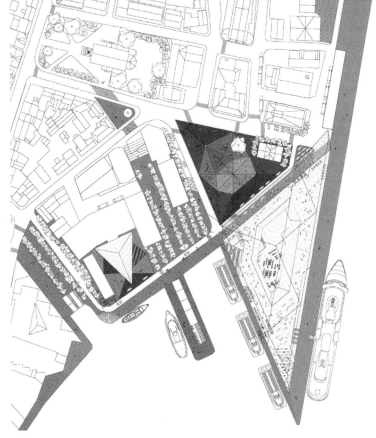

circulate around all sides of the core, sometimes through it, circumnavigating areas temporarily occupied by special functions, exhibitions or events that extend from the core or occupy one of the corners of the building.

Structural Concept and Construction
Similar to the internal organisations of crystals, the formal organisation of the project is based on a strict order and structural grid layout. This provides an economic solution utilising mass fabrication techniques wherever possible while making optimum use of the possiblities of complex computer modelling optimisation. Reinforced concrete is proposed as the principle material from the substructure level to the first
floor level and auditorium walls. The structural concept creates a large "triangular" floor plate at the first floor level. This floor is supported on walls and columns which typically form a 9m x 7.5m grid supported by pile caps and cast-in place 600mm dia piles. Over the car parking zone short "transfer beams" are necessary to allow the required number of spaces, minimise spans and avoid deeper excavation.
In line with the architectural concept the central "auditorium" is considered as a "black box". The six side walls above the first floor are conceived as "structural walls" with penetrations which span as deep beams. This is consistent with the acoustic and thermal isolation that will be required. The auditorium walls are then supported under by a triangular grid of column and walls. The roof structure for the terminal building forms a key part of the overall structural strategy. The surface proposed is partly clad with a "triple" glazed system. The underlying approach is to provide a light-weight column-free unobtrusive structure,

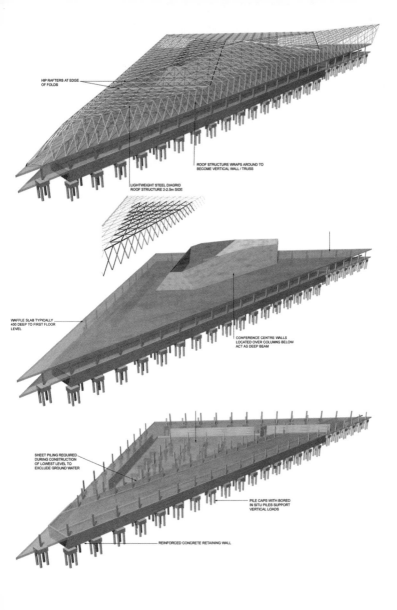

HIP RAFTERS AT EDGE
OF FOLDS

ROOF STRUCTURE WRAPS AROUND TO
BECOME VERTICAL WALL / TRUSS

LIGHTWEIGHT STEEL DIAGRID
ROOF STRUCTURE 2-2.5m SIDE

WAFFLE SLAB TYPICALLY
400 DEEP TO FIRST FLOOR
LEVEL

CONFERENCE CENTRE WALLS
LOCATED OVER COLUMNS BELOW
ACT AS DEEP BEAM

SHEET PILING REQUIRED
DURING CONSTRUCTION
OF LOWEST LEVEL TO
EXCLUDE GROUND WATER

PILE CAPS WITH BORED
IN SITU PILES SUPPORT
VERTICAL LOADS

REINFORCED CONCRETE RETAINING WALL

with maximum pre-fabrication to achieve a high quality.

The geometric constraints result in a "facetted" surface which allows a good drainage and prevents large "snow drift" build-up. The roof surface is supported by the perimeter of the building and in addition internally by the auditorium walls. The structure proposed is a "diagrid folded plate", whereby folds provide stiff "hips" allowing the introduction of line elements of structural rafters. The plate then spans in two directions between the "hips", the "auditorium" and "perimeter structure". By folding the plate vertically on the facade additional stiffness is achieved whilst transferring roof loads in a direct way to the reinforced concrete structures. Where the facade leans significantly additional stiffening will be introduced at the knee joint.

The diagrid is formed of a triangular structural module of approximately 2m length. From the outset the components are intended to provide maximum transparency, be small enough to allow ease of fabrication and erection, achieve a balance of minimum glass thickness and shallow structural depths. Durability, maintenance and cleaning issues are simplified with this approach. At present a closed steel "box" section is proposed for the diagrid, however further investigations would be undertaken to explore the use of purpose made triangular or shaped aluminium extrusions to further reduce maintenance costs. This would be undertaken once the geometry is developed and extent of repetition/variation established.

The building captures the positive climatic forces of daylight whilst minimising solar heat gain and encouraging the movement of air through the site to increase external comfort and shed heat gains.

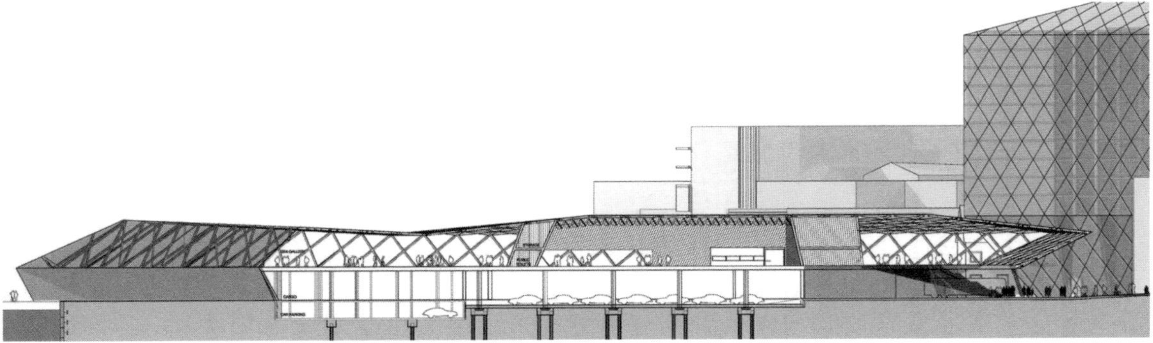

Longitudinal section

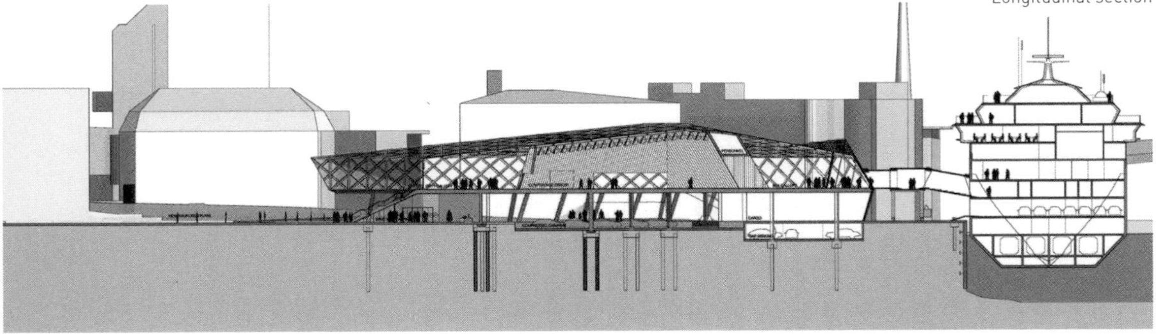

Transverse section

The building has been divided into a number of zones representing the necessary means of climate conditioning needed to maintain a comfort environment. Close condition zones are limited to the conference area which requires more constant environmental conditioning and is equipped with radiant floor heating. Bioclimatic zones will constitute the majority of the public areas and comfort is provided to a microclimate zone which is where people will be in the building.

The bulk of the heat needs are met by passive solar gain and the thermal storage properties of the massive floors. Ventilation rates are determined by fresh air needs and heat and cooling loads to reduce the discomfort from the façade surface temperatures. In summer, external air is tempered by a heat exchanger in the sea to provide cold fresh air to the space, countering solar gains, which are also reduced by the specified glazing. The floor and radiant cooling remove heat gains from the façade to ensure comfort. The air is passed through heat recovery systems on extraction to reduce the energy required to cool the space. The façade controls the interaction between the austere external climate and the internal environment. The ambition is to not only to utilise solar gains in winter whilst reducing them in summer, but also to shift these in time, so that peak solar gains do not coincide with the peak fresh air cooling requirements thereby limiting consequential impact on plant duty.

The strategy is to adopt highly insulated glazing including thermally broken frames, with an airtight fabric construction and controlled ventilation rates which is combined with displacement ventilation and climate control to form a conditioned comfort zone at low level only, obviating the need to heat a large volume.

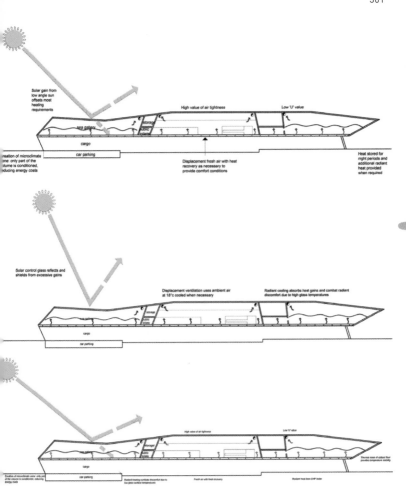

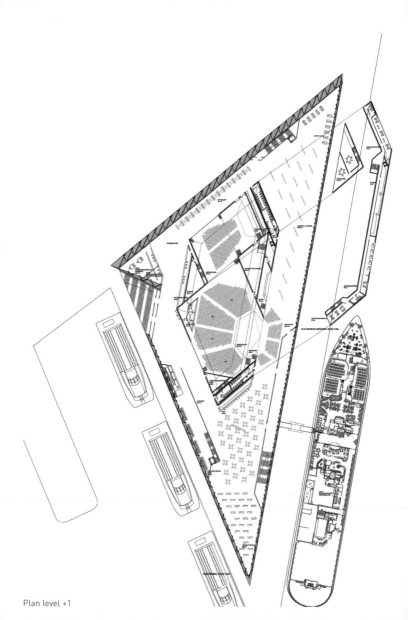

Plan level +1

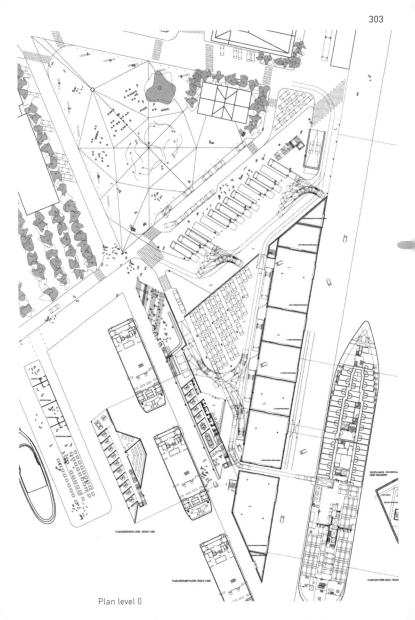

Plan level 0

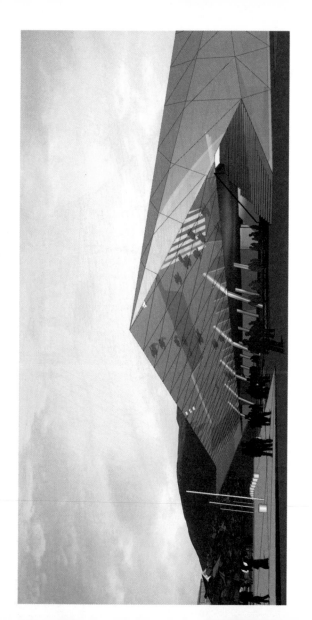

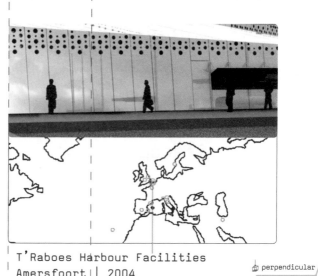

T'Raboes Harbour Facilities
Amersfoort | 2004

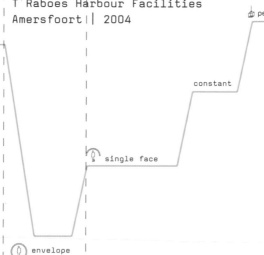

perpendicular

constant

single face

envelope

[ensifacoper_pladis_traboes]

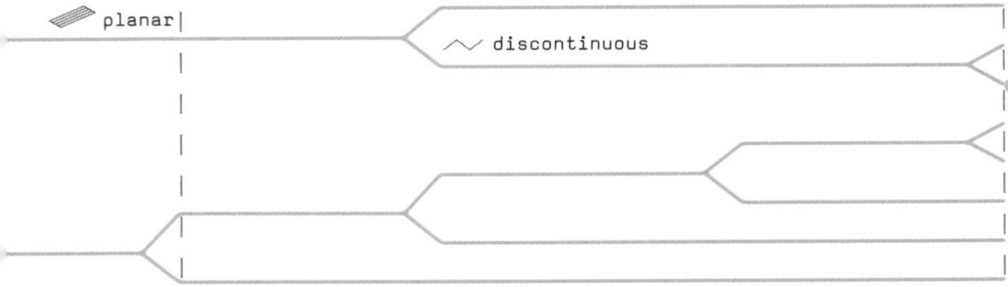

planar

discontinuous

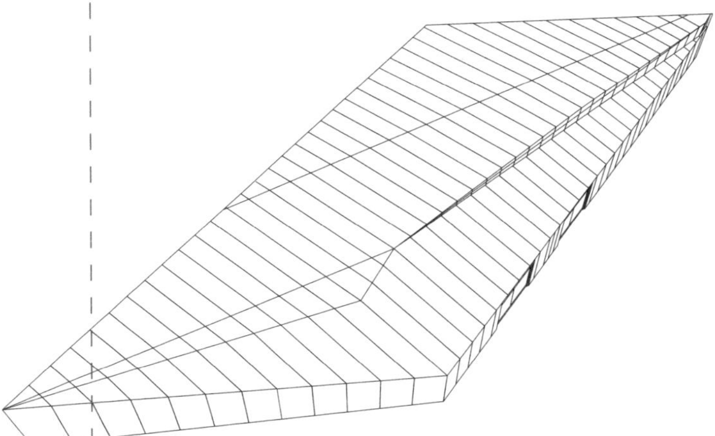

The building is located in Amersfoort, on the border of the water gulf that occupies the center of the Netherlands, in the middle of a beautiful rural landscape, where construction is severely limited. T'Raboes used to be a small harbor for the vessels used for the construction of different fluvial infrastructures in the area. Currently, the harbor has been re-used to host sports and recreative boats, and it is being enlarged from 100 to 200 vessel capacity. The commission included the organisation of the new harbor facilities, and the location and design of a central facility building. The areas around the harbor had to include:
- A hard platform serving for parking of automobiles — the only transport possibility into the site —, boat repair and temporary storage. What we called the industrial platform.
- A green surface for recreational activities and sports.
- A forested surface for resting, strolling, and location of resi-dential units.
The building has been located in between the limit between the hard-surfaced platform and the grass surface. The brief for the project required a large variety of complementary, diverse and unusual programs, including the ability to house cows and boats over the winter and provide kitchen, recreational and service facilities such as meeting rooms, canteen, offices and workshops for the harbor in the summer. All had to be housed in a single, 5m high volume because of the limitations in the plan-ning permission. Our proposal combines these programs into a unified envelope, a monolithic object shaped in its perimeter considering the movement to bring the maximum amount of boats into the storage. Hence the skewed figure of the building in plan. The building acquires a differentiäted roofscape through the demands of the various programs intended to be hosted in

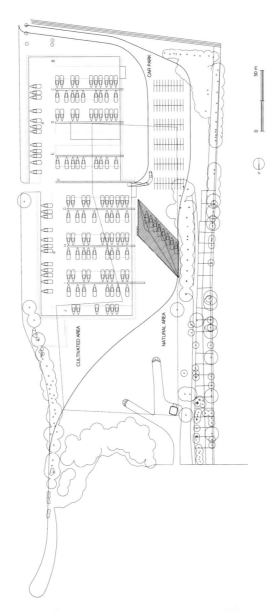

CAR PARK

CULTIVATED AREA

NATURAL AREA

0   50 m

N

the volume, using their requirements as an argument to differ-
entiate the otherwise simple form of the container. The skin
will be made with highly reflective stainless steel panels in order
to diffuse the pristine shape in the reflections of the different
elements in the landscape. In order to do this, the section is
also skewed to produce a reflection of the sky on the waterside
and a reflection of the green surface and trees on the rural side.
The steel plates on the facade will be pierced with differentiated
patterns to allow for a penetrable enclosure keeping views
and the privacy during the summer while providing the ability
for complete closure during the winter months, when use and
inhabitation will be sparse.

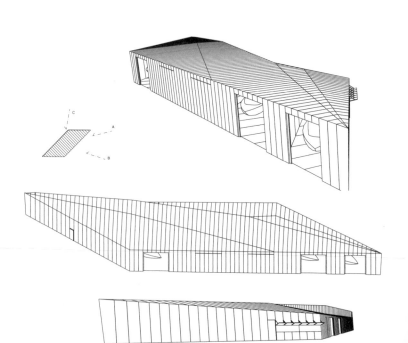

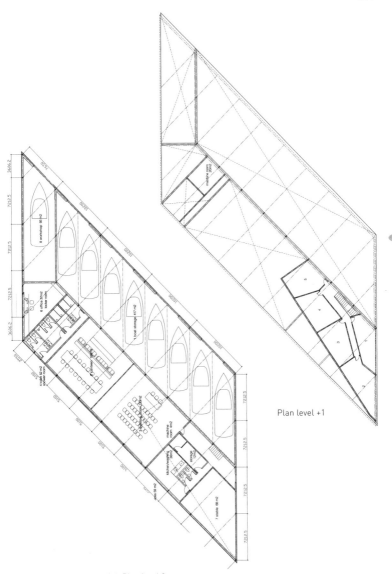

Plan level +1

Plan level 0

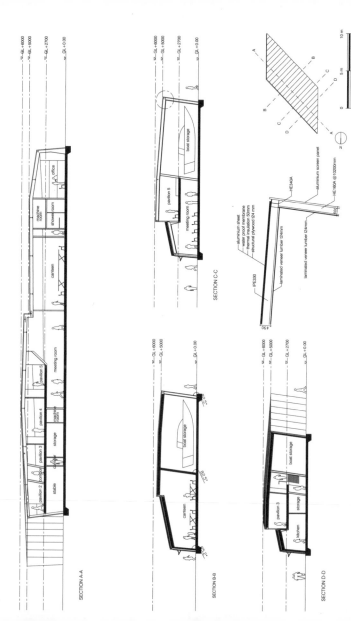

SECTION A-A

SECTION B-B

SECTION C-C

SECTION D-D

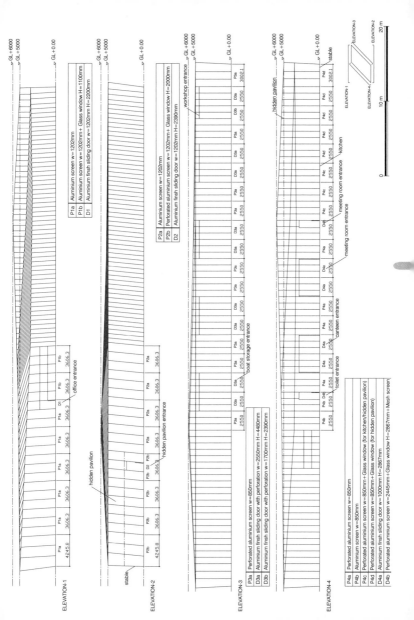

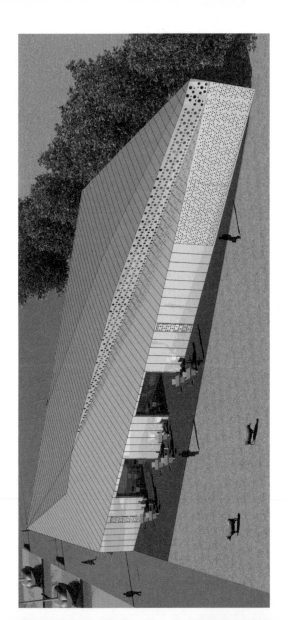

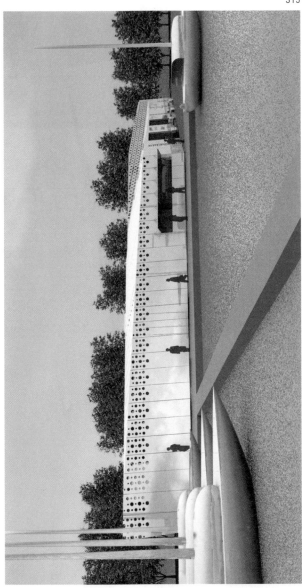

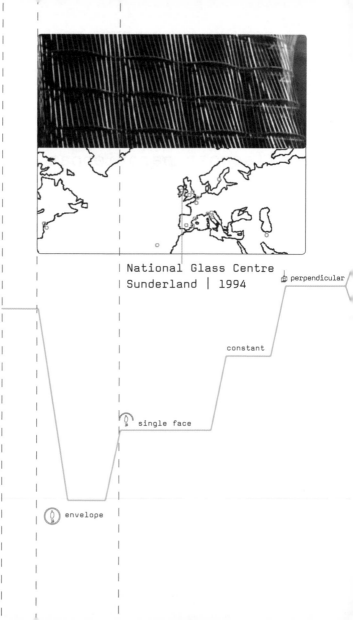

National Glass Centre
Sunderland | 1994

perpendicular

constant

single face

envelope

[ensifacoper_peroricopat_vitrum]

Confronted with a site of low urban density, we decided that the proposed Glass Centre had to provide the simultaneity of activities that the surrounding environment lacks. The building had therefore to concentrate the program instead of spreading it on the site, bringing closer to each other the various activities occuring within the building, making possible the kind of interaction that will be required for the success of a public program on the proposed site.

The brief required a programmatic hybrid condition: a structure to host industrial uses and cultural activities. A factory for the production of glass had to share space with a museum of glass. The brief also suggested that the building may have to undergo programmatic changes and become part of the facilities of the university adjacent to the site. This suggested that the building could not be functionally determined. It would instead have to be conceived as a differentiated topography where the forms of occupation are not determined rigidly, being able to be reconfigured in different fashions. In the proposed building, the leisure and industrial functions would not be assigned through rigid segmentation and yet determine specific domains. The building would become like a drop of glass in semi-fluid state, programmatically and as a topography.

The difference in levels (10.5m) between the road access, either through the roundabout or through the university complex, and the river walk suggested the need for complex topographical articulation. We tried to produce the articulation without turning the existing topografical levels into determinant factors, by using a continuous surface as a device to increase the continuity between the different levels of the site, to de-stratify the structure of the program.

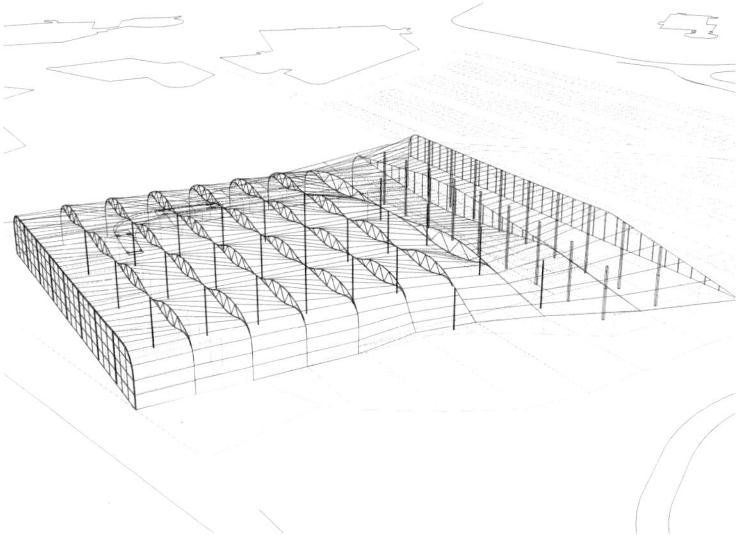

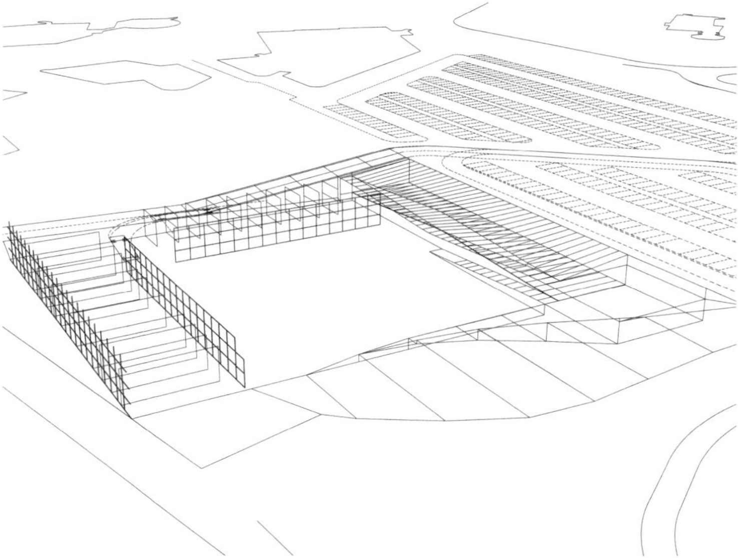

The circulation of the building is arranged as a single route linking the visitors' facilities and the production facilities. The public side of the building is developed as an extension and is continuous with the parking facility. From this area, visitors can enter the reception area, the temporary exhibition and cafeteria. A sloping extension of that same floor will take them through the Harley Woof factory into the 'History of Glass' located below the reception area. After this, visitors might wish to continue down the factory floor to see the demonstration area and the Hot and Cold studio, from where they could exit either through reception, or through the retail area. Access to the industrial facilities is organized in the reverse way, starting on the lower level with the loading bays, and climbing through the museum, as the products become finished.

Following a strategy of blending programmatic and tectonic factors into a consistent structure, we hybridized both tectonic components, the ground and the envelope. A deformed surface, striated in bands orientated in parallel to the site's natural slope and to the north orientation, became the device for the structuring both the access and circulation system, and the enveloping structure and daylight penetration. This continuous surface produces both the enclosure and the topography that articulates the different levels on the site, blurring the segmentation between the different parts of the program. The coupling of the openings in the enveloping surface with the structure that had to sustain the roof bands formed the basis for the tectonic system, blending the roof and the ground into a single system. The skylights in the shed were made by cutting and deforming the surface rather than by piercing it. Orientated to capture the light from the north, the eye-shaped openings were filled with trusses that increased their depth in proportion to the contour of the bend. Structural stresses are handled through the singularities of the surface itself.

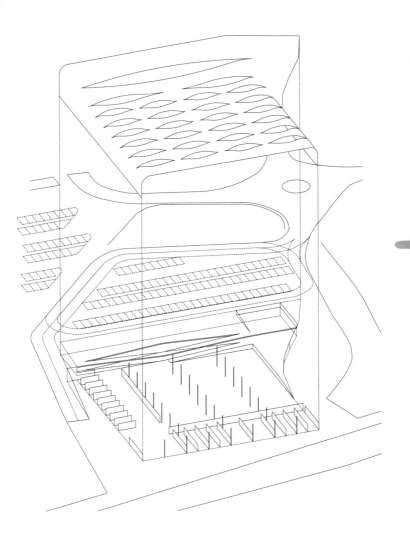

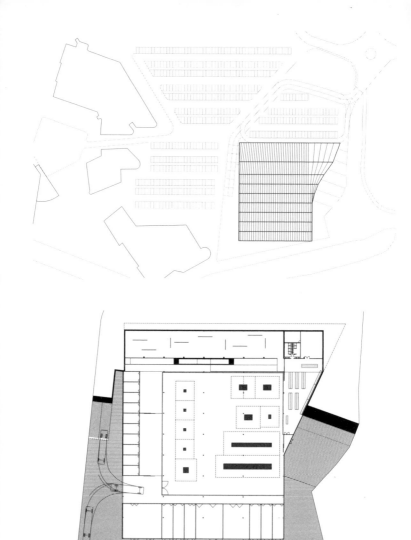

Plan level 0

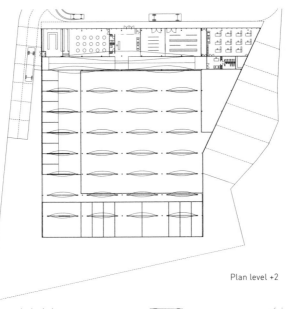

Plan level +2

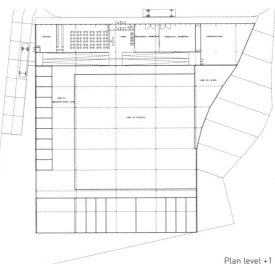

Plan level +1

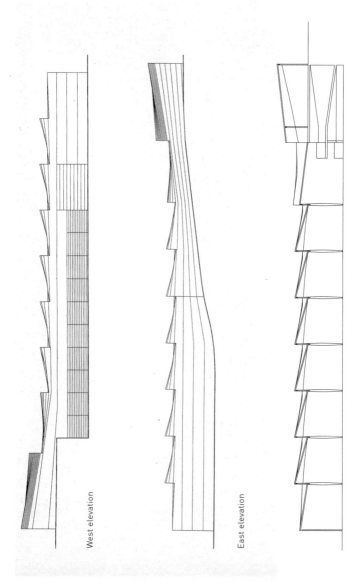

West elevation

East elevation

Longitudinal section

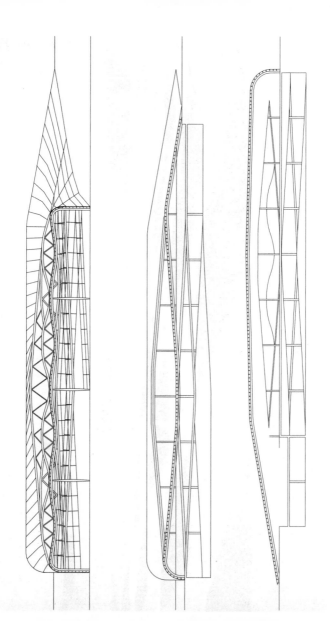

Transverse sections

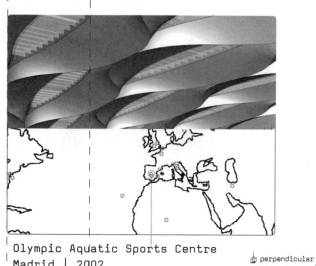

Olympic Aquatic Sports Centre
Madrid | 2002

perpendicular

constant

single face

envelope

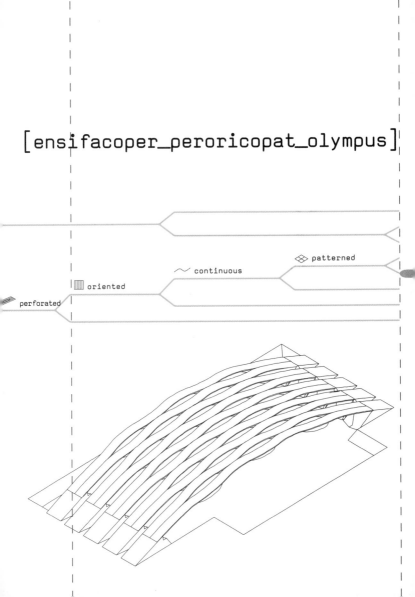

[ensifacoper_peroricopat_olympus]

⬦ patterned

∼ continuous

▦ oriented

perforated

Our proposal is to concentrate the project in a single large physical gesture capable of solving the spatial questions posed by the programme.

Our analysis of the needs programme shows that the fundamental issue of this project lies in the resolution of a sports complex that, under normal conditions, would serve for a range of training and leisure sporting activities and as a venue for a series of sporting events with up to 20,000 spectators, if Madrid were to become the next host city of the Olympic Games.

The architectural gesture that will distinguish the complex – just as the raised stands distinguish "La Peineta" – is a suspended arch 160m in span and 84m wide covering lengthwise the series of pools, leaving space for the stands on either side of the containers, such that, with a system of temporary stands, the seating capacity can be expanded from the 8,000-seat fixed structure to a total of 20,000.

The roof arch is made with ten prefabricated steel ribs – like the number of lanes in an Olympic pool – similar to those used in the construction of the deck of a bridge. The geometry of the surface ribs undulates the length of the section along the plane of the arch, in reference to water, the medium for the chief activities of the complex.

By arranging the string of containers in the east-west direction, perpendicular to the two service axes that delimit the three central buildings of the Olympic Ring, we establish a connection below the public access level, which will notably improve the functioning of the service accesses during peak use periods, providing for fluid and differentiated accesses for the press, athletes and VIPs. There is the possibility of locating a fifth container, for simultaneous training uses, at the east end of the

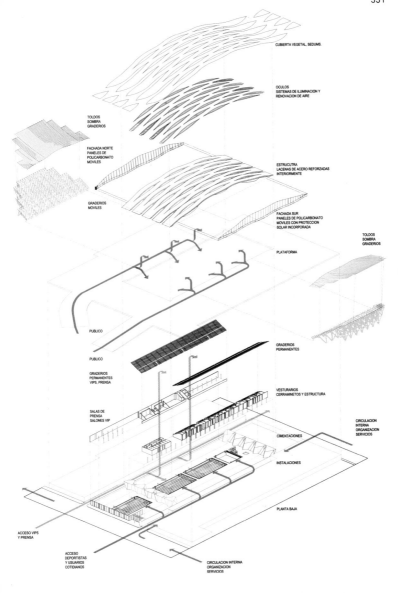

CUBIERTA VEGETAL, SEDUMS.

OCULOS
SISTEMAS DE ILUMINACION Y
RENOVACION DE AIRE

TOLDOS
SOMBRA
GRADERIOS

FACHADA NORTE
PANELES DE
POLICARBONATO
MOVILES

ESTRUCUTRA
LACENAS DE ACERO REFORZADAS
INTERIORMENTE

GRADERIOS
MOVILES

FACHADA SUR
PANELES DE POLICARBONATO
MOVILES CON PROTECCION
SOLAR INCORPORADA

TOLDOS
SOMBRA
GRADERIOS

PLATAFORMA

PUBLICO

PUBLICO

GRADERIOS
PERMANENTES

GRADERIOS
PERMANENTES
VIPS, PRENSA

VESTURARIOS
CERRAMINETOS Y ESTRUCTURA

CIRCULACION
INTERNA
ORGANIZACION
SERVICIOS

SALAS DE
PRENSA
SALONES VIP

CIMENTACIONES

INSTALACIONES

PLANTA BAJA

ACCESO VIPS
Y PRENSA

ACCESO
DEPORTISTAS
Y USUARIOS
COTIDIANOS

CIRCULACION INTERNA
ORGANIZACION
SERVICIOS

complex, but we feel that four containers should be enough to accommodate the Olympic programme.

The users' entrance is from the access way along the length of the West side of the complex, directly to the lower level.

Off the central waiting and control area, to the left, is the changing room area of the training container, which, lit directly from outside, acts as a filter between the "dry" area of the entrance and the "wet" area of the pools. Once inside the wet area of the training container, direct access is provided through the monumental portico formed by the dados of the arch over the main pool hall. The entrance from the control point, changing rooms and the massage and work-out rooms is through the distribution corridor, parallel to the line of the containers, from which the flow to the wet area is distributed. The bay for the changing, massage, work-out and therapy rooms is located on the South side of the line of containers, immediately below the line of stands. To provide light from above, the covering over the stands is to be of translucent glass. On the North side, under the corresponding line of stands, the press, administration and VIP rooms and the other services not related with the direct use of the facilities will be housed. The accesses to the press, guest and VIP boxes will also be from the North side of the containers.

A two-lane road for vehicle traffic, with the VIP entrances and docks for the mobile TV units, will also be on the North side. All the spectator entrances are located at the +665 level. That level is accessed from the drop-off point on the West side of the complex, the metro and the car park located on the West side by means of two access ramps that cross the service road, or else from the commuter train station located at the North gate to the Olympic Ring.

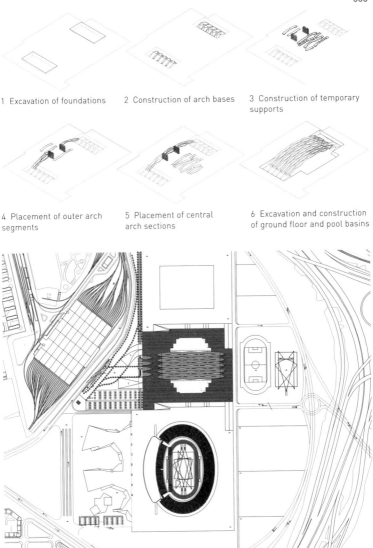

1 Excavation of foundations

2 Construction of arch bases

3 Construction of temporary supports

4 Placement of outer arch segments

5 Placement of central arch sections

6 Excavation and construction of ground floor and pool basins

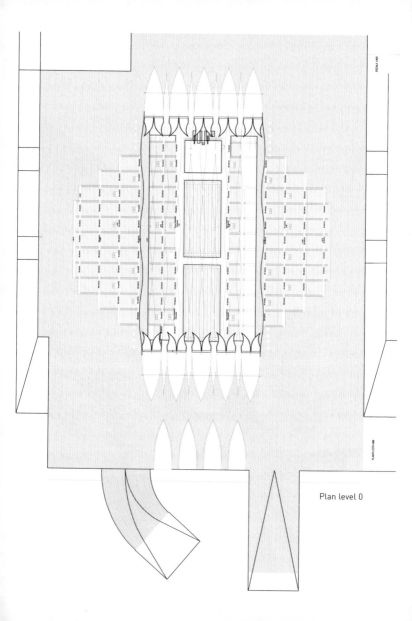

ESCALA 1/400

PLANTA COTA 000

Plan level 0

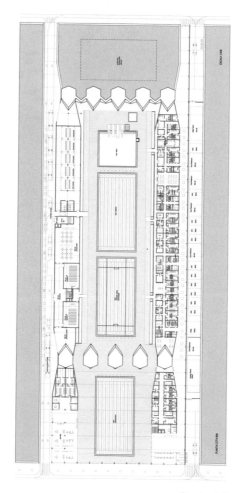

Plan level -1

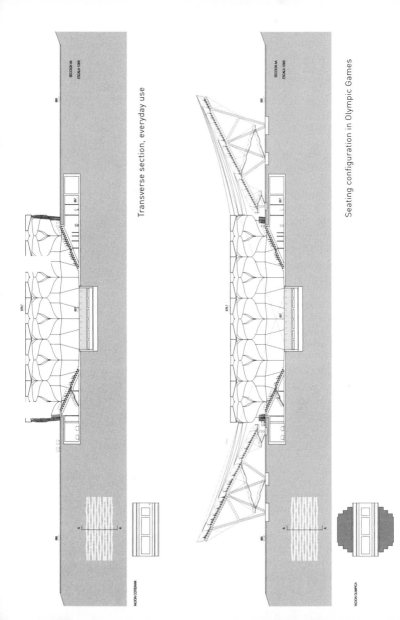

Transverse section, everyday use

Seating configuration in Olympic Games

339

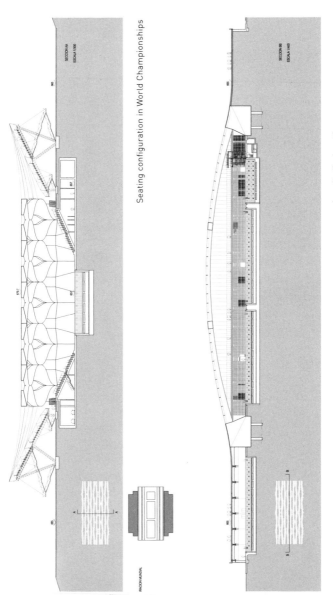

Seating configuration in World Championships

Longitudinal section

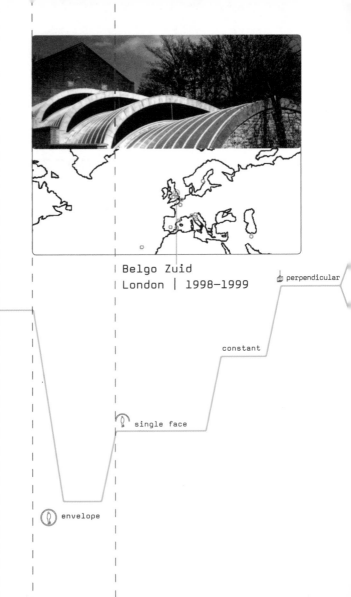

Belgo Zuid
London | 1998–1999

perpendicular

constant

single face

envelope

[ensifacoper_peroriconco]

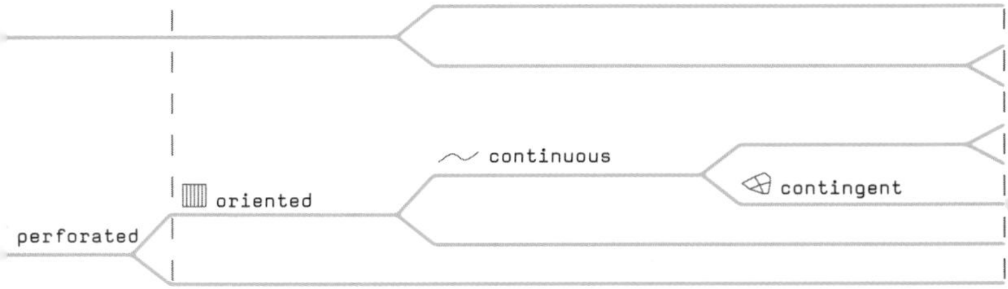

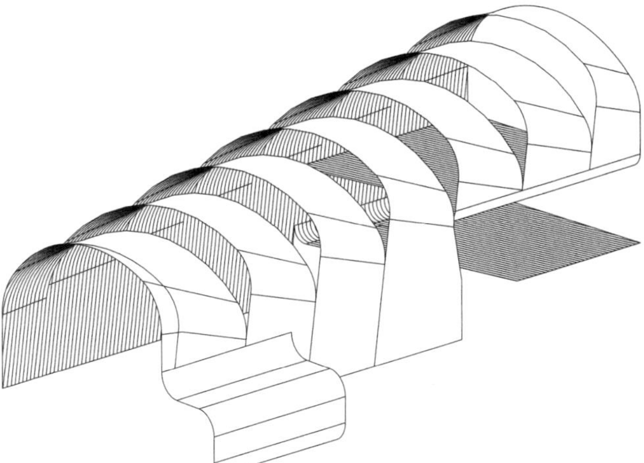

perforated

oriented

~ continuous

contingent

Belgo is an international restaurant chain that serves Belgian food: moules, frites and biere, and exploits the Belgian idiosyncrasies as a theme. Our design strategy was to play with our client's themes, trying to exploit their formal, structural and organisational qualities, beyond their intentionally kitsch origins. Mussel shells, velodromes, stomachs and intestines, bier barrels, medieval vaults, stained glass, Breughel, Bosch, became our form-making devices.

Belgo Zuid is placed in a former dance hall/small theater in Notting Hill Gate in London. Due to the poor condition of the existing building, a large part of it had to be demolished and replaced by a structure that would match the requirement of its new use. The walls and the roof of the main dining hall were rebuilt as structures both structural and enclosing. Their geometry is complex, due to the views of neighbours over the roof and the distribution of skylights, and exploits the theme of the shell and its material continuity. The wall and the roof of these surfaces have become a single element clad in stainless steel on the outside, and wrapped with oak planks on the inside. The surface presents three cuts that open the main space to daylight. Both the geometry of the space and its superficial texture is designed to maximise the deflection of gravity. On the north face of the main space, we have maintained the opening of the old proscenium, to expose the kitchen operation, and a bar that is placed above the kitchen. The kitchen is finished in stainless steel, and lit with red neon, while the bar has a sky-blue lighting, forming a medieval diptych representing hell and heaven, as in Bosch. The façade of the building is three meters wide and four stories high and is occupied by a 12m- high rotating sign placed above the entrance. The entrance opens to a 3m-wide and 20m-long corridor, clad in beer bottles, that in turn opens to the main dining hall.

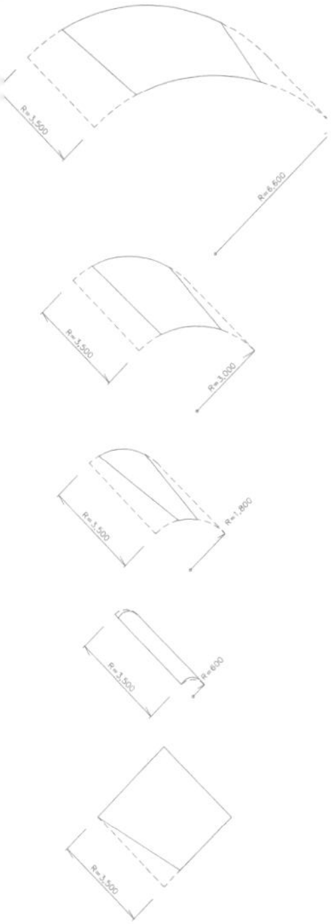
R=3,500
R=6,500
R=3,500
R=3,000
R=3,500
R=1,800
R=3,500
R=600
R=3,500

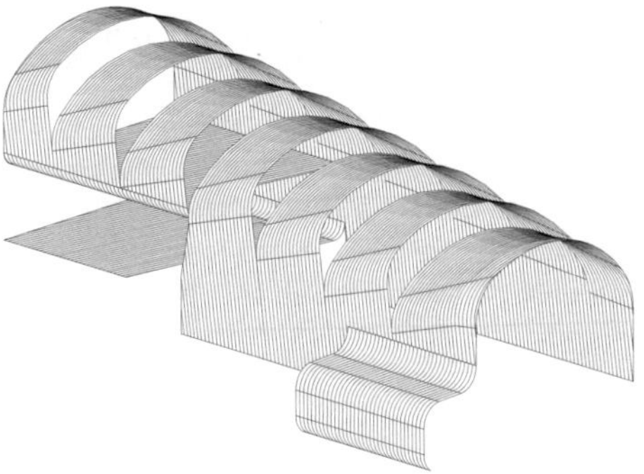

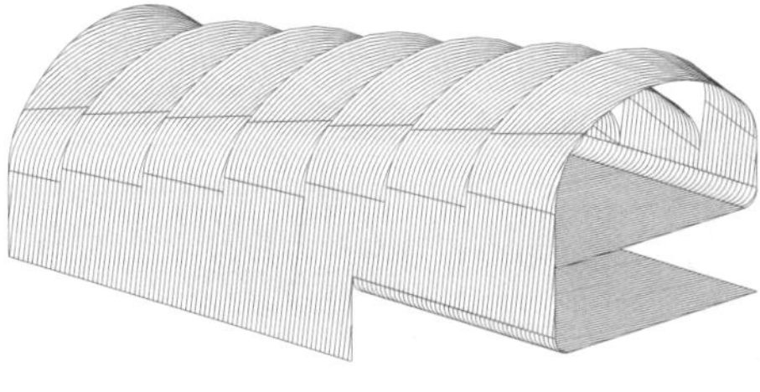

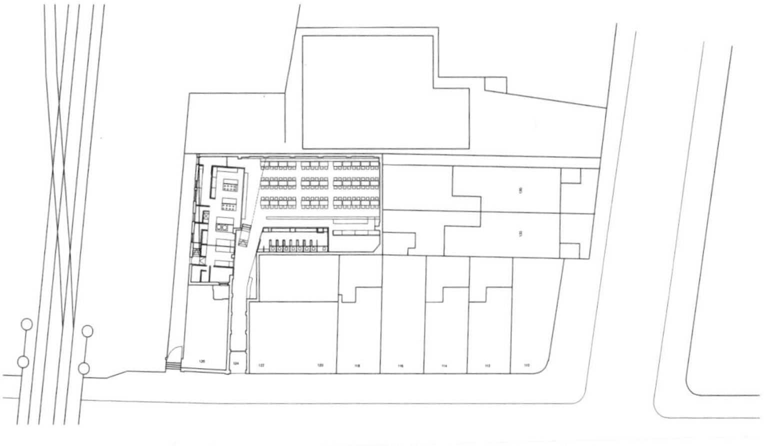

Transverse section through access

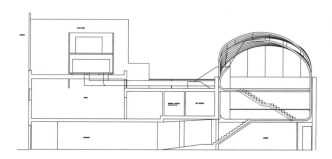

Plan level 0

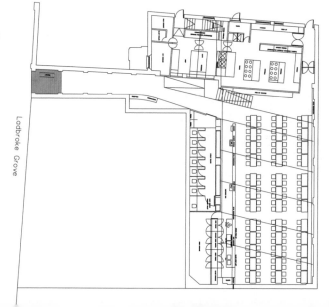

Ladbroke Grove

Plan level +2

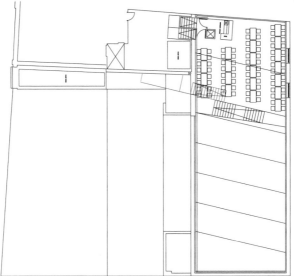

Plan level +1

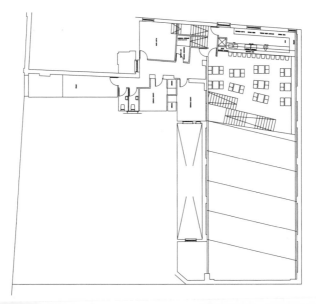

Longitudinal section

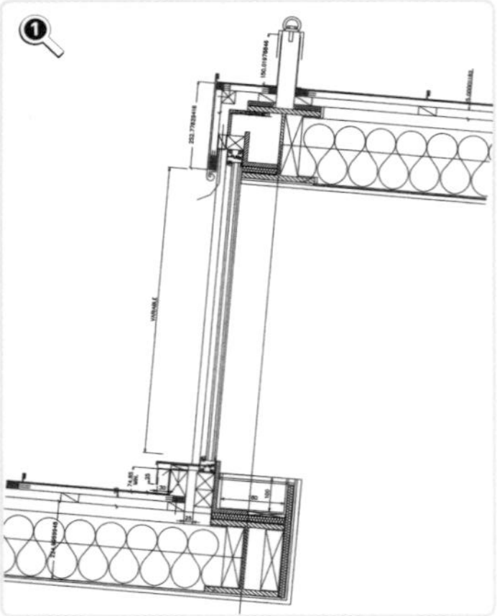

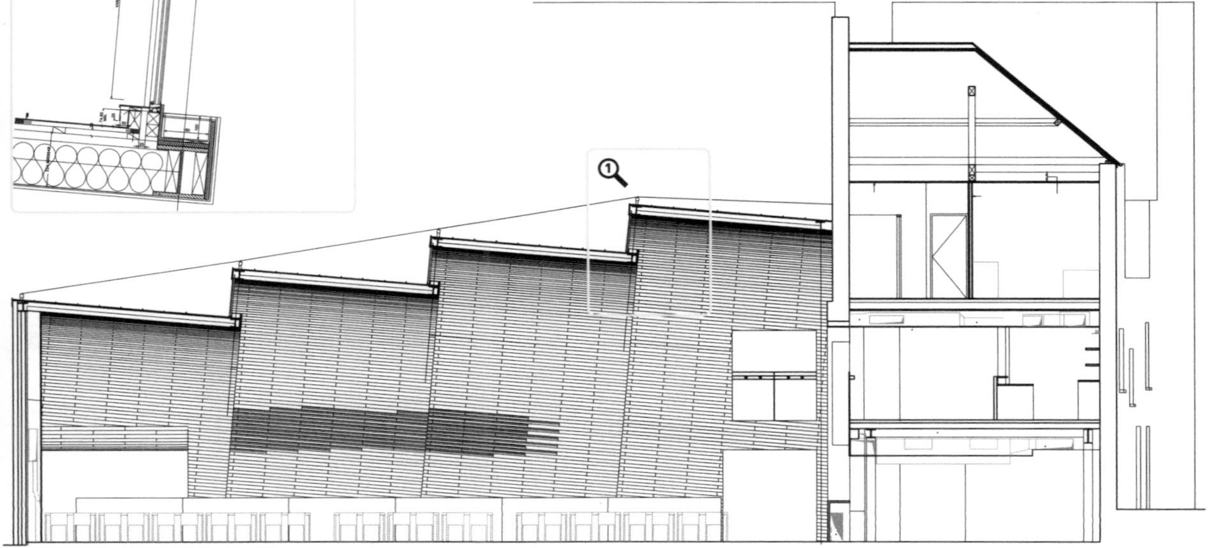

Transverse section through
main dining hall

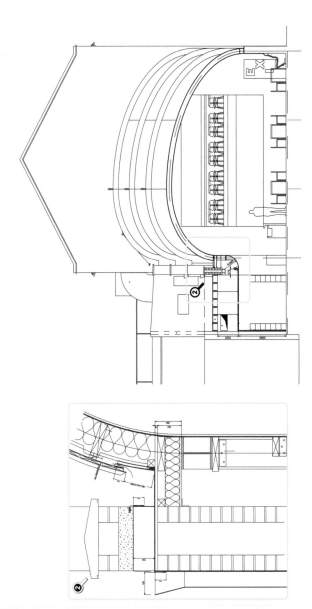

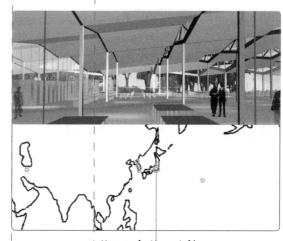

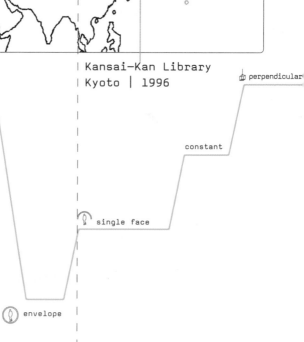

Kansai-Kan Library
Kyoto | 1996

perpendicular

constant

single face

envelope

[ensifacoper_perordis]

oriented

discontinuous

erforated

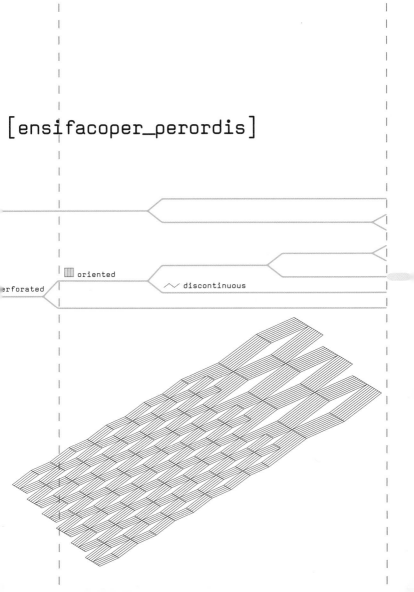

The National Diet Library is the only Japanese library that collects books and other library materials and also offers library services to the executive and judicial branches of the National Government as well as to the general public. Its basic function is to preserve the library materials of Japan on a permanent basis. Due to current developments in information technology, the importance of the library as a primarily local, urban and institutional facility is diminishing: today, the library is becoming a centre for information-processing, a 'site' that is entered from remote locations, and that does not pertain to any local community. The library as a global infrastructure, rather than as a local public institution, is the main rationale behind the project. The location of the building seems to already address this change in the typology, in which the public 'significance' of the building is abandoned in favour of an instrumentalization that does not address the critical mass of a metropolitan community, but rather the vast and abstract population of the whole country, or even the whole world. And so, our approach has been to design the library as if it were a factory or a bridge, by trying to pragmatically solve the technical problems, rather than by focusing on the problems of image and signification traditionally associated with this type.

The project is organised by placing the entire public area of the program on the ground floor. The position of the underground archive was judged to be optimal, in order to preserve it from climatic change and potential earthquake damage. All other programs were located around the archive 'box' in order to provide a climatic and structural buffer. The ground surface was formed by the top of the box structure of the archive, mostly sunken underground, as if the new ground were formed by the pilling-

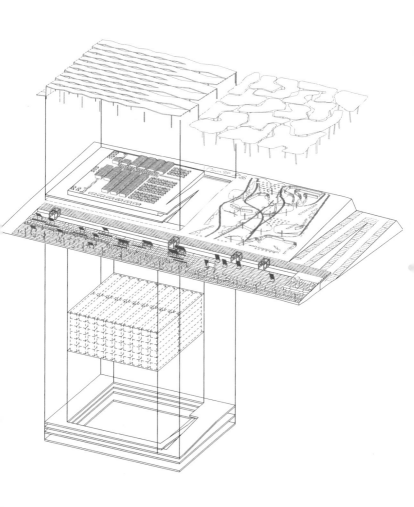

up of the archives in four layers. The envelope of these public areas is a canopy extending the foliage of the pre-existing forest. The canopy was designed as a folded membrane with openings towards the north light, and extending the reading rooms and public accessed areas towards the forest.

The structure of the single-layer program was produced as a combination of two fields, formed as gradients close to the two access roads. The resulting gradated field was mirrored by the pattern of cuts on the roof membrane, and in order to produce differentiated lighting conditions on the ground plane. We took the orthogonal structure of the book-stacking system as a given determinant in the organisation of the building. To minimise the perimeter-to-surface ratio of the building the limits of the space were determined as a square, the most efficient form for preserving a highly controlled environment and minimising delivery time of books given the use of a mechanical archive system.

East-west elevations

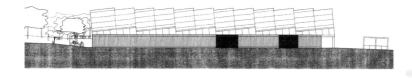

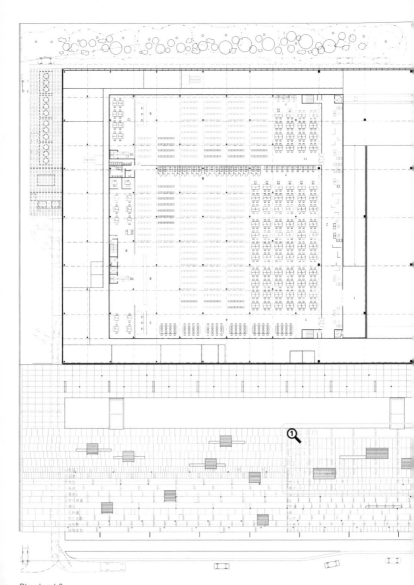

Plan level 0

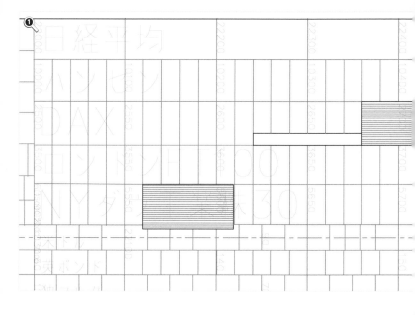

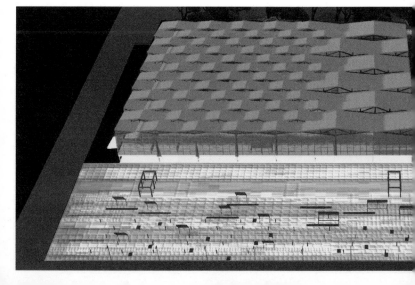

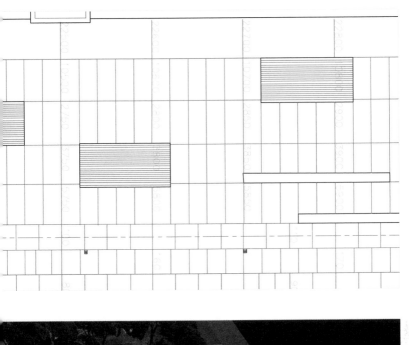

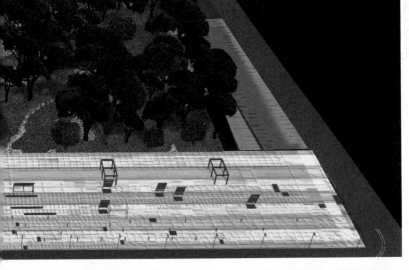

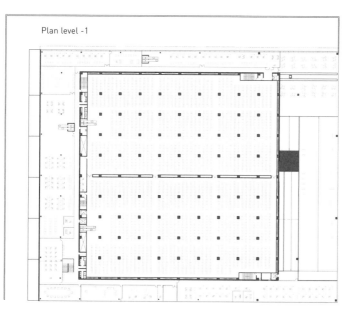

Plan level -1

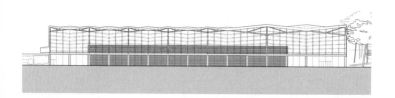

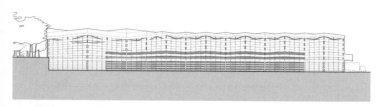

North-south elevations

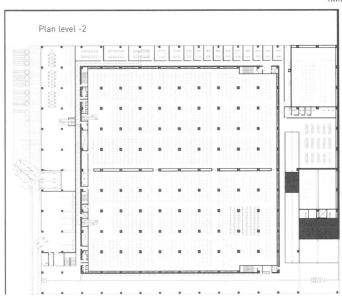

Plan level -2

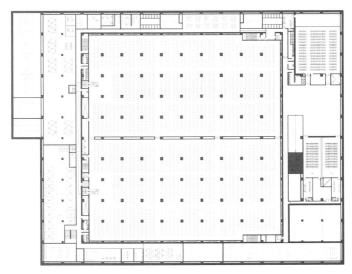

Plan level -3

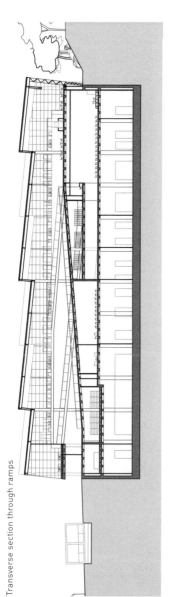

Transverse section through ramps

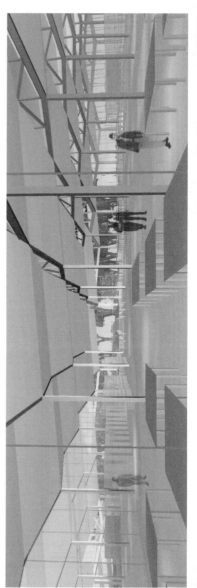

Longitudinal section through archive

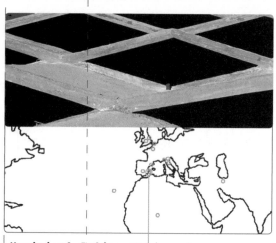

Municipal Police Headquarters
La Vila Joiosa | 2000–2003

perpendicular

constant

single face

envelope

[ensifacoper_pernonor]

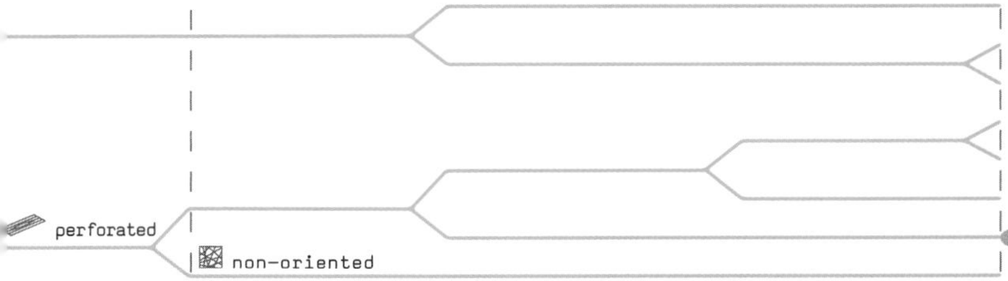

perforated

non-oriented

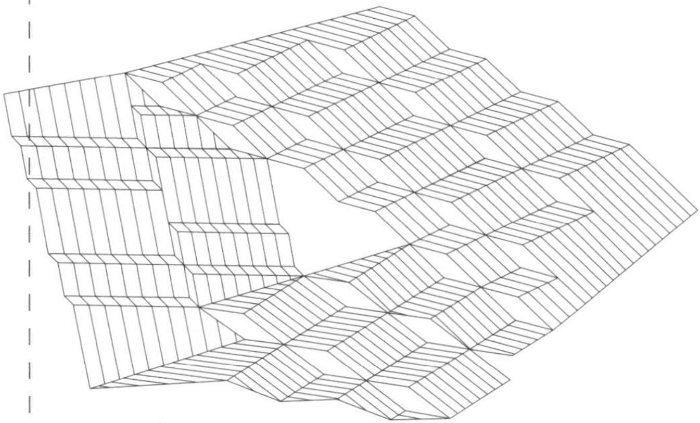

La Vila Joiosa is the one remaining undeveloped spot on the Costa Blanca between Benidorm and Alicante on the Spanish White Coast. As the town braces for the imminent invasion of tour-operators and developers, the local authorities have devised a series of planning operations and projects to upgrade the local infrastructure to cope with the emerging needs and control of the developments.

This project aims at the design of a strategic site to the future development, a triangle limiting with the railroad tracks, the main highway access to the town, and the areas for future growth of the urban centre, where a new train stop has to be located, next to the new Municipal Police Headquarters.

The building obtains its form – an irregular pentagon – from the alignment with the neighbouring streets and views. The centralised plan tries to keep the building as compact and internal as possible, aiming to minimise the blockage between the city and the northern development: a core of stability in the vortex of circulation. With a background dominated by a large mountain and the remnants of the local farmland, we have tried to keep the mass as low as possible, as if it was another wall in the rural landscape. The plan is organised in three bays around a secret courtyard that brings light into a detention center in the basement level. One band is dedicated to public interface, with an auditorium, a library and a testifying office. The second is dedicated to the administration and direction of the complex. The third is dedicated to the officers quarters and the different brigades. In the basement there is also a parking for the police vehicles, a shooting gallery for training and an archive area.

The mass is clad with a concrete plate that folds to enclose the facilities, and produces a series of skylights for the different rooms. The exteriors walls are pierced by series of holes that vary in density to produce lattices for the windows.

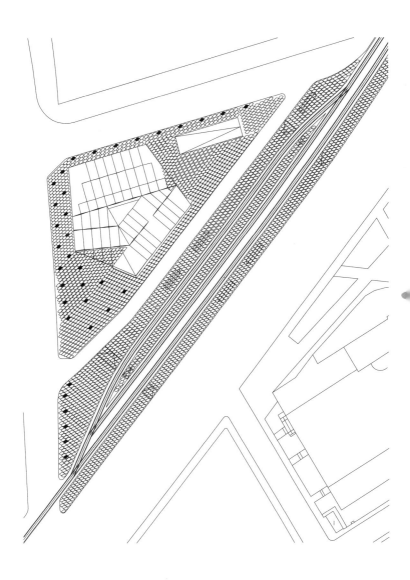

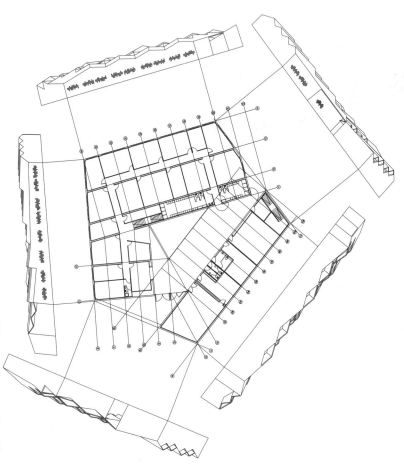

Elevations

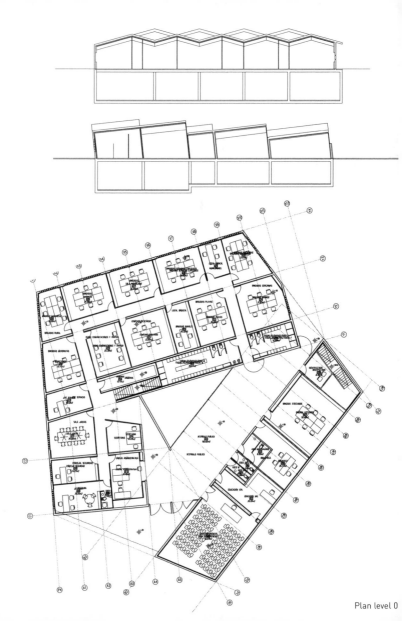

Plan level 0

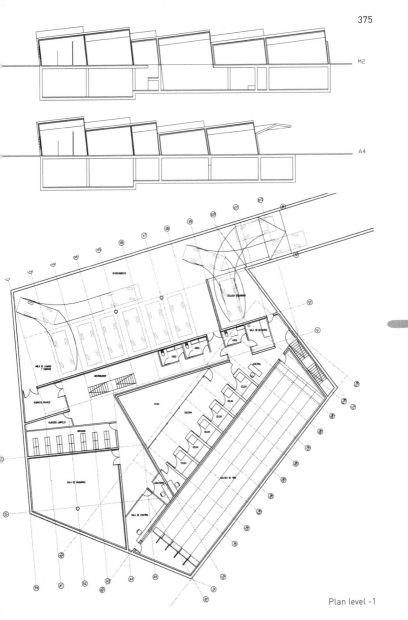

M2

A4

Plan level -1

Towards a Non-Standard Mode of Production
Patrick Beaucé, Bernard Cache

Under what conditions can a term like "non-standard architecture" have meaning? Perhaps it's easier to begin by answering in a negative way. If, indeed, a non-standard architecture consists of generating more or less soft surfaces which will then be called a building by transferring them onto a battery of production software in order to create very expensive kinds of sculpture which no longer have any relationship with the historical and social sedimentation that makes up a city, then we are only perpetuating the Romantic myth of the artist-architect.

Over and above any polemical intention, this negative exordium must serve us for making a list of a series of criteria to which we would wish to try and positively respond, so as not to allow what is really in play within the possibility of a non-standard architecture at the present time escape us. It is a question of form, city and productivity.

Let's begin by form, since why deny it? this is where the "fascination" lies. And sure enough an extraordinary feeling of power consumes any architect to whom the modelers of CAO[1] give the means to generate surfaces that he or she generally cannot design with a ruler and compasses. In that respect we may consider three sorts of shape. The feeling of all-powerfulness may come in the first instance from such highly ergonomic modelers as Rhino, which provides the means to readily design surfaces sufficiently complex for us to no longer be certain, even, of their spatial coherence. The man in the street still has no idea of this, but delineating the control points

[1] Conception Assistée par Ordinateur (Computer-Assisted Design).

of a Nurbs surface in order to generate a fluid surface is now within the range of any user after an apprenticeship of just half an hour, and that's how it should be. That on the other hand it may then be a question of controlling these surfaces, of modifying them by intervening on their coordinates, of giving them a thickness and of fabricating them, that's a whole new ballgame: namely, to shift the problems onto someone else while multiplying the budget. Whence the adage, repeated time and again by lucid architects like Alejandro Zaera Polo: nothing gets built that isn't transposable onto Autocad.

The second sort of shape: the use of complex generators such as simulators of particle movements that we find on imagery software programs like Maya, Softimage and others. Software programs that are not criticizable in themselves, but which were never intended for fabricating concrete objects, and which therefore hardly concern themselves with assuring, for example, that the four corners of a flat board are coplanar. In the first instance, the fascination grows out of the simplicity of an extremely transparent interface; in the second this feeling comes, on the contrary, from the fact of us having available motors so complex that we no longer control the generation drive, and that the result gets to us as if covered with a mantle of innocence, so to speak: that of randomness or of accident. In the event, this chaos is entirely determinist, but as we don't understand the algorithmic determinants the forms are stamped with a sort of aura conferred by their alleged aleatoriness.

Lastly, there's a third and finally much more honest instance which consists of dispensing with the computer black box and simply twisting sheets of paper, like a time-honored sculpture sketch, a process that has the advantage of creating developable surfaces, namely of nil curvature, which boils

down to saying that these surface are intrinsically Euclidian.[2]
The paper model will then have to be digitalized in order
to transfer it onto a software program that regularizes its
surfaces, before turning over the files to virtuoso outfits in
architectural prêt à porter like Permasteelisa[3].
In its three strategies the "non-standard" amounts to saying
"original" or "complex", but in all these instances we remain
stuck in a Fine-Arts state of mind which seeks to turn the
architectural project into a work of individual creation.
And from this point of view non-standard architecture is
inscribed within a tradition of the unicum cutting across all
sorts of output: artisanal, artistic, industrial or digital.
The alternative viewpoint is the series: the object as a
particular instance on a continuum. Yet even here things need
to be clarified. Because today we know, through the magic of
the workings of morphing, that anything can be transformed
into something else. In seeking to avoid Charybdis and
the unicum, we quickly fall into the Scylla of transformations
lacking proper consistency that guarantee an artificial
continuity between forms that are unrelated to each other.
Morphè, indeed. What is a shape? What must two objects
have in common for one to be able to say that they have
the same shape? The answer lies in a basic concept
of architectural theory, but also in the modern axiomatics
of geometry as formulated by Hilbert in Grundlage der
Geometrie.[4] Two objects have the same shape when,
independently of their size, their elements form between them

[2] On all surfaces developable on a plane, the sum of the angles of a triangle remains
constant and equals 180°.
[3] An Italian company, the market leader in facade facings for oddly shaped buildings
of great size.
[4] David Hilbert: Fondements de la géométrie (1899); see the chapter devoted to the
theory of proportions.

the same angles, and above all abide by the same proportions. The word is slipshod the preoccupation with shape is nourished by a theory of proportions that it is essential to understand if we want
to avoid the dangers which have all too often beset the course of architectural thinking from neo-Pythagorean acoustics to the Modulor of Le Corbusier. In fact the philosophy that poses the problem most clearly, and this in relation to architecture, is Plato's The Sophist.
What's involved here? Plato is preoccupied with these people, the Sophists, who profess all things and their contrary, and who give lessons in overturning all arguments in order to defend theses that are totally opposed to them. In short, the Sophists are image-makers who practise morphing by means of rhetoric. As is his wont, Socrates dialogues and arrives at an examination of two major positions. On the one hand, it isn't difficult to reject the notion of Heraclitus, for whom everything is in movement. Because if everything was change, and change alone, how could we even give a name to the things we speak of? The possibility of the logos presupposes that the invariant exists. On the other hand, however, the position of Parmenides seems hardly more tenable, for he wants Being to be One and that only the One is. This second thesis is all the more difficult to sustain if we keep to Parmenides's famous dichotomy, according to which "one must be absolutely or not be at all." For, then, how do we address the Sophist's discourses, discourses that at once "are" and yet are "false"? In The Sophist Plato comes to recognize that we live in a world which is an intertwining of being and non-being. The Greek word is extremely precise: sumplokè means "intertwining" in contexts that extend from the intermingling of bodies in lovemaking or combat to the combinations of letters in the forming of words.

A world of images and simulacra is involved. The visible world is a copy of Ideas, which are the only entities that escape immanence and corruption. But all these copies are worthless since they don't necessarily have the same relationship to their model. There again, Plato is very precise and refers to the visual arts and to architecture. On the one hand we have good copies that respect the proportions of the model, and on the other we have simulacra: shadows and reflections which do not do justice to proportion. In Latin proportion was called "ratio" and in Greek, "logos". We are at the very foundation of rationality and of discourse. For Plato every physical thing is manifestly corrupted by the future. So much so that no physical model can equal the Idea. The perfect relationship in Plato is the one which will convert identity into an ideal proportion: the isometric relationship of sameness, the ratio of 1:1.

There it is, we have everything necessary for constructing a philosophy of the image that was certainly not foreseeable in Plato's time, but which nevertheless creates the technical specifications of it. Ideas, those abstract events, are so many invariants that escape corruption. In the first rank we find identity, the relationship of sameness which enables the thing to be superposed upon the image, or rest upon movement. The same goes for those perfect forms the circle or the sphere, which remain identical to themselves in the movement of rotation around their center. In rotating invariants the same measurements are preserved. And next we have those somewhat degraded copies that reproduce the model while altering its dimensions. These copies remain good, however, to the degree in which the painter, sculptor or architect has respected the correct proportions of the model. These artists will have produced a number of "similitudes" which preserve both angles and proportions. The ratio is invariant through homothety (similarity), this being the leitmotif of Greek philosophy after Thales. The shadow of the pyramid varies according to the hour, day and season, but the relationship of the pyramid to its shadow remains identical to the relationship between the gnomon planted in the ground and its own shadow these relationships are variable invariants, intertwinings of being and non-being. Plato also keeps back his criticisms for attacking those sculptors who alter the proportions of statues placed on temple acroteria in order to correct their optical deformations. And sure enough the apparent angle of the different superposed parts changes very quickly when statues are seen from below, in perspective. We enter, here, into the realm of optical corrections adopted by Vitruvius and repeatedly relayed since then by different writers of treatises on architecture. But let's be ultra careful here. Plato doesn't question the raison d'être of these deformations. In that respect he adopts an attitude very different to that of a Perrault, who as a good Cartesian will categorically reject the idea that our senses may be deceived. A circle will always be perceived as a circle, even though its apparent profile is an ellipse when seen sideways on. The devil take those people who, like Caramuel de Lobkowitz, intend to deform the real section of the columns on Saint Peter's Square so as to take account of their perspectival deformation. Cartesian rationalism remains wholly within this rejection of the hypothesis of the evil genius. Here, there is total incompatibility between Descartes and Desargues, both of who wrote their fundamental texts in 1638. And in point of fact we would have to take the time to look closely at whether there wasn't just as wide a gap between the two great projectivists, Desargues et Pascal, the latter totally commanding the thought of the former, but in a sense that leads to a mystique of the infinite,[5] unlike a Desargues, who treats the vanishing point as an ordinary point.

This "hic et nunc" of French rationalist philosophy between 1638 and 1640 is not dependent on any Zeitgeist: we are in the presence of highly divergent lines at the core of so-called "classical" thinking.

But let us return to Plato, who himself recognizes the validity of optical corrections. He doesn't deny artists their reasons for minimizing the importance of the model what he objects to is the result. A statue placed atop a column has to be distorted, yet this copy with altered proportions is the very prototype of the simulacra discredited by Plato. This is because, in comparison with the mathematics of his time, Plato lacks the means to cogitate Ideas that, due to projective deformation, remain invariants. In order to see something other than corruption in this, it would have been necessary for Plato to have projective invariants available to him, and in particular the relationship of relationships, that second-degree logos Spanish mathematicians rightly call razón doble, which expresses the number of that which is conserved in projective deformations. We observe, as well, how the discourse of science proceeds. The primitive invariant is the relationship of identity, an isometric relationship of sameness. Next we come to that second variable invariant which articulates Greek rationality and of which we do not take our leave until 1638, at least as far as its translation to geometrical space goes: the homothetic relationship. Desargues makes his entrance here, followed

---

[5] To us it seems important to note that the theorem of the mystical hexagon was invented long before Pascal was connected with Port-Royal. There would thus have been a mystical process of Pascal's own that had nothing to do with his relations with his sister and her entering the convent. Was Guarini, who rejected the secular implications of Arguesian geometry, aware of this?

closely by Pascal, the two of them creating the first geometrical projective invariants, alignment and intersection, prior to the invention of the numerical bi-relationship. Following Desargues only a dozen years or so will be necessary before Euler produces, in 1736, the first topological invariants, which are preserved through surface deformations of any kind, insofar as their continuity is respected. Euler's famous formula, which established the invariability of the sum of the number of vertices and faces reduced by the number of edges for any polyhedron, constitutes the first topological invariant, based on which an area of investigation opened up which is far from being exhausted, since, for example, the theory of invariants characterizing knots remains a very active subject of research within contemporary mathematics. But it is in 1872 that it will be given to Félix Klein,[6] better known for his bottle, to grasp this movement of geometric reason, which progresses by inventing increasingly sophisticated invariants enabling us to manipulate ever greater variations.

What relationship can this very brief historical survey of geometry have with the opportunities to be sure, right now, of creating a genuine non-standard architecture? What relationship can it have with both architecture and the non-standard? We will evoke an altogether classical definition of architecture: to order the diversity of space in such a way as to guarantee maximum freedom for the collectivity that frequents or colonizes it. Arranging means providing a diversity that is not naturally livable in with an invariant. Absolute space is an exterior that is scarcely more inhabitable than the hyper-grid of a totalitarian architecture. We are seeking devices that

[6] Félix Klein was to expound his general conceptions of geometry in the following texts: Ueber die so-genannt Nicht Euklidisch Geometrie (1871); Au sujet des géométries dites non-euclidiennes: Programme d'Erlangen (1872).

guarantee the invariants necessary to the supplest possible varieties. It is here that we are concerned by a non-standard architecture, to which we think that digital technologies might permit a threshold to be crossed, without the notion being completely new in itself. Because, in fact, if we set aside the extreme forms that architectures with isometric invariants (like Newton's cenotaph or the totalitarian spaces of a Hilberseimer) have constituted, architectural thinking has always turned, for preference, towards proportional invariants. To the point that a Le Corbusier still goes back to proportion when attempting to elaborate a universal system of industrial standardization. That he then invokes an harmonic, neo-Pythagorean conception invented all of a pice by 19th-century German ideologists,[7] does not detract in the least from the pertinence of the concept of proportion in architecture; on the contrary, this modern error proves just how difficult it is to imagine architecture without proportion. Also, when the theorists of the Italian Renaissance attempt to interpret the perspective system invented by Brunelleschi in 1420, it is to the system of proportions that they will repeatedly have recourse, striving in vain to reduce the projective coordinates by establishing simple ratios between the diminishing segments of a paved area seen in perspective, even though this is a canonic case of projective bi-relation.

The fact is that architecture was never to understand projective ratios except in a highly ambiguous way. Even though project-ive geometry was prepared and finally invented by architects: a filiation that extends over two hundred years, from Brunelleschi to Desargues, and including Philibert De L'Orme, which is prolonged at least as far as Monge, and whose first area of application was the military fortifications at the École Mézières.

[7] Le Nombre d'or, anatomie d'un mythe.

Even though architects are the ones who worked out the projective coordinates, the stereotomic works integrating this geometry in the production of architecture itself always remained secondary: at the very most the magnificent vaults in the Hôtel de Ville in Arles,[8] but more often than not simple additions such as the pendentives of Philibert De L'Orme. And the place of topological invariants, strap-work and the like, is presented under a still more problematic light: the knot[9] or foliated scroll[10] performing the role of a basic ornamental motif, a register from which, prior to very contemporary designs, these topological forms hardly ever deviate, aside from a few specific applications such as the extraordinary staircase schemes Philibert De L'Orme created for the Château des Tuileries.[11] This formal analysis needs, of course, to be refined, but the more we consider the history of architecture from the CFAO angle,[12] the more it seems to us that tradition has always incorporated, albeit in very different dosages, these four types of invariant: isometric, homothetic, projective and topological. What happens today is that we have the means at our disposal which allow the implicit system of hierarchy between these different registers to be repeatedly called into question, to the future profit of more sophisticated invariants, both projective and topological. Yet we don't believe in a merely topological architecture an aleatory, fluid, moving or virtual, not to mention non-Euclidian one, or whatever any more than we once did in an isometric architecture that was central, orthogonal and panoptic. We are on the lookout, much more, for a just and

[8] Probably built by Hardouin-Mansart around 1640.
[9] Gottfried Semper, Der Stil, 1861.
[10] Alois Riegl, Stilfragen (1893); French translation: Questions de style, Hazan, 1992.
[11] See the reconstruction drawing in Philippe Potié, Philibert De L'Orme, Figures du projet.
[12] Conception et Fabrication Assistée par Ordinateur (Computer-Assisted Conception and Fabrication).

ordinary environment that incorporates the different registers of invariants, since in order to grant even more space to the grid/chaos alternation in the suburbs the media consensus is increasingly in favor of spatial ruptures in certain privileged locations. Generally speaking, and apart from a situation in which certain invariants are formulated by the actual context of the building, architecture will order the diversity of space that much better when it brings each of the four invariants into play by deterritorializing their traditional register of application: the isometry of central planes, the homothetism of a proportional architectonics, the projectivity of complex solids, and the topology of intertwining ornaments. This reinterpretation of traditional registers takes in a rereading of historical urban typologies. An architecture based on variable invariants allows us to return, in effect, to typology in a way other than the neo-Platonist mode[13] of the identically or proportionally reproducible model.[14] The city thus becomes a field for the varying of historical invariants.

In point of fact, relationships in the city being determined, at least in part, by the relations of production, what is to be done in order for a non-standard architecture to become a social fact different from the latest form of distinction of a clientele which has the means to augment standard budgets? How do we prevent the non-standard from collapsing into original formalism? How do we see to it that the object is genuinely conceived and produced as a single instance in a series?

[13] At the level of problems, Platonist philosophy seems much more open than most of the interpretations given of it by epigones.
[14] See the series of illustrations at the end of this text in which a regular hexagon, archetype of the central plan, is varied so as to progressively transform it into a figure certain Californian architects would not disown, while preserving the projective invariants of the theories of Brianchon and Pascal: a convergence of diagonals, an alignment of the intersections of opposite sides.

How do we integrate the architectural object in the urban fabric? To all these questions there is, in our opinion, one basic response: the productivity of agencies of various architectures, of conception keeping track of fabrication. From this point of view, the question of non-standard architecture is no different from the basic problem of postindustrial societies, namely the productivity of services in general.[15] The architect is a worker whose mode of production is conditioned by digital technologies, but the development of these has nothing natural about it. In that respect the writing of software programs is at once the major genre of contemporary culture[16] and at the same time the privileged terrain of a confrontation of the forces which organize production in our societies. In this field it is a strategic concept that will determine the form standard architecture will take in the years ahead: this is the concept of associativeness. What are we to understand by associativeness? Associativeness is the software method of constituting the architectural project in a long sequence of relationships from the first conceptual hypotheses to the driving of the machines that prefabricate the components that will be assembled on site. Designing on an associative software program comes down to transforming the geometrical design in a programming language interface. Thus, to create a point at the intersection of two lines no longer consists of creating a graphic element, but in establishing a

[15] Paul Krugmann, L'Àge des rendements décroissants, Economica, and La Mondialisation n'est pas coupable; vertus et limites du libre échange, La Découverte. Moreconjunctionally, one may refer to the article by Patrick Artus, under the heading of "Economiques des Rebonds" in Libération, 31 March 2003, called "Des finances pour la croissance de l'Europe".

[16] We can only render homage here to the developers of the MisslerCompany, who go on developing theTopSolid software program on which the Objectile application is based. We wish to thank Christian Arber and Jean-Luc Rolland, along with their whole team of collaborators, foremost among whom we have to mention Jean-Louis Jammot and Charles Claeys.

relationship of intersection on the basis of two relationships of alignment. Here, the reader will recall that this involves two basic projective invariants, as well as two primitive gestures in space: aiming and intercepting. The whole interest of associative CFAO software programs lies in translating this geometrical relationship into a program which will see to it that the point of intersection is recalculated as it should be when we displace the end points of the segments of the lines we intersect. Of course, only an elementary link is involved here and all this only has architectural interest provided we are able to set up long sequences of subordinates on the basis of a small number of primitive elements called, in technical jargon, "original parents". The first consequence of associativeness is the need to rationally formalize the architectural project, taking great pains to distinguish antecedents and dependents, at the risk, if not, of creating circular references or all kinds of other logical incongruities. Associativeness constitutes, then, a filter obliging us to rationally think through the architectural project and to explicate its hypotheses. Ultimately, this ought to encourage clear thinking in both the procedures and concepts of architecture. We might also be surprised that this concept has awakened so little interest among those who once flaunted themselves as the champions of rational architecture. What we have just described concerns the activities of conceiving the project alone. Now, the whole difficulty of non-standard architecture lies in the sheer quantity of data that has to be generated and manipulated in order to industrially fabricate components that are totally different to each other at a price that is not necessarily higher than if they were standardized. In order to efficiently manage these data flows and to guarantee full and entire associativeness between conception and fabrication, it is essential above all else to work on the same nucleus, or control program, which will enable us, among other things, to ensure size control of the components following the conception stage, and this up to and including the generating of the programs (code ISO) that will drive the digital machines ensuring the production of the objects. On these grounds the technical specifications of a CFAO associative system includes at least four basic elements. The first has to do with the need to handle vast groups of complex elements, all of them different, elements that it is no longer possible to design one by one. This causes us to have recourse to a process known in technical terms as the "insertion of components". The designing of a project using an insertion of components obliges us to first think up a "model" of relation that can be applied in all the situations in which we will have to create a component of this type. The model is, as it were, an invariant that must cope with all the variations to which the terms we have established relations between will be submitted. That Platonism bears the seed of all the technological developments of our Western societies is an assertion that for us is no longer the object of theoretical speculation, but instead the result of empirical verification. And we have indeed experienced situations in which the implementation of this logic of components in a non-standard project has been able to generate gains in productivity of a factor of 100! Furthermore, it is only on the express understanding of gains in productivity of this order of grandeur that the term "non-standard architecture" has meaning.

Another aspect of the technical specifications is the need to work in distended flows and in a state of provisional information up until the very last moment, and this in a delocalized way. It was Moholy-Nagy who said in the 1920s that the criterion of modernity of a work was of its being able to be transmitted by telephone. This is even truer today. The multiplicity and dispersion of interlocutors, the volatility of decisions, oblige us to begin formalizing the project on the basis of uncertain information. Some values that are capable of being easily corrected must be able to be given by default, some points must be able to be defined in a geometric location without receiving a definitive positioning on this location, manufacturing programs must be able to be brought up to date the evening before their execution. Prior to taking shape as constructed buildings, non-standard architecture proceeds from an abstract architecture that orders the flow of data necessary for digital production, and this in a much more automated way since there is no longer an intermediary between conceiver and machine. The modification of one of the original parents of the project has to automatically set in motion the updating of the entire sequence of information because human intervention is always subject to error.

As it is, a truly non-standard architecture will only emerge on condition that it reproduces in the realm of construction what has already occurred in the realm of edition. Just as it is possible today to write and lay out graphic documents that can be put on line on Internet by their conceiver and be printed on demand by a distant reader, so non-standard architecture presupposes that the conceiver of a building is capable of producing all the documents necessary for the distant production of architectural components without the a posteriori intervention of any office of control or office of business studies filtering out the errors from them.

Lastly, in order for all this not to remain at the utopian stage, this automated sequence of data must include the documents that serve as backup to the economic transactions necessary to the production of the structure: specifications, estimate,

production and delivery orders, assembly plans, etc.
To be sure, all these technical specifications turn associativeness into a mechanism that is at once very powerful and very complex. CFAO software programs are only beginning to implement computerized architecture in such spheres as mechanics. But there's nothing to suggest that this full and entire associativeness may never see the light of day, except in very compartmentalized and exceedingly limited industrial applications. Many factors of a social, legal and cultural kind are involved, which may be summed up in a single formula: in order for associativeness not to become mere technological prowess and for it to be inscribed within economic reality, it is necessary for conception and production to be strongly integrated. Indeed, what point is there in developing highly sophisticated software tools if we don't encounter users and architects, in particular who are ready to understand the functioning of these? The ability and rigor necessary to using such software programs means that they are by nature aimed at well-informed users endowed with a certain level of logical and geometrical reasoning. What use is it, too, to develop an associativeness between conception and fabrication if in practice order-placers and producers do not manage to establish relationships that enable them to make the most of the continuity of the flow of information? As long as each of the two parties doesn't encounter the arrangement that makes it advantageous to collaborate and not to artificially break this chain and blame the other party, associativeness will be a mere software producer's marketing ploy, or worse still, a strategic error of development. More than ever, architecture will benefit from the opportunities offered by the non-standard only on condition that it progressively and patiently constructs a genuine culture of digital production.

In 1810 the mathematician Brianchon invented a theorem which is deduced from Pascal's theorem through a simple permutation of the terms of its wording (for example, by replacing the word "point" by the word "line" and vice versa). In the classic case, Brianchon's theorem seems a commonplace, almost, since it states that the diagonals of a regular polygon intersect at the center of the circle inscribed; a typical case of a Renaissance central plane. The interesting thing is that this property remains constant whatever the polygon inscribed in a conic of any kind may be, whether a convex polygon inscribed in an ellipse (image 2) or an intersecting polygon, again in an ellipse (image 3). This property gives way, then, to a much greater variety than classical architecture. On the other hand, this property is not transposable as such when the conic inscribed degenerates into a pair of lines.

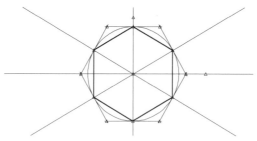

1. A classic presentation of Brianchon's theorem (Pascal is non-representable, then).

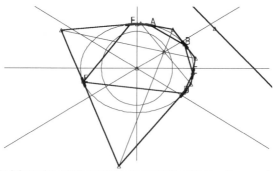

2. A slight deformation, which permits a representation of the two theorems to be made.

Pascal's theorem, a dual of Brianchon's theorem, finds itself in a converse situation as to its representability in classical and degenerate extreme cases. Pascal stated that the pairs of opposite sides of all polygons inscribed in any conic intersect at three collinear points; a dual property which appears clearly on image 2 and which remains constant in the case of an intersecting polygon such as the one in image 3. In Pascal the conic may even degenerate into a pair of lines, and we then obtain the time-honored theorem of Pappus (image 4). On the other hand, Pascal's theorem is no longer representable in the event of the conic being transformed into a simple circle (image 1): the line then extends into infinity. It should be said that this theorem was articulated in 1639, long before Pascal had dealings with Port-Royal.

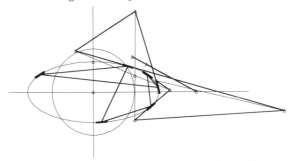

3. A strong deformation, which alters the two theorems beyond recognition.

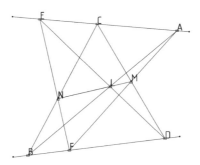

4. A degeneration that supports Pascal's theorem alone: we then obtain Pappus' theorem.

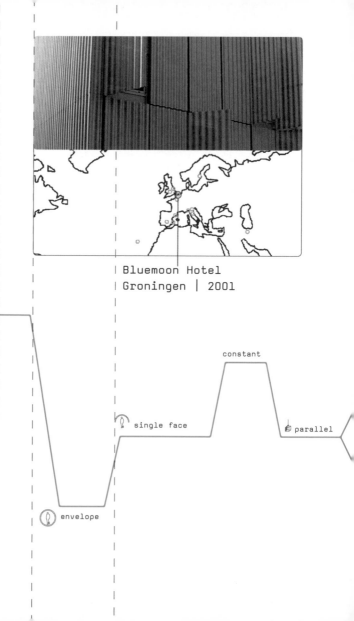

Bluemoon Hotel
Groningen | 2001

constant

single face

parallel

envelope

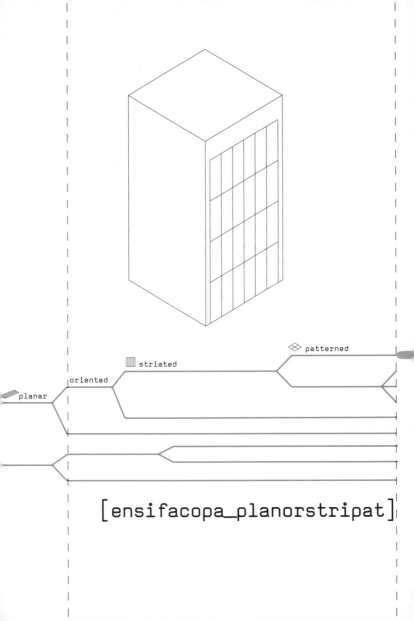

planar

oriented

striated

patterned

[ensifacopa_planorstripat]

After commissioning Wiel Arets with a masterplan extension as big as itself, the City of Groningen decided to commission Toyo Ito with a super-masterplan aimed at turning both halves into one again. Toyo Ito proposed Bluemoon, an operation where one project in the inner city and another in the future extension will be commissioned to four different architects to trigger virtual links between both extensions to stitch them back together.

The first site is in the Schuitenwerksquartier, an area historically characterised by boat traffic, sluices, docks, and pensions and facilities for the travellers and the merchandises arriving to the city, to be used for residential use. Programmatically, our proposal was to create facilities for the travellers, the temporary inhabitants of Groningen, traders, tourists or drifters. Tectonically, we will use the quality of the paradigmatic nomadic material: fabric.

The skin of the inner city site project was treated homogeneously in the use of the cladding, with a resulting facade almost like a steel cloth wrapping the volume of the building.

This site, a 5x5m, four story tower by regulation, became an aparthotel with two open plan suites, clad in corrugated steel panels that in the front facade are perforated. The front facade allowing its relation with the outside through the perforation of the steel panel, has the possibility of finding further relations with the outside by mean of a opening system that can range from total enclosure to total openness and all other configurations operated by the dweller.

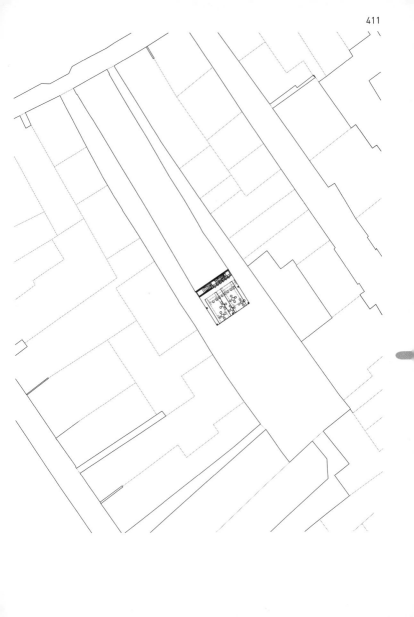

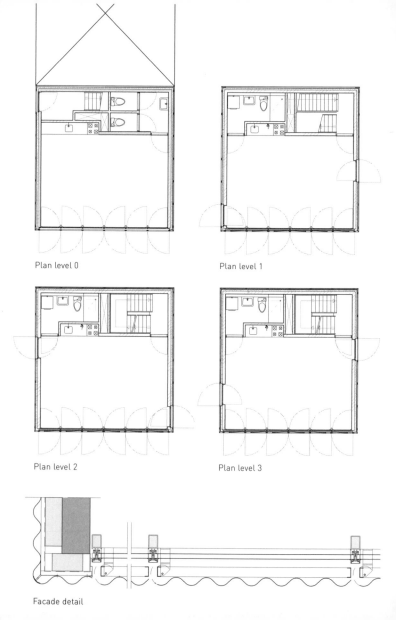

Plan level 0

Plan level 1

Plan level 2

Plan level 3

Facade detail

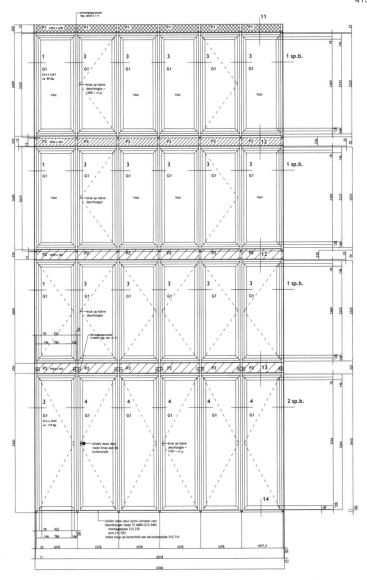

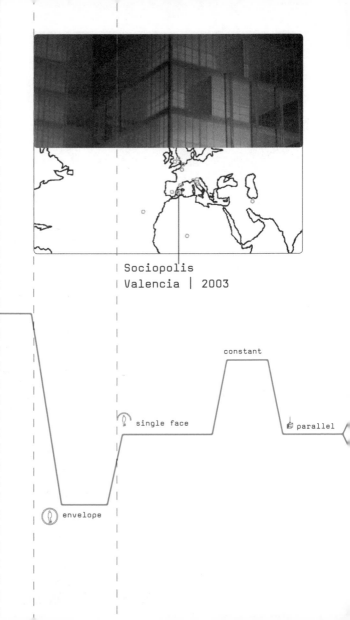

Sociopolis
Valencia | 2003

constant

single face

parallel

envelope

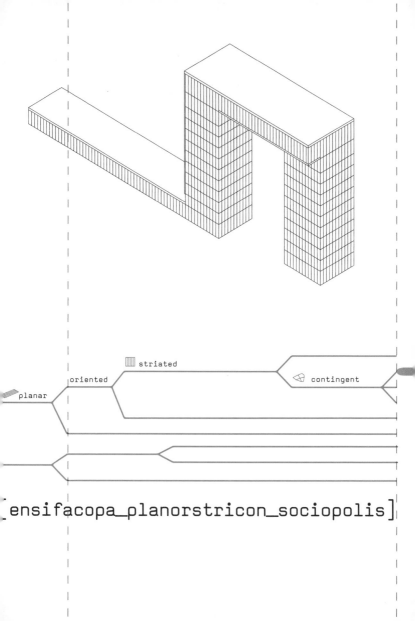

planar   oriented   striated   contingent

[ensifacopa_planorstricon_sociopolis]

The *huerta* (area of orchards and citrus groves) has always combined land and technology. Where oranges had once grown, later grew hands and now brains...

Our proposal for Sociópolis is an attempt to transfer to this new medium some of the patterns and topographies of the past: the extensive area of the huerta, the vertical structure of the trees, the rhythm of the irrigation system and the mechanisms that regulate it: the water tanks, the pumps, the sluices... Production, storage, distribution...

Lifts: Where once there were pumps to raise the water we have put lifts that take people, able or disabled, up to the housing units. The housing units are the new water tanks, the new silos for storing production. The housing units grow out from the lift, which is the most efficient system for vertical accessibility. According to the local code, above nine floors we have to provide for two fire escapes. To avoid this impact on the construction in height, we take nine floors as our limit.

Around the core, the living space is organized in a continuous ring that can be freely compartmentalized to accommodate manifold housing-unit types to meet the specific needs of the residents. The façade, a sort of "x-ray" of the community within, will be designed as the residents move in.

Trees: The housing units form a ring of space growing around the nucleus of vertical communication. Residents live like oranges, exposed to the sun and air. The façade is generous and the protruding galleries are closed with curtains, a minimal diaphragm integrated into the metal perimeter cage structure that complements the nucleus. It's like living in a garden.

Huerta-Garden: Where once there was huerta, now there is a garden. The ground is still soft and orange trees remains, but

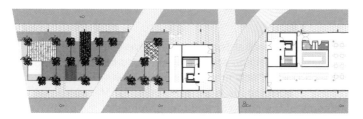

Housing types

A yuppie

B soltero

C dinkies

D estudiante

E divorciado con hijos

F madre soltera

G just married

H artista

I matrimonio con hijos

J inmigrantes

k profesional autonomo

L oficina

VIVIENDAS TIPO

estar	dormitorio	aseo	comedor
cocina	trabajar	estar-dormir	dormir-trabajar-comedor-estar

the area now serves as a recreational landscape. We have tried to minimize the footprint of the building, thus constructing on less land: we "tiptoe" through the huerta... We've divided the mass into two towers, to allow for more open space, for the sake of lightness...

The inhabitants of Sociópolis live in the huerta, with which they maintain a direct connection. The production is no longer massive. The residents' associations manage their huerta-garden units cooperatively. Orange, almond, medlar and cherry trees... mingle with vegetable beds... with recreational spaces, retreats for reading, play areas ...

City: The city looms above the horizon. It enjoys the landscape of the huerta from above; it looks out over the mountains and sea. The public gathering spaces are located in the garden to encourage active use of the space. The workspaces of the complex have been raised to the highest point, and act as storage space for urban activity, which, rather than encroaching on the huerta, reveals in it a new urban form.

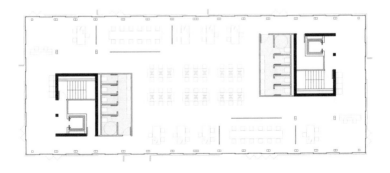

Office level

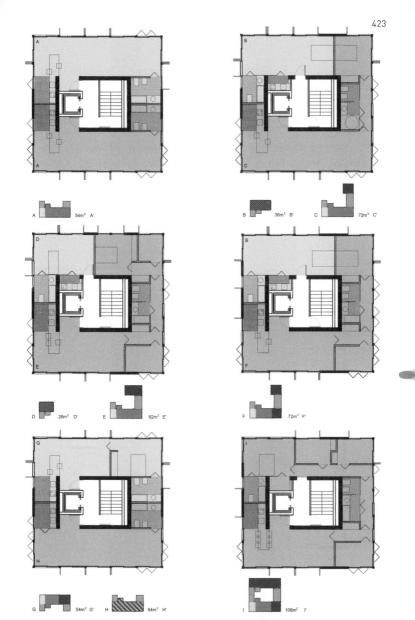

A   54m² A'

B   36m² B'   C   72m² C'

D   26m² D'   E   82m² E'

F   72m² F'

G   54m² G'   H   54m² H'

I   108m² I'

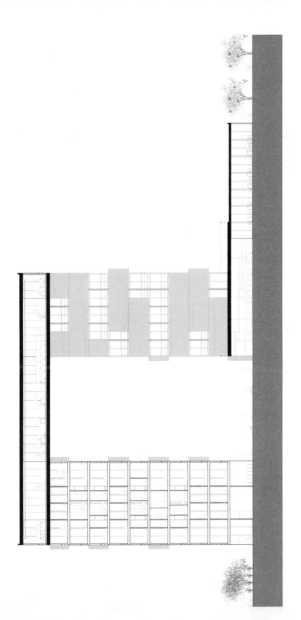

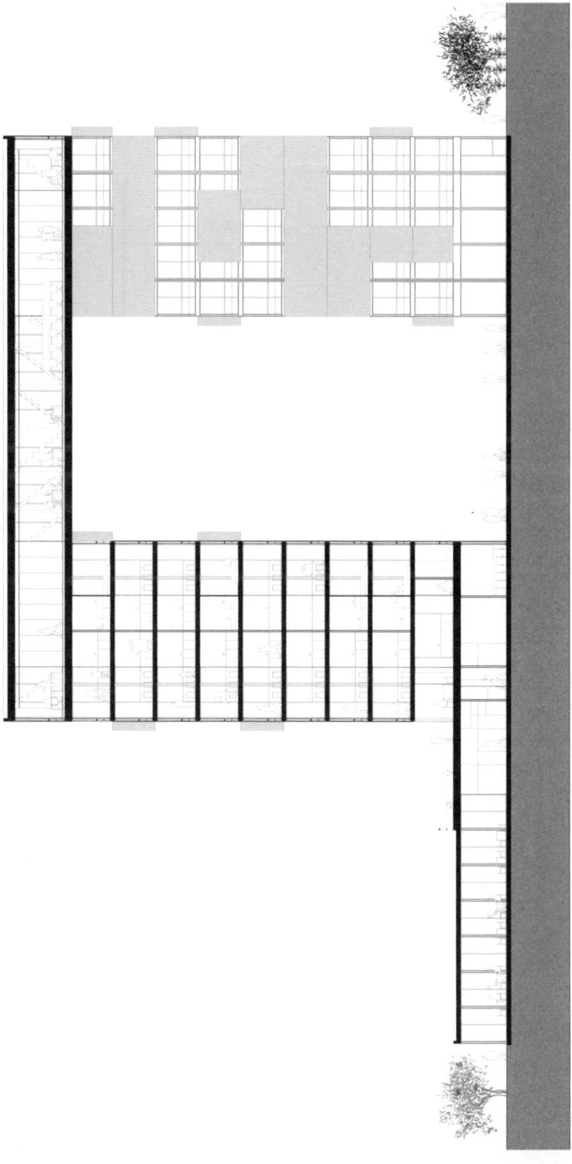

Longitudinal sections

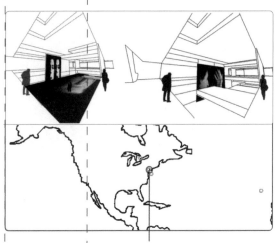

Eyebeam Museum of Art and Technology
New York | 2001

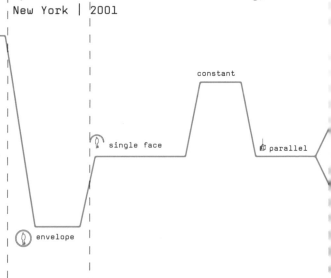

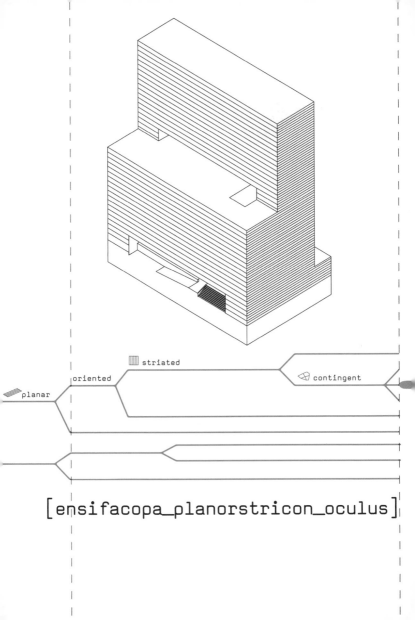

planar · oriented · striated · contingent

[ensifacopa_planorstricon_oculus]

What is the specificity of an institution that is dedicated to exploring the relationship between Art and Technology? Arts have always been about the manipulation of a particular media with specific techniques. In fact, a media is usually produced by a particular technique. Art has always been about the production of the virtual in different media. Eyebeam's program reads as an institution devoted to the production, discussion and dissemination of Art based in New Media.

By its own definition, "New Media" is an ever changing field, difficult to pin down unless a certain temporal bracket is introduced into the equation. If we think about what New Media are likely to be in the beginning of the 21st Century, we could conclude that New Media are characterised by the convergence of different media and fields of experience into information technology. Sound, image, form, space, motion... once fields of organisation and experience characteristic of a particular media and constructed by certain techniques have been abstracted and trans-coded into a milieu – the informational sequence – of such simplicity and abstraction that it has become a plane of consistency for all these once independent domains.

The informational sequence is an infrastructure, that is, the organisation, the field that precedes the formation of a structure. Moreover, recent advances in mechanised and numerically controlled production of sound, image and manufacturing have also shifted towards a mediated output. The specificity of contemporary New Media resides in their capacity to extend the possibilities of operation way beyond the original fields of experience and organisation. By operating on a phase space different from the space or medium of effect, contemporary New Media

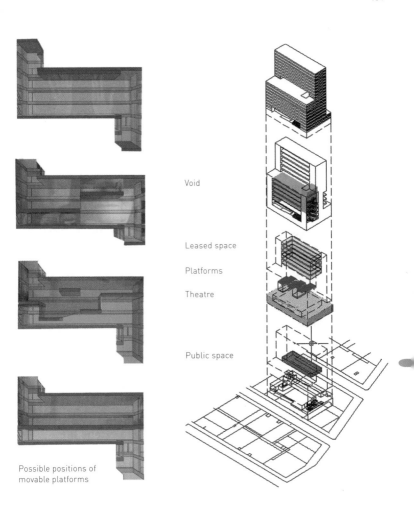

Possible positions of
movable platforms

Void

Leased space

Platforms

Theatre

Public space

are able to produce virtuality beyond the different fields'
original dimensions, material resistance, cultural signification...
To propose a space to produce and exhibit New Media's Art
is probably an impossible task, such is the degree of indetermination of that program. Like in natural systems, a specific,
complex form emerges as the degree of determination increases. As media evolve to remain new, the determinations of an
adequate space are constantly in evolution. Rather than trying to
explore experientially or structurally the spatial and formal possibilities that computer aided design could provide, our proposal
is to comply to the site's underlying urban structure, spatially
and constructively, as a default infrastructural condition for the
project. In the absence of a clear determination for the project,
we have defaulted – like in the binary sequence – to the most
basic form of architectural organisation: the orthogonal grid.
To try to link, either experientially or structurally, the building to
the contemporary computer technology will most likely handicap
the possibilities for it to host the constantly evolving shape of
new media. In this sense, our proposition for the future museum
is a void as large as the program and the structure of the site
can host, in order to be reconfigured into an infinite variety of
spatial arrangements in the future. This approach has also
the advantage of being able to concentrate the budget of the
building in the provision of technical systems, such as movable
platforms, escalators, and especially, sophisticated façades for
lighting control and image projection. In a high-rise museum,
the quality of the vertical surfaces is critical, as it is the element
that control the relation with the outside, both in terms of
lighting control, and image.

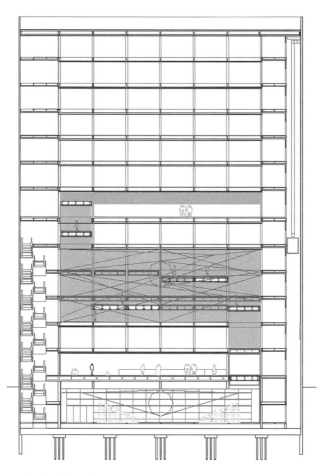

Longitudinal section

Located inside the building the exhibition space features a
9,50x32x11m void space, where 6 mechanically operated platforms can be located in multiple positions inside the space.
Through the use of these movable platforms (vertically and hori-
zontally) we can reconfigure the scale and distribution of the
exhibition space and establish changing relationships between
the production spaces and ateliers located around it. Like in a
computer CPU, blocks of activity can be permanently re-
organised, re-connected into multiple spatial arrangements.
It will be the exploration of the resident artists or the exhibitors
that will have to explore the infinite possibilities of the space of
new media in the future.
Eyebeam's idea of an atelier-museum is embedded in this
organisation through the literal wrapping of the exhibition
space in a crust of production spaces. This idea of the museum
as a place of production has also reinforced our infrastructural
approach to the project, that we see very much as a factory,
a silo or an office: a container of a certain amount of generic,
blank, non-differentiated space, without any attempt at signification. It will be the work of the artists, in their appropriation
of these generic spaces, and in their display onto the façade-
screen that will provide the building with a specific quality.
In the same way, the production space have defaulted to the
most generic type of informational production space in New
York, a series of platforms separated approximately 13', containing an inhabitable layer and a technical space to provide
environmental conditioning, power and data supply, and with a
depth of approximately 20' to an exterior opening. Architecture
as an infrastructure for informational production rather than

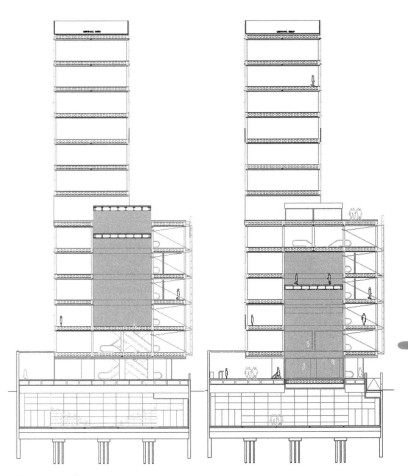

Transverse sections

as structure or an experience. The office slab is configured as a double-fronted, 12m slab with north and south oriented façades with diagonal views to the river and the city.

As for the performance space, a similar approach has been followed: a 32x27m, 6m high structure-free space is located under the public access lobby, where infinite arrangements are possible with the re-configuration of a variety of screens and temporary stands. A flytower/lift will provide the possibility to bring very large objects into the room, both from the entrance lobby and from the museum/production studios, crossing through the public space. In this way, that atelier-like experience of the performance space will also be immediately given to spectators, as the theater's foyer is surrounding the flytower, looking down onto the scene, when the platform is removed.

Given the organisation of the uses into these three blocks for production, exhibition/production and administration, distribution and archive, we have organised the section of the building in three structures separated by two public spaces. The two most public uses, the performance space and the exhibition/production block are closest to the access lobby on the ground floor. As we have tried to minimise the presence of structure through the void spaces that define these two blocks, we have concentrated all the circulation systems, and the vertical load-bearing structures towards the east and west firewalls, so that the three blocks span 32m between them. This allows to provide two structure-free public spaces, one on a raised ground level (+1.80) where the access lobbies for tenants and museum, ticketing and control, museum store and café/restaurant will be located. The second is a roof terrace located at level +26.00,

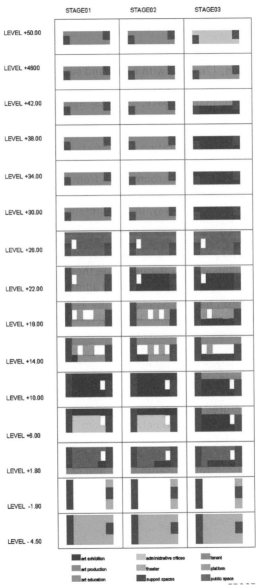

Distribution of programs in plan

between the exhibition/production block and the administration/ archive/research/education/distribution upper slab. This open-air roof terrace can be used as an open-air gallery or event space, or just a relax space for the museum and tenant staff. The distribution of the vertical circulation spaces on both ends of the building will ensure two means of egress for every floor in the building. From both cores, the eastern one will be dedicated in the first two phases to tenant's access, then to administrative/ research/education/distribution access. The western one will include a mechanical escalator providing access to the most public spaces in the museum. Finally, the façades will be the most sophisticated element in the building, and the element that will concentrate the "expressive" qualities of the building, as a display board for the museum's ongoing activities. It will also provide adequate environmental conditioning, and views to the city and the river. The south façade is built with horizontal bands of filtering glass and of photovoltaic panels. The glazing will allow views over the city and the river, without excessive solar gains, and the photovoltaic panels will act a a collector of energy for the maintenance of the building's systems. The north façade will be made with photochromic glass panels, able to control the light intensity through the day, but also able to become a screen for the images projected from inside the ateliers or the exhibition areas, becoming a mosaic display of the changing activities inside the museum.

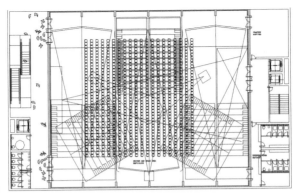

-5.40m

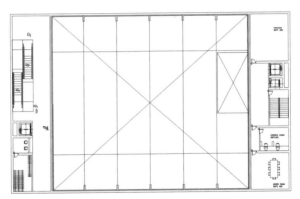

-1.80m

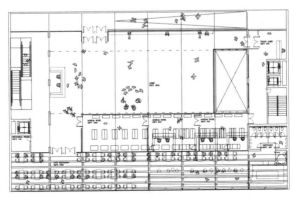

+1.80m

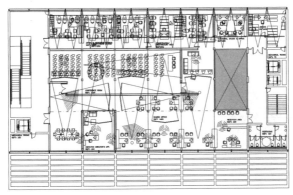

+6.00m

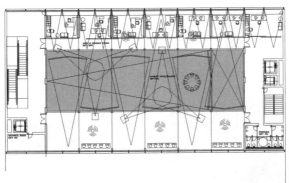

+10.00m

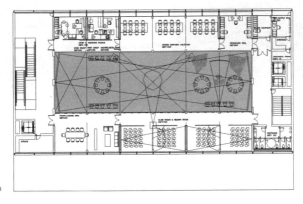

+18.00m

441

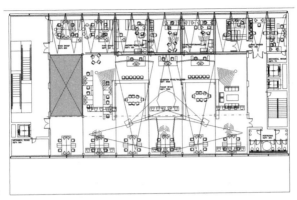

+22.00m

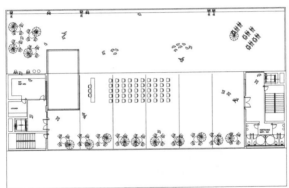

+26.00m

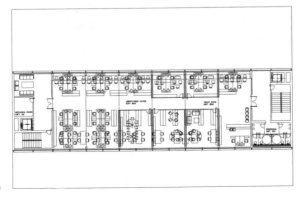

+30.00m

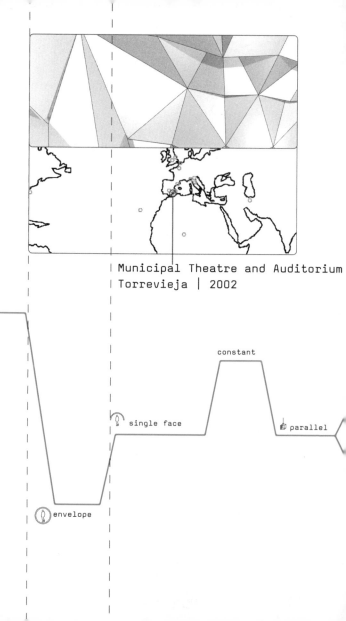

446

Municipal Theatre and Auditorium
Torrevieja | 2002

constant

single face

parallel

envelope

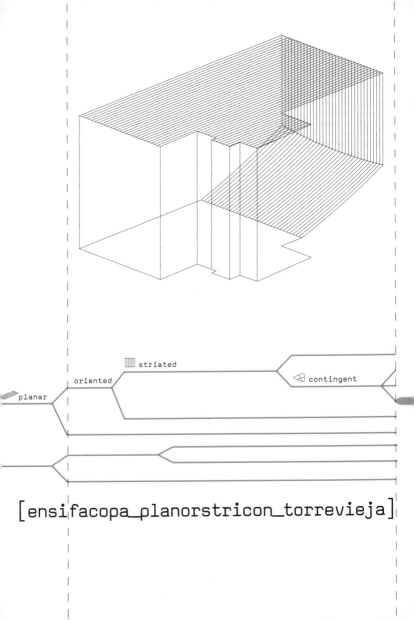

planar   oriented   striated   contingent

[ensifacopa_planorstricon_torrevieja]

Torrevieja is one of the main tourist towns in south-east Spain, and is now involved in an ambitious program of infrastructural improvements aimed at raising the profile of the town beyond its current mass tourist destination. This commission is to implement one of these new urban infrastructures, a 650-seat theatre and auditorium in a corner site inside one of the town centre blocks, and the redevelopment of a neighbouring existing plaza. Given the scarce amount of space in the plot in respect to the required program, our proposal is to lift the auditorium from the ground level, letting the plaza penetrate the plot, becoming a foyer that sits underneath the cantilevered mass of the building. The public space becomes an incision into a solid mass, clad in local limestone, that completes the volume of the block's corner. The auditorium is proposed to entirely fill the available plan, and to become a single black box with the scenic tower, in order to allow for the maximum flexibility of use of the theatre. The geometry of the auditorium is exploited as a feature of the cantilevered, carved mass.

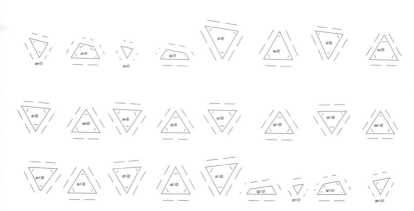

Tile catalogue

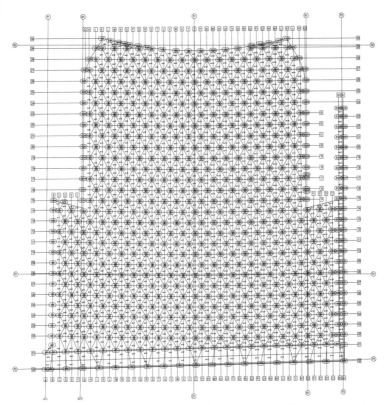

Tile classification plan

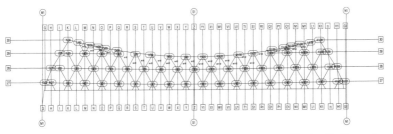

Tile classification section

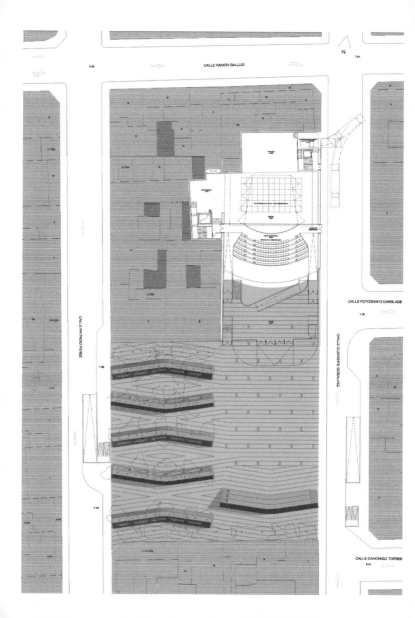

CALLE RAMON GALLUD

CALLE PATRICIO PEREZ

CALLE FOTOGRAFO GARBILADE

CALLE CLEMENTE GOSALVEZ

CALLE CANONIGO TORRES

N

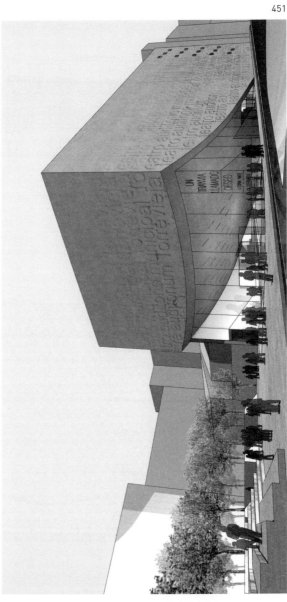

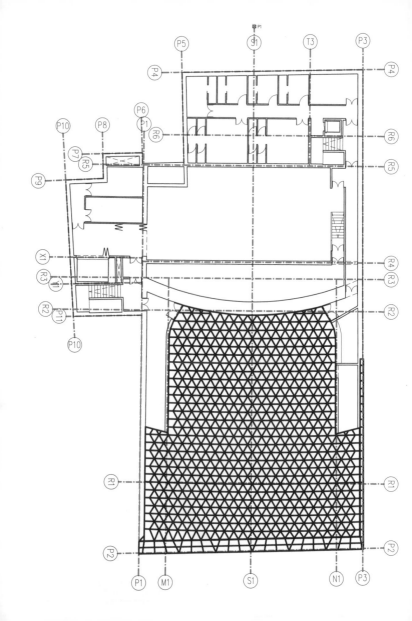

453

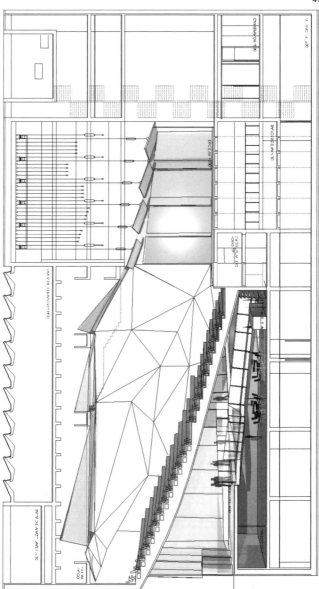

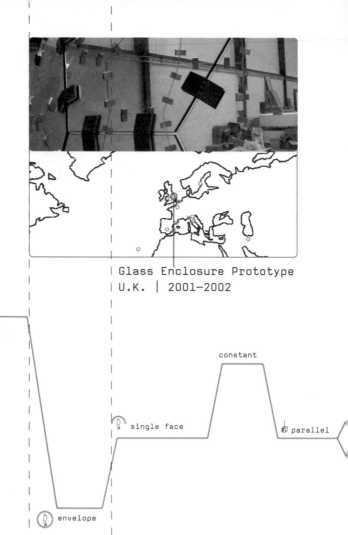

Glass Enclosure Prototype
U.K. | 2001—2002

envelope

single face

constant

parallel

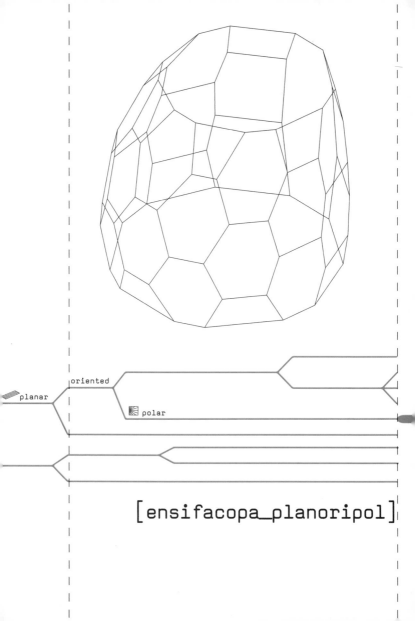

planar

oriented

polar

[ensifacopa_planoripol]

The brief consisted of two spatial components: open areas and rooms of different scales throughout the building, designed to host group presentations, private offices, meeting rooms, conference and board rooms. In these, we attempted to produce a single prototype able to adapt in size to cater for the scale of different functions that the building will offer.

We developed a glass prototype that will allow maximum light at the same time as visual privacy in the necessary areas, and acoustic privacy from the open spaces. We began by exploring circular rooms as the most efficient form with a circular meeting table, and a geometry that will minimise the restriction of flow and impose less structure on the surrounding open space. This structure generates spatial differences without producing segmentation.

The glass prototype has been developed at five different scales (using five different radii for the setting of the geometry for each) to accommodate the various functions that require enclosed spaces throughout the building.

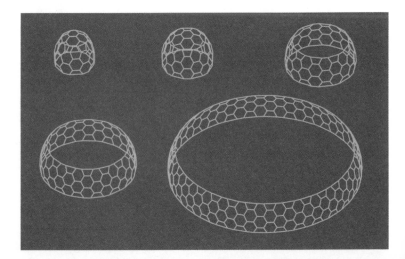

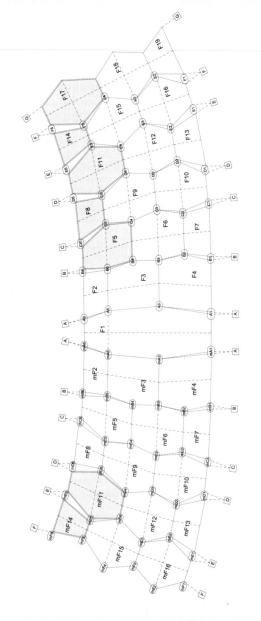

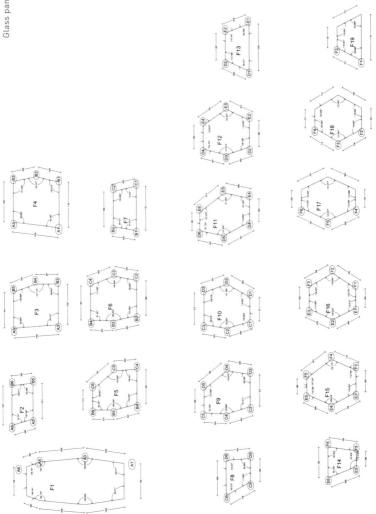

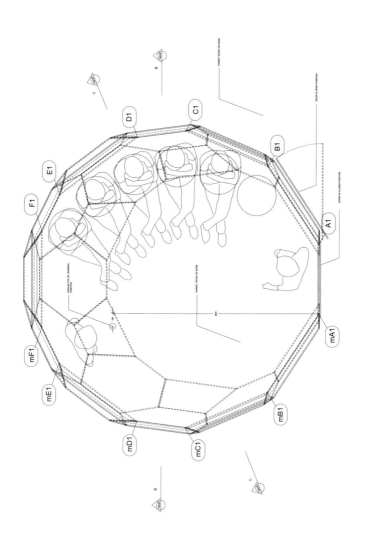

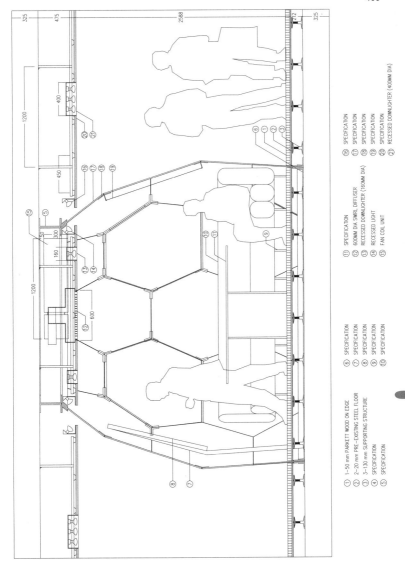

① 1–50 mm PARKETT WOOD ON EDGE
② 2–20 mm PRE-EXISTING STEEL FLOOR
③ 3–130 mm SUPPORTING STRUCTURE
④ SPECIFICATION
⑤ SPECIFICATION

⑥ SPECIFICATION
⑦ SPECIFICATION
⑧ SPECIFICATION
⑨ SPECIFICATION
⑩ SPECIFICATION

⑪ SPECIFICATION
⑫ 600MM DIA SWIRL DIFFUSER
⑬ RECESSED DOWNLIGHTER (160MM DIA)
⑭ RECESSED LIGHT
⑮ FAN COIL UNIT

⑯ SPECIFICATION
⑰ SPECIFICATION
⑱ SPECIFICATION
⑲ SPECIFICATION
⑳ SPECIFICATION
㉑ RECESSED DOWNLIGHTER (400MM DIA)

325
475
2588
272
325
400
1200
450
50 100
160
1200
600

463

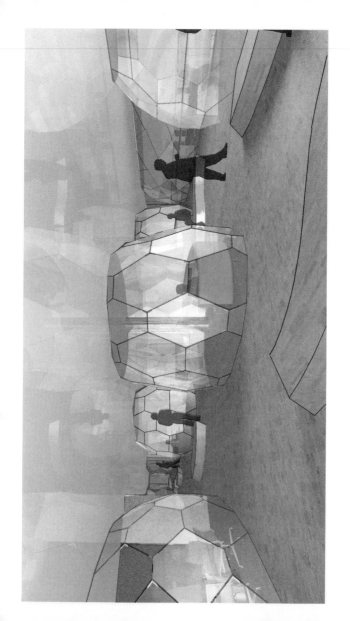

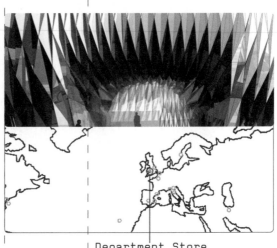

Department Store
Bristol | 2002

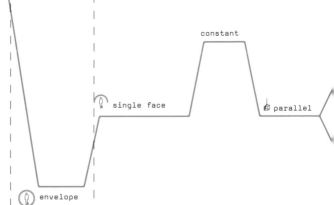

constant

single face

parallel

envelope

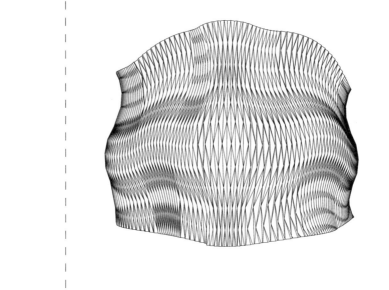

planar

non-oriented

[ensifacopa_planonor]

This project is to be located in a new complex in the Broadsmead area in central Bristol, now being extended into a large shopping centre. The building is a free-standing volume on the eastern side of the future development, on the main road access to the city, and in a most prominent position in terms of views from the road. The building needs to be accessed on two different ground levels, and connected a further higher level above the surrounding highway, connecting to a parking structure on the other side of the road. The program included 17,000m^2 of commercial space in 5 levels including administrative spaces of 1300m^2, to be distributed in floor plates of approximately 3600m^2, into an approximately 25 m high volume. The plan was organized as a ring around an atrium, around which the interior structure concentrates, and where the main public circulation is located, limiting the presence of structure to that ring and the facade line.

The architectural features of the project come out of an attempt to capture the prominent perspective from the road access, and exploit the physical isolation of the volume to dress it as a jewel, as a gem that reflects the light in multiple angles and colors. The process is inspired literally in the processes of diamond cutting, where a stone is faceted to obtain its maximum brightness by applying a precise geometry. The envelope has been generated from the irregular footprint geometry of the site, a 3.5 m deflection of the facade that will generate a canopy to cover people walking around the building watching the shopwindows, the upper level walkways, and the vertical service cores on the edge of the building. Out of these surface singularities, we create the basic envelope geometry, that then is tessellated in facets generated by a process of optimization of edges. The surface is meant to be clad with holographic film laminated on a light metal facade.

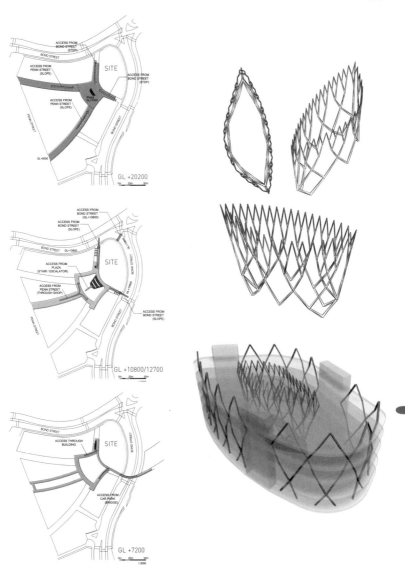

Site access routes

Tubular structure of facade and atrium

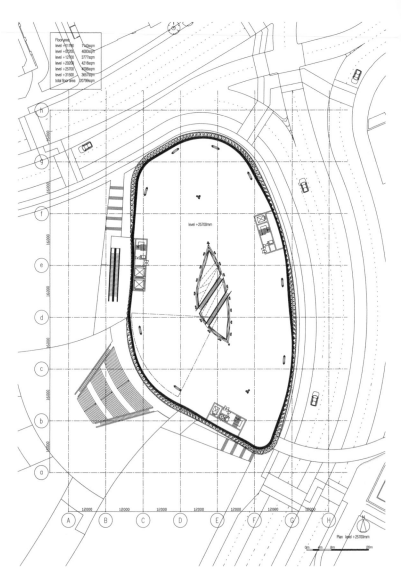

Pleated plan

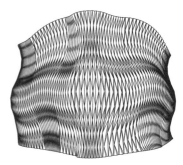

Facade option A: Pleated

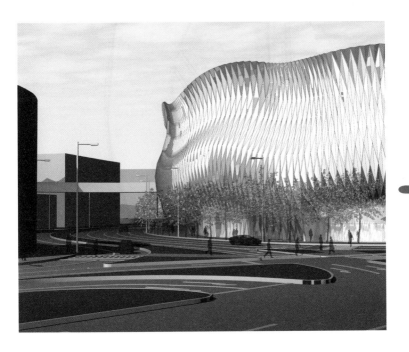

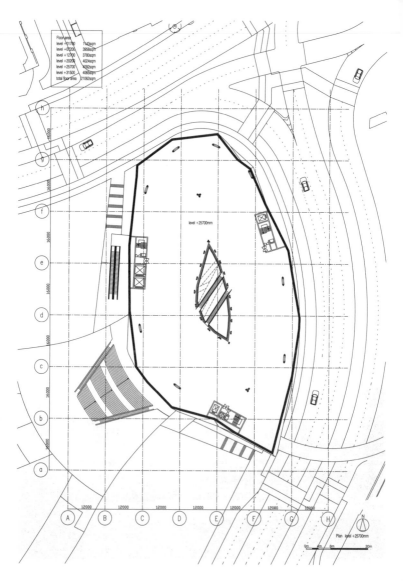

Diamond option plan

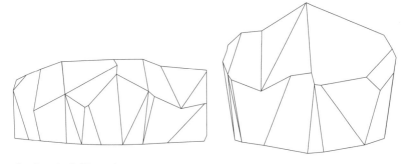

Facade option B: Diamond

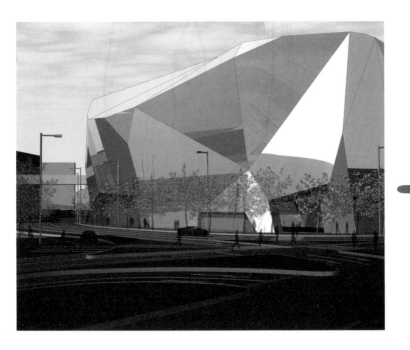

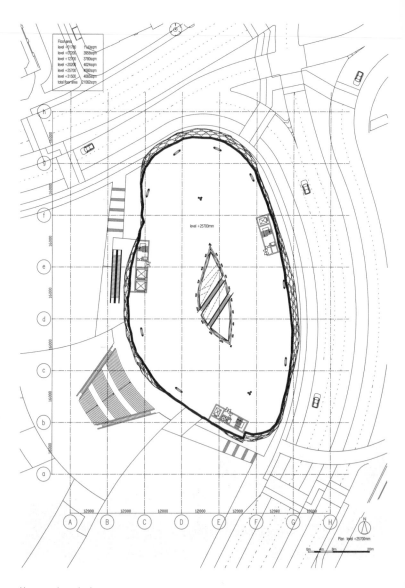

level +25700mm

Plan level +25700mm

0m   4m   8m   20m

Hexagonal mesh plan

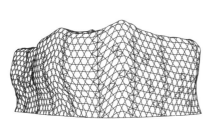
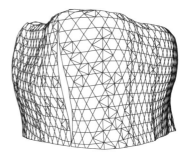

Facade option C: Hexagonal mesh

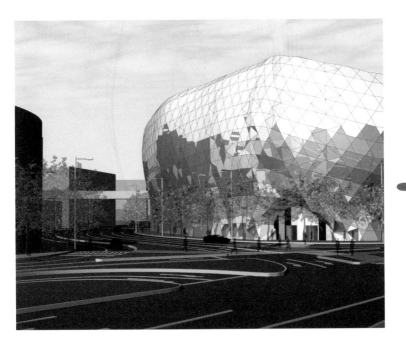

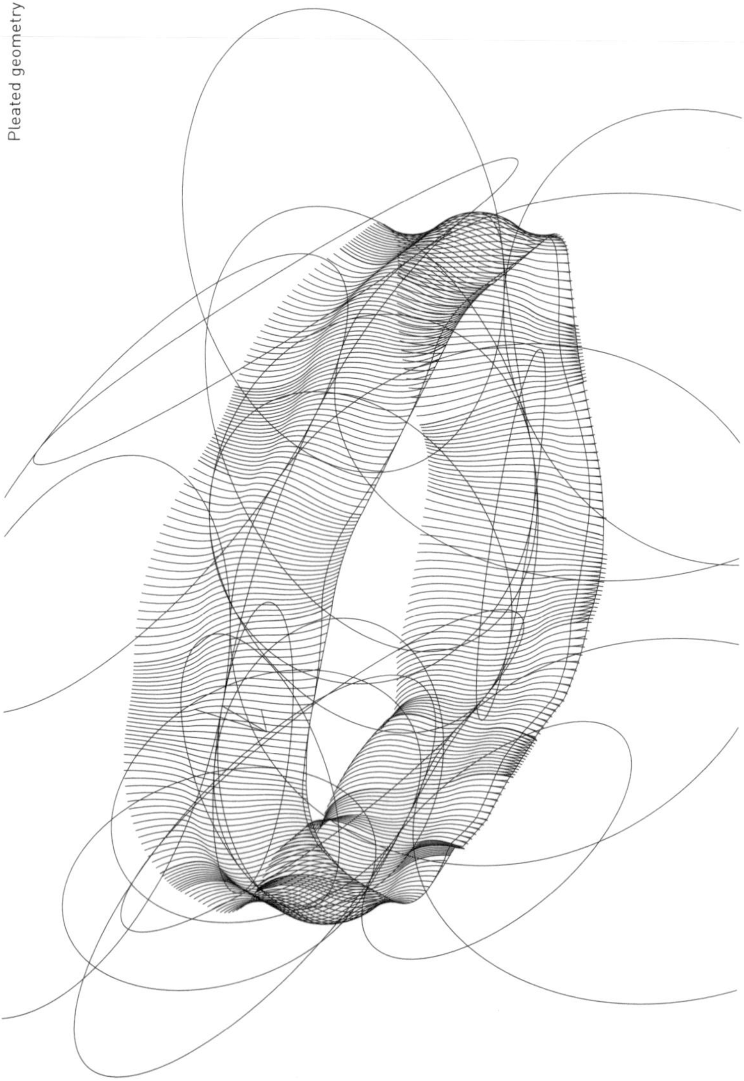

Diamond geometry

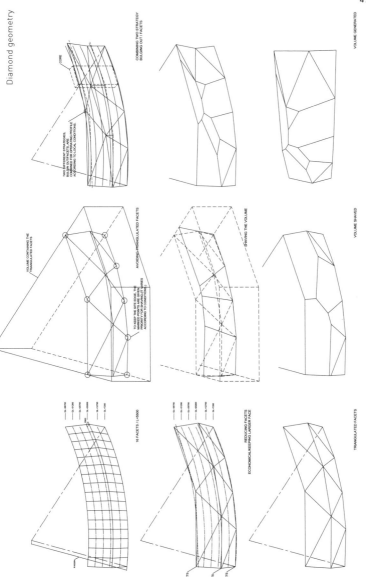

TWO DIFFERENT STRATEGIES,
BULGING OUT/FACETS, ARE
COMBINED FOR OPERATING PROFILE
ACCORDING TO LOCAL CONDITIONS.

CORE

COMBINING TWO STRATEGY
BULGING OUT / FACETS

VOLUME GENERATED

VOLUME CONTAINING THE
TRIANGULATED FACETS

AVOIDING TRIANGULATED FACETS

TO KEEP THE SITE EDGE, THE
MARKED POINTS ARE GIVEN
PRIORITY FOR SHAVING BUT VARIES
ACCORDING TO CONDITIONS.

SHAVING THE VOLUME

VOLUME SHAVED

16 FACETS / L=5600

REDUCING FACETS
ECONOMICAL/KEEPING LARGER FACE

TRIANGULATED FACETS

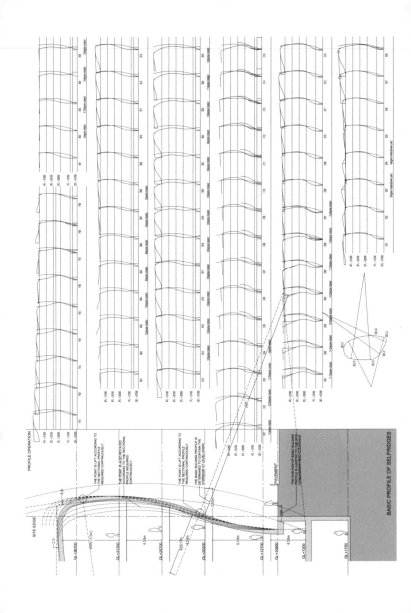

PROFILE OPERATION

SITE EDGE

THE POINT IS LEFT ACCORDING TO THE SECTIONAL PROFILE REQUIRED CONTINUOUSLY.

THE POINT IS ALSO ROTATED ACCORDING TO THE SECTIONAL PROFILE REQUIRED CONTINUOUSLY.

THE POINT IS LEFT ACCORDING TO THE SECTIONAL PROFILE REQUIRED CONTINUOUSLY.

THE BASIC BUILDING PROFILE IS DETERMINED TO CLEAR THE CORRIDOR AT LEVEL +20200.

PAVEMENT

THE POSITION OF BASIC BUILDING PROFILE IS ADAPTED TO THE SITE, CEILING AND HEAD CLEARANCE.

BASIC PROFILE OF SELFRIDGES

Hexagonal mesh geometry

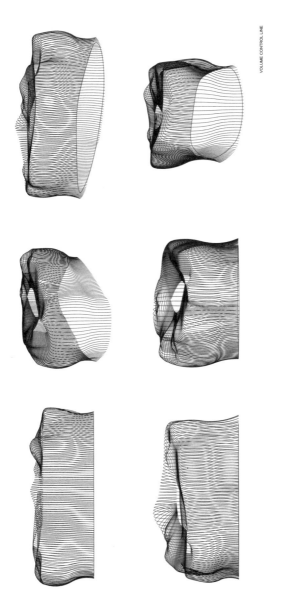

VOLUME CONTROL LINE

UNFOLDED CONTROL LINE

GL +31200
GL +25700
GL +20000
GL +12700
GL +7200

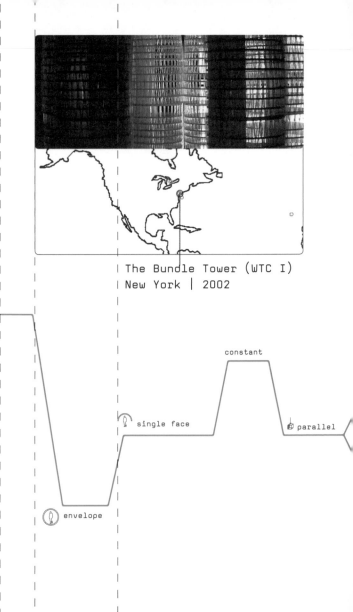

The Bundle Tower (WTC I)
New York | 2002

constant

single face

parallel

envelope

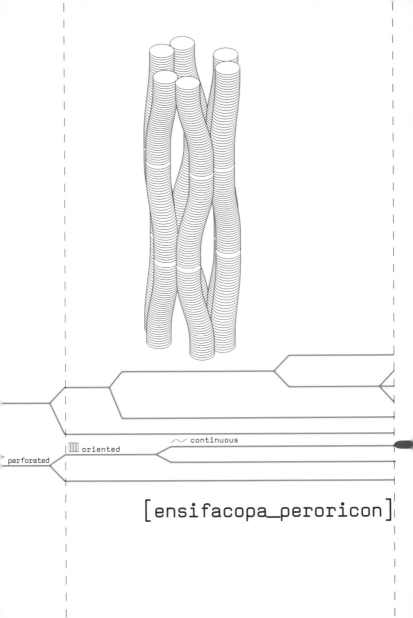

perforated ▥ oriented 〜 continuous

[ensifacopa_peroricon]

The Bundle Tower was born as an answer to the reconstruction of Ground Zero and is revisited here as a free-floating, atent utopia to be built in place of the late WTC, or somewhere else. Beijing, London, Mexico, Paris, Seoul, Singapore, Shanghai, Tokyo... could also become the recipients of this operative celebration of the global and dynamic processes that were the object of the WTC attack.

The Bundle Tower is presented here in its most generic form, devoid of local specificities, possible differentiations between towers or sectors of towers and potential negotiations with ground structures. The Bundle Tower is described here as a species in the most diagrammatic form, grown in a generic ecosystem, awaiting the specificity of a situation to actualise its potentials. It has been provisionally scaled to match the size of the original WTC complex (1.3M m^2), but to reach higher to become the tallest building in the world.

The world's tallest building requires a new high-rise typology. If we look at the evolution of the skyscraper type we can see a process in which the increase in height of the structure results in a tendency of the organisation to concentrate increasingly capable materials in the periphery of the plan. As the lateral forces become stronger than the gravitational ones, it becomes necessary to maximise the moment of inertia of the structure. This process has evolved the post and beam typology, which distributed structure evenly across the plan, into different types of tubular organisations, concentrating structure in the periphery of the mass.

But as the structure grows taller, the strength of the material is not sufficient to provide stability to lateral forces, so the only solution is to keep increasing the depth of the plan proportionally.

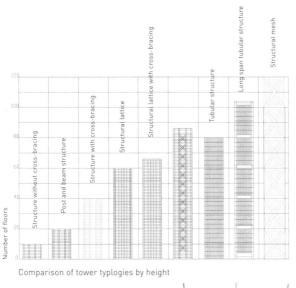
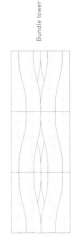

Structure without cross-bracing

Post and beam structure

Structure with cross-bracing

Structural lattice

Structural lattice with cross-bracing

Tubular structure

Long span tubular structure

Structural mesh

Bundle tower

Number of floors

Comparison of tower typlogies by height

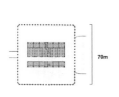

Original WTC

70m

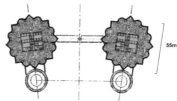

Petronas Towers

55m

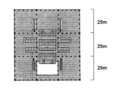

Sears Tower

25m
25m
25m

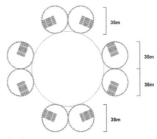

Bundle tower

35m
35m
35m
35m

Comparison of tower floor plans

This leads into building types that become extremely deep, and therefore heavily dependent on artificial light and mechanically controlled ventilation.

In order to generate a new type of high-rise, our proposal is to operate with the building massing, rather than with just the distribution of the structure. Instead of splitting the complex into two independent towers, like in the former WTC or in the Petrona towers, to avoid excessively deep workspaces, our proposal is to maintain the physical continuity of the whole mass, and to use it as a structural advantage. Our proposal is to form the complex as a bundle of interconnected towers that provide a flexible floor size and that buttress each other structurally, being able to increase the moment of inertia of the structure without necessarily increasing the floor depth and the total area. The average workspace floor size in New York City is 1000m², and we have taken that as our quantum of space, or bundle scale in the new WTC NY: the floor plan of the bundle towers will be approximately that size. As our target is to reach approximately 500m in height, we are aiming at approximately 110 floors with a conventional floor to floor height of 4.5m. If we take the size of the former complex as a measure of total floor size, we have:

884,000 m²/110 floors = 8036 m²/floor, which equals approximately 8 towers of 1000 m² per floor.

In order to maximise the ratio between floor area and perimeter, and to improve the structural performance of the building, we have opted for a tubular structure with a circular profile with an 18m diameter, where the structure is concentrated in a structural lattice on the fasade of each tower. The tubes, organised in a circle, bend vertically to buttress each other approxi-

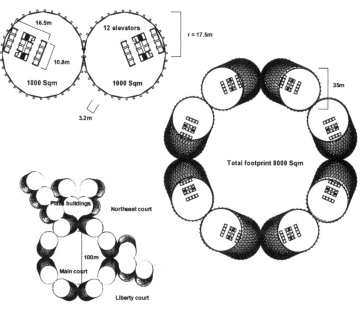

16.5m

12 elevators

r = 17.5m

10.8m

1000 Sqm

1000 Sqm

3.2m

35m

Total footprint 8000 Sqm

Plaza buildings

Northeast court

100m

Main court

Liberty court

Total Area 1.3M Sqm

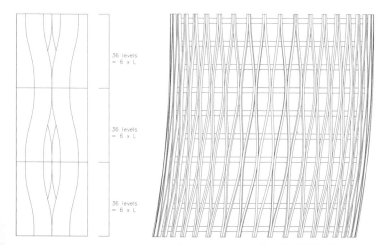

36 levels = 6 x L

36 levels = 6 x L

36 levels = 6 x L

mately every third of the total height of the building, cutting the bending length of the towers to approximately 165m.
In order to maximise the resistance of the structural lattice of the tubes, the geometry of the columns will also bend, balancing the transmission of weight and the resistance to buckling and lateral stresses. The lattice of the tower structure and the geometry of the bunch tower are self-similar structures.
Every tower, with an approximate area of 110,000m^2 will be provided with a battery of 12 high speed lifts that will provide access primarily to the floors in the tower, but will form part of a network of skylobbies that every tower shares with the two neighbouring ones every 36 floors. The fire escape system is organised also through these vertical cores, allowing transfers between six different fire escapes for every tower through the skylobbies (two stairs per tower). Raisers for HVAC, fire-suppression systems electricity and telecommunications are contained also in the system of vertical cores, allowing every tower to access supplies from the two neighbouring ones.
As the vertical structure is always concentrated in the periphery of the tubes, the slabs inside the towers are column-free circles of 36m diameter, made with a lattice that increases depths as the bending moment in the floor increases. As the tower envelope bends to touch the neighbouring towers, the vertical circulation core, remains vertical, providing with periodical variations in the depth of workspace between the envelope and the circulation core. This offers a higher variety of work-space types.

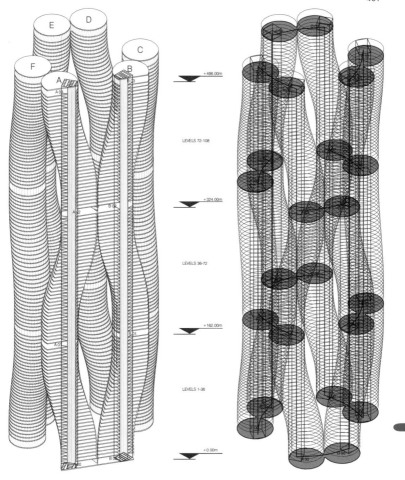

Sky lobby system and vertical cores

LEVELS 72-108

+486.00m

+324.00m

LEVELS 36-72

+162.00m

LEVELS 1-36

+0.00m

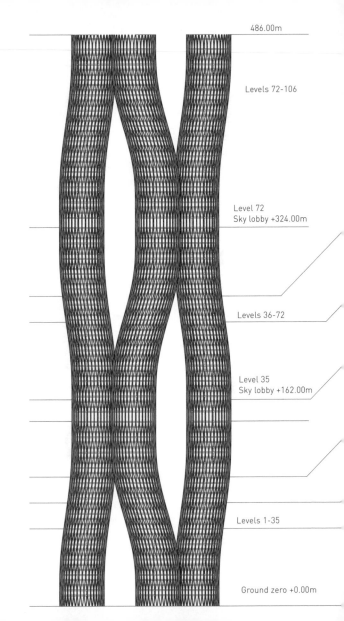

486.00m

Levels 72-106

Level 72
Sky lobby +324.00m

Levels 36-72

Level 35
Sky lobby +162.00m

Levels 1-35

Ground zero +0.00m

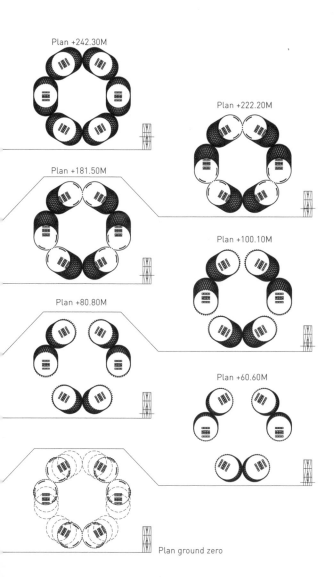

Plan +242.30M

Plan +222.20M

Plan +181.50M

Plan +100.10M

Plan +80.80M

Plan +60.60M

Plan ground zero

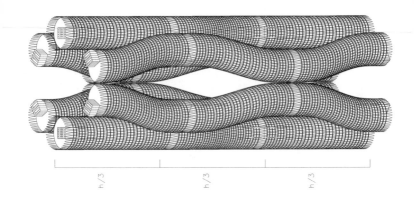

h/3   h/3   h/3

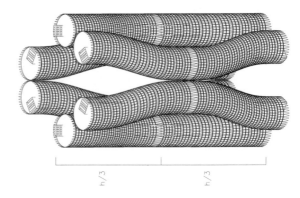

h/3   h/3

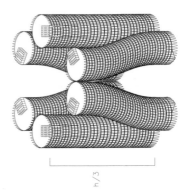

h/3

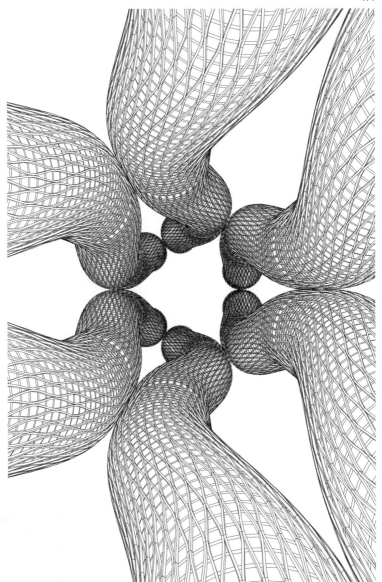

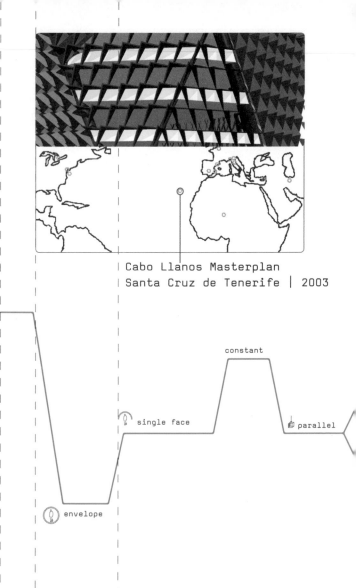

Cabo Llanos Masterplan
Santa Cruz de Tenerife | 2003

constant

single face

parallel

envelope

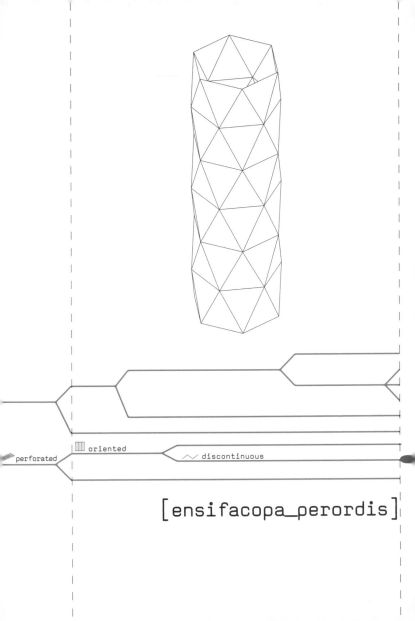

perforated ▦ oriented ⌒ discontinuous

[ensifacopa_perordis]

Cabo Llanos is the largest urban development in Santa Cruz de Tenerife, a large area formally used by an oil refinery which is now being developed as a new central business district, very near to the city centre. This development has been occurring for the last ten years and, due to a very insufficient and unimaginative planning strategy, evolved into a new, crammed and unattractive residential district very near to the town centre. Our commission consisted in redefining the urban planning strategy in an attempt to improve the urban environment to allocate the remaining 90,000m2 of offices, commercial and hotel, and 4,500 parking spaces dictated in the general masterplan for the city of Santa Cruz.

Our proposal had also to consider the integration of the El Tanque Cultural Centre, an institution located in the last remaining oil tank in the site.

Our plan is an attempt to alter dramatically the environment by proposing a dissolution of the rigid orthogonal and symmetrical grid of the existing development into an urban structure more able to deal with the remarkable differences on the borders of the site, and the specificity of its topography and climate. With this in mind, our strategies have been twofold:

- To declare the whole block as an "environmental zone", with no traffic flow on ground level.
- To structure the parking socle using a split-level system in order to adjust to the sloped topography of the site. The socle will be sloped, replicating the existing topography in the site as a positive contribution towards a more theatrical public space.
- To dissolve the repetitive orthogonal grid into a continuous public space, uninterrupted by roads, where the buildings are allowed much higher freedom to be located.

- To propose a change of typology towards high-rise buildings that will have a much smaller footprint, therefore allowing for a substantial increase in the amount of public space, and a more dramatic skyline for the new buildings.
- To treat the public level with an intensive planting strategy that will produce a green canopy across the entire public space to provide shadow and humidity. This green canopy will be differentiated to match the wind, sun and rain protection required by the different circulation and activity patterns on the plaza. The proposed buildings occupy footprints of no more than 1,000m2 and their plan is centralized, either in the form of a square, a circle or another polygon with polar symmetry, in order to maximize the multidirectional flow across the plaza. The effect on the skyline will be dramatic, especially in the multi-purpose building for the Government of the Canary Islands, which will occupy the central position in the plan, articulating the east-west axis that connects with the Urban project and the city centre on one side and with the fair grounds on the other, and the north-south axis, that links the site with the waterfront. Due to the footprint restrictions, this building will rise to nearly 30 stories, with a skin of brise-soleil that change orientation depending of the sunpath, forming a scale-like skin that resembles the skin of a palm tree trunk.

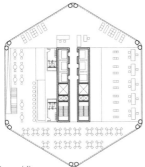

Ground floor
1039 m²

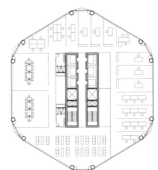

Floors 9 / 19
1090 m²

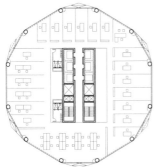

Floors 10 / 20
1116 m²

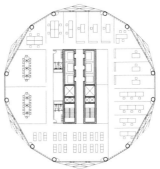

Floors 1 / 14 / 21
1116 m²

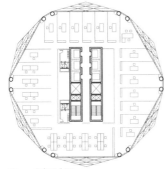

Floors 2 / 12 / 22
1090 m²

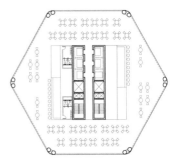

Floor 23
1039 m²

	8.00	9.00	10.00	11.00	12.00	13.00	14.00	15.00	16.00	17.00	18.00	19.00	20.00	21.00	22.00	23.00
Edificio para la Agencia Tributaria																
Edificio M3																
Edificio para la autoridad portuaria																
Edificio de oficinas																
Hotel																
SPA																
Restaurante Hotel																
Cafetería interior																
Cafetería exterior																
Auditorio M3																
Auditorio al aire libre																
Zona de exposiciones al aire libre																
Zona de juegos																
Gimnasio al aire libre																
Paseo																
Circuito de footing																
Zona de lectura, descanso																
Mercadillo																

Diario — — — Fin de semana

Fin de semana

Temperaturas en Tenerife: min 17-18 (Ene); max 28-30 grados centígrados (Sept)

Horas de sol: 5.8 h en (Enero), 10.7 h en Agosto

VISTAS AL MAR
PENDIENTE SUAVE/PRONUNCIADA
DOMINANTE DEL NORESTE
EXPOSICION/RESGUARDO A VIENTO
SOL/SOMBRA

Location of buildings based on site conditions

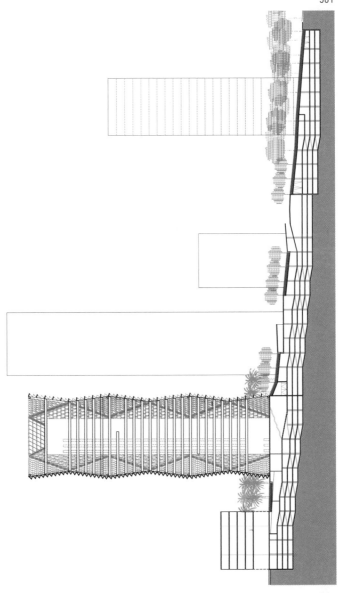

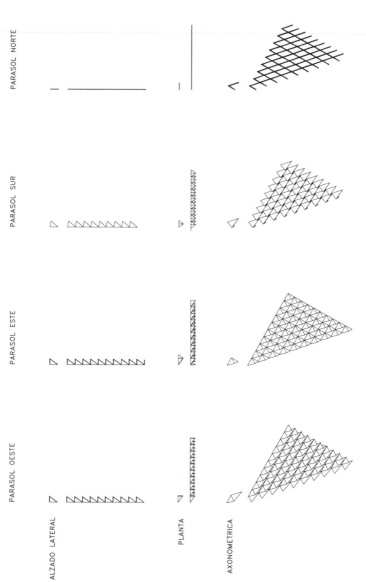

PARASOL OESTE   PARASOL ESTE   PARASOL SUR   PARASOL NORTE

ALZADO LATERAL

PLANTA

AXONOMETRICA

Facade system

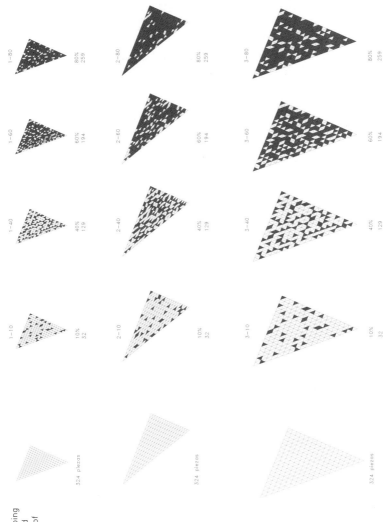

Plant grouping types based on density of vegetation

506

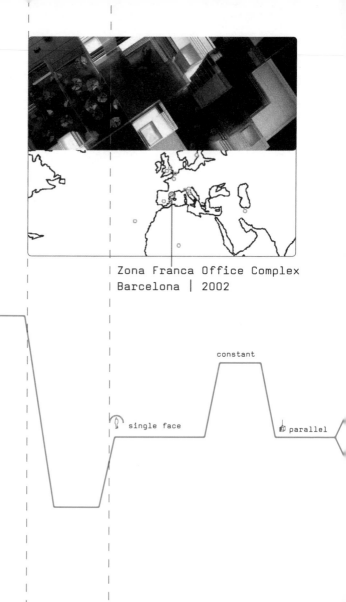

Zona Franca Office Complex
Barcelona | 2002

constant

single face

parallel

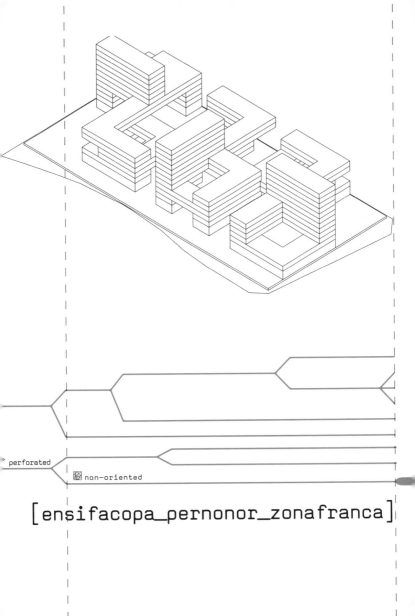

perforated

non-oriented

[ensifacopa_pernonor_zonafranca]

This project is aimed to operate in a similar way in which a gothic fabric or a Mediterranean village grew, by defining a series of rules and regulations that will ensure that a certain urban and spatial quality is produced, rather than by producing a final design. The final design will be produced by the interplay between those series of rules and parameters of control and the indeterminate forces of the market to enter into the process during the implementation of the project.

The qualities of the fabric that we aim to enforce through our project are aimed at three fundamental targets:

1 To ensure that the new office complex provides not only office space in an important area in the future of Barcelona, but that it provides public space and urban quality, becoming an adequate urban scenario within the future developments in Zona Franca. In this sense the project will enforce the maximum liberation on ground level for public use and the maximum coverage of public space to provide shadow and shelter on it, producing a tight spatial integration between the buildings and the public space.

2 To ensure that the future complex generates a new type of urban fabric that does not reproduce the existing models of tertiary urban development, originating a new type of urban fabric with the advantages of the traditional Barcelona city block and the gothic fabric. In this sense the proposal attempts to produce more a continuous and differentiated fabric of buildings rather than a series of architectural icons. The quality of the fabric will be in the consistency of the fabric more than in the qualities of the individual buildings, and the buildings should tend to appear as a continuous structure, rather than independent objects on a field.

3 To develop a new typology of tertiary space able to host an

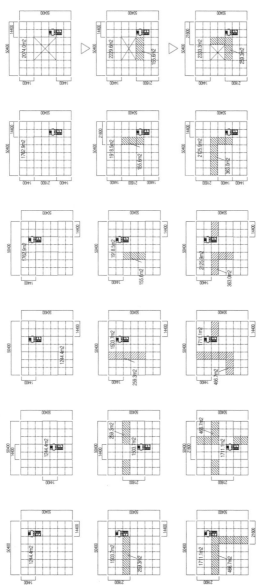

Volume study

infinite variety of workspaces, from professional small bureaus, to conventional 2-bay cellular offices, to "Kombi" types, to deep plan offices for large organisations, to trading floors... surmounting the limitations of conventional office typologies.
This new typology should be able to establish formal consistency across the different workspace types and at the same time allow for differentiation and incorporate in the design the variations in demand across the different phases, making possible to adjust the plans in time.
In this respect, we have identified a number of parameters of control and regulations that will target at the production of the before mentioned qualities:
1 In order to ensure the provision of public space design will set
a The footprint of the buildings as a percentage of the site.
b The occupation of the site including footprints and cantilevered volumes.
c A percentage of cantilevered or bridged volumes to cover the public spaces.

2 In order to achieve consistency in the fabric, the design will set
a The maximum height to ensure a consistent density within virtual volumes.
b The percentage of fasade alignment between the maximum envelop and the built mass.
c The percentage of continuity of the cornice level

3 In order to ensure the flexibility of the new typology we have developed an optimum grid dimension of 7,50x7,50 that will allow to make the parking grid and the office space consistent. By declaring a maximum floor plate of 7x7 modules of the grid, we allow the different phases to absorb the floor depth that the later workspace type demand may require, and keep consistency with a flexible parking layout.

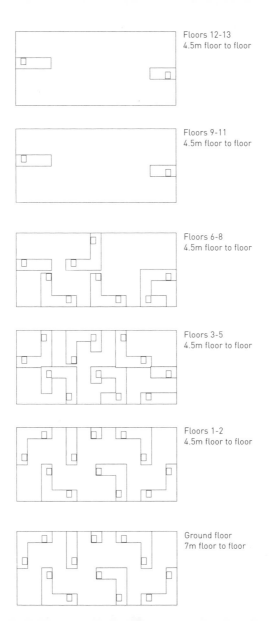

Floors 12-13
4.5m floor to floor

Floors 9-11
4.5m floor to floor

Floors 6-8
4.5m floor to floor

Floors 3-5
4.5m floor to floor

Floors 1-2
4.5m floor to floor

Ground floor
7m floor to floor

CARRER DE L'ENCUNY

PASSEIG DE LA ZONA FRANCA

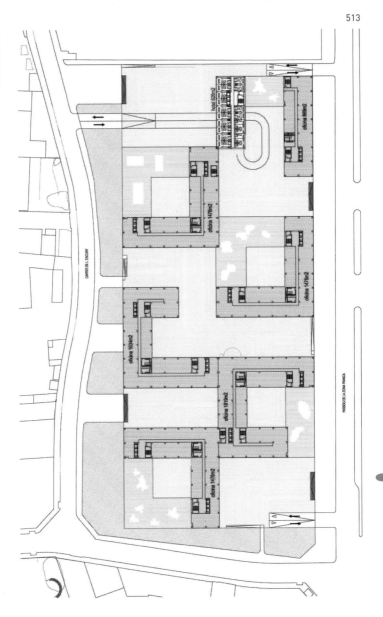

Plan levels 6-8

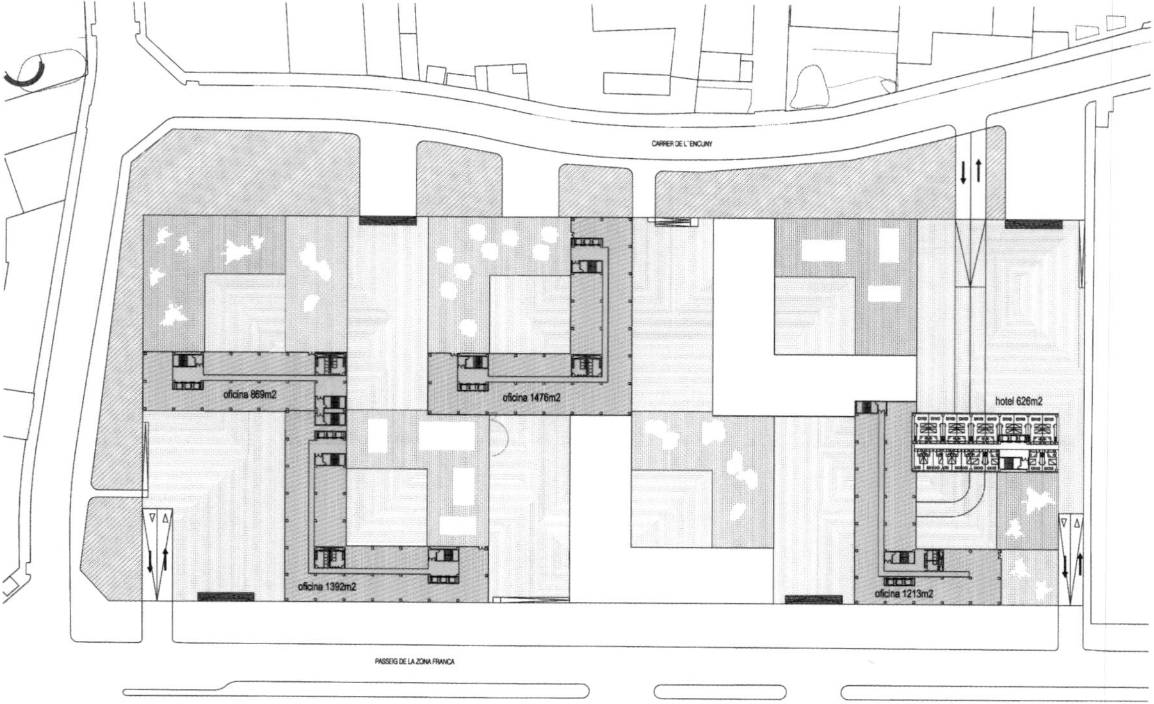
CARRER DE L'ENCUNY
oficina 869m2
oficina 1476m2
hotel 626m2
oficina 1392m2
oficina 1213m2
PASSEIG DE LA ZONA FRANCA

hotel 626m2

oficina 895m2

CARRER DE L'ENCANY

PASSEIG DE LA ZONA FRANCA

Deleuze and the Use of
the Genetic Algorithm in Architecture
Manuel de Landa

The computer simulation of evolutionary processes is already a well established technique for the study of biological dynamics. One can unleash within a digital environment a population of virtual plants or animals and keep track of the way in which these creatures change as they mate and pass their virtual genetic materials to their offspring. The hard work goes into defining the relation between the virtual genes and the virtual bodily traits that they generate, everything else–keeping track of who mated with whom, assigning fitness values to each new form, determining how a gene spreads through a population over many generations is a task performed automatically by certain computer programs collectively known as "genetic algorithms". The study of the formal and functional properties of this type of software has now become a field in itself, quite separate from the applications in biological research which these simulations may have. In this essay I will deal neither with the computer science aspects of genetic algorithms (as a special case of "search algorithms") nor with their use in biology, but focus instead on the applications which these techniques may have as aids in *artistic design*.

In a sense evolutionary simulations replace design, since artists can use this software to breed new forms rather than specifically design them. This is basically correct but, as I argue below, there is a part of the process in which deliberate design is still a crucial component. Although the software itself is relatively well known and easily available, so that users may get the impression that breeding new forms has become a matter of routine, the space of possible designs that the algorithm searches needs to be sufficiently rich for the evolutionary results to be truly surprising. As an aid in design these techniques would be quite useless if the designer could easily foresee what forms will be bred. *Only if virtual evolution can be used to explore a space rich enough so that all the possibilities cannot be considered in advance by the designer, only if what results shocks or at least surprises, can genetic algorithms be considered useful visualization tools.* And in the task of designing rich search spaces certain philosophical ideas, which may be traced to the work of Gilles Deleuze, play a very important role.

I will argue that the productive use of genetic algorithms implies the deployment of three forms of philosophical thinking (populational, intensive, and topological thinking) which were not invented by Deleuze but which he has brought together for the first time and made the basis for a brand new conception of the genesis of form.

To be able to apply the genetic algorithm at all, a particular field of art needs to first solve the problem of how to represent the final product (a painting, a song, a building) in terms of the process that generated it, and then, how to represent this process itself as a well-defined sequence of operations. It is this sequence, or rather, the computer code that specifies it, that becomes the "genetic material" of the painting, song, or building in question. In the case of architects using computer-aided design (CAD) this problem becomes greatly simplified given that a CAD model of an architectural structure is already given by a series of operations. A round column, for example, is produced by a series such as this: 1) draw a line defining the profile of the column; 2) rotate this line to yield a surface of revolution; 3) perform a few "Boolean subtractions" to carve out some detail in the body of the column. Some software packages store this sequence and may even make available the actual computer code corresponding to it, so that this code now becomes the "virtual DNA" of the column. (A similar procedure is followed to create each of the other structural and ornamental elements of a building.)

At this point we need to bring one of the philosophical resources I mentioned earlier to understand what happens next: *population thinking*. This style of reasoning was created in the 1930's by the biologists who brought together Darwin's and Mendel's theories and synthesized the modern version of evolutionary theory. In a nut shell what characterizes this style may be phrased as "never think in terms of Adam and Eve but always in terms of larger reproductive communities". More technically, the idea is that despite the fact that at any one time an evolved form is realized in individual organisms, the population not the individual is the matrix for the production of form. A given animal or plant architecture evolves slowly as genes propagate in a population, at different rates and at different times, so that the new form is slowly synthesized within the larger reproductive community.[1] The lesson for computer design is simply that once the relationship between the virtual genes and the virtual bodily traits of a CAD building has been worked out, as I just described, an entire population of such buildings needs to be unleashed within the computer, not just a couple of them. The architect must add to the CAD sequence of operations points at which spontaneous mutations may occur (in the column example: the relative proportions of the initial line; the center of rotation; the shape with which the Boolean subtraction is performed) and then let these mutant instructions propagate and interact in a collectivity over many generations.

To population thinking Deleuze adds another cognitive style which in its present form is derived from thermodynamics, but which as he realizes has roots as far back as late medieval philosophy: *intensive thinking*. The modern definition of an intensive quantity is given by contrast with its opposite, an extensive quantity. The latter refers to the magnitudes with which architects are most familiar with, lengths, areas, volumes. These are defined as magnitudes which can be spatially subdivided: if one takes a volume of water, for example, and divides it in two halves, one ends up with two half volumes. The term "intensive" on the other hand, refers to quantities like temperature, pressure or speed, which cannot be so subdivided: if one divides in two halves a volume of water at ninety degrees of temperature one does not end up with two half volumes at forty five degrees of temperature, but with two halves at the original ninety degrees. Although for Deleuze this lack of divisibility

---

[1] First....the forms do not preexist the population, they are more like statistical results. The more a population assumes divergent forms, the more its multiplicity divides into multiplicities of a different nature....the more efficiently it distributes itself in the milieu, or divides up the milieu....Second, simultaneously and under the same conditions....degrees are no longer measured in terms of increasing perfection....but in terms of differential relations and coefficients such as selection pressure, catalytic action, speed of propagation, rate of growth, evolution, mutation....Darwinism's two fundamental contributions move in the direction of a science of multiplicities: the substitution of populations for types, and the substitution of rates or differential relations for degrees.
Gilles Deleuze and Felix Guattari. A Thousand Plateaus. (University of Minnesota Press, Minneapolis, 1987). Page 48.

is important, he also stresses another feature of intensive quantities: a difference of intensity spontaneously tends to cancel itself out and in the process, it drives fluxes of matter and energy. In other words, differences of intensity are productive differences since they drive processes in which the diversity of actual forms is produced.[2] For example, the process of embryogenesis, which produces a human body out of a fertilized egg, is a process driven by differences of intensity (differences of chemical concentration, of density, of surface tension).

What does this mean for the architect? That unless one brings into a CAD model the intensive elements of structural engineering, basically, distributions of stress, a virtual building will not evolve as a building. In other words, if the column I described above is not linked to the rest of the building as a load-bearing element, by the third or fourth generation this column may be placed in such a way that it cannot perform its function of carrying loads in compression anymore. The only way of making sure that structural elements do not lose their function, and hence that the overall building does not lose viability as a stable structure, is to somehow represent the distribution of stresses, as well as what type of concentrations of stress endanger a structure's integrity, as part of the process which translates virtual genes into bodies. In the case of real organisms, if a developing embryo becomes structurally unviable it won't

[2] Difference is not diversity. Diversity is given, but difference is that by which the given is given...Difference is not phenomenon but the nuomenon closest to the phenomenon... Every phenomenon refers to an inequality by which it is conditioned...Everything which happens and everything which appears is correlated with orders of differences: differences of level, temperature, pressure, tension, potential, difference of intensity. Gilles Deleuze. Difference and Repetition. (Columbia UniversityPress, New York, 1994). Page 222.

even get to reproductive age to be sorted out by natural selection. It gets selected out prior to that. A similar process would have to be simulated in the computer to make sure that the products of virtual evolution are viable in terms of structural engineering prior to being selected by the designer in terms of their "aesthetic fitness".

Now, let's assume that these requirements have indeed been met, perhaps by an architect-hacker who takes existing software (a CAD package and a structural engineering package) and writes some code to bring the two together. If he or she now sets out to use virtual evolution as a design tool the fact that the only role left for a human is to be the judge of aesthetic fitness in every generation (that is, to let die buildings that do not look esthetically promising and let mate those that do) may be disappointing. *The role of design has now been transformed into* (some would say degraded down to) *the equivalent of a prize-dog or a race-horse breeder.* There clearly is an aesthetic component in the latter two activities, one is in a way, "sculpting" dogs or horses, but hardly the kind of creativity that one identifies with the development of a personal artistic style. Although today slogans about the "death of the author" and attitudes against the "romantic view of the genius" are in vogue, I expect this to be fad and questions of personal style to return to the spotlight. Will these future authors be satisfied with the role of breeders of virtual forms? Not that the process so far is routine in any sense. After all, the original CAD model must be endowed with mutation points at just the right places (an this involves design decisions) and much creativity will need to be exercised to link ornamental and structural elements in just the right way. But still this seems a far cry from a design process where one can develop a unique style.

There is, however, another part of the process where stylistic questions are still crucial, although in a different sense than in ordinary design. Explaining this involves bringing in the third element in Deleuze's philosophy of the genesis of form: *topological thinking*. One way to introduce this other style of thinking is by contrasting the results which artists have so far obtained with the genetic algorithm and those achieved by biological evolution. When one looks at current artistic results the most striking fact is that, once a few interesting forms have been generated, the evolutionary process seems to run out of possibilities. New forms do continue to emerge but they seem too close to the original ones, as if the space of possible designs which the process explores had been exhausted.[3] This is in sharp contrast with the incredible combinatorial productivity of natural forms, like the thousands of original architectural "designs" exhibited by vertebrate or insect bodies. Although biologists do not have a full explanation of this fact, one possible way of approaching the question is through the notion of a "*body plan*".

As vertebrates, the architecture of our bodies (which combines bones bearing loads in compression and muscles bearing then in tension) makes us part of the phylum "chordata". The term "phylum" refers to a branch in the evolutionary tree (the first bifurcation after animal and plant "kingdoms") but it also carries the idea of a shared body-plan, a kind of "abstract vertebrate" which, if folded and curled in particular sequences during embryogenesis, yields

[3] See for example: Stephen Todd and William Latham. Evolutionary Art and Computers. (Academic Press, New York, 1992).

an elephant, twisted and stretched in another sequence
yields a giraffe, and in yet other sequences of intensive
operations yields snakes, eagles, sharks and humans.
To put this differently, there are "abstract vertebrate" design
elements, such as the tetrapod limb, which may be realized
in structures as different as as the single digit limb of a
horse, the wing of a bird, or the hand with opposing thumb
of a human. Given that the proportions of each of these
limbs, as well as the number and shape of digits, is variable,
their common body plan cannot include any of these details.
In other words, while the form of the final product (an actual
horse, bird or human) does have specific lengths, areas and
volumes, the body-plan cannot possibly be defined in these
terms but must be abstract enough to be compatible with
a myriad combination of these extensive quantities. Deleuze
uses the term "abstract diagram" (or "virtual multiplicity") to
refer to entities like the vertebrate body plan, but his concept
also includes the "body plans" of non-organic entities like
clouds or mountains.[4]
What kind of theoretical resources do we need to think
about these abstract diagrams? In mathematics the
kind of spaces in which terms like "length" or "area" are
fundamental notions are called "metric spaces", the familiar
Euclidean geometry being one example of this class.
(Non-Euclidean geometries, using curved instead of flat
spaces, are also metric). On the other hand, there are

[4] An abstract machine in itself is not physical or corporeal, any more than it is semiotic; it
is diagrammatic (it knows nothing of the distinctions between the artificial and the natural
either). It operates by matter, not by substance; by function, not by form... The abstract
machine is pure Matter-Function—a diagram independent of the forms and substances,
expressions and contents it will distribute.
Gilles Deleuze and Felix Guattari. A Thousand Plateaus. Op. Cit. Page 141

geometries where these notions are not basic, since these geometries possess operations which do not preserve lengths or areas unchanged. Architects are familiar with at least one of these geometries, projective geometry (as in perspective projections). In this case the operation "to project" may lengthen or shrink lengths and areas so these cannot be basic notions. In turn, those properties which do remain fixed underprojections may not be preserved under yet other forms of geometry, such as differential geometry or topology. The operations allowed in the latter, such as stretching without tearing, and folding without gluing, preserve only a set of very abstract properties invariant. These topological invariants (such as the dimensionality of a space, or its connectivity) are precisely the elements we need to think about body plans (or more generally, abstract diagrams.) It is clear that the kind of spatial structure defining a body plan cannot be metric since embryological operations can produce a large variety of finished bodies, each with a different metric structure. Therefore body plans must be topological.

To return to the genetic algorithm, if evolved architectural structures are to enjoy the same degree of combinatorial productivity as biological ones they must also begin with an adequate diagram, an "abstract building" corresponding to the "abstract vertebrate". And it is a this point that design goes beyond mere breeding, with different artists designing different topological diagrams bearing their signature. The design process, however, will be quite different from the traditional one which operates within metric spaces. It is indeed too early to say just what kind of design methodologies will be necessary when one cannot use fixed lengths or even fixed proportions as aesthetic elements and must instead rely on pure connectivities (and other topological invariants). But what it is clear is that without this the space of possibilities which virtual evolution blindly searches will be too impoverished to be of any use. *Thus, architects wishing to use this new tool must not only become hackers* (so that they can create the code needed to bring extensive and intensive aspects together) *but also be able "to hack" biology, thermodynamics, mathematics, and other areas of science to tap into the necessary resources.* As fascinating as the idea of breeding buildings inside a computer may be, it is clear that mere digital technology without populational, intensive and topological thinking will never be enough.

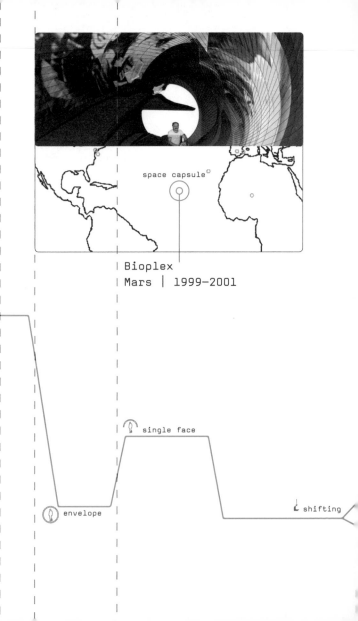

space capsule

Bioplex
Mars | 1999–2001

single face

envelope

shifting

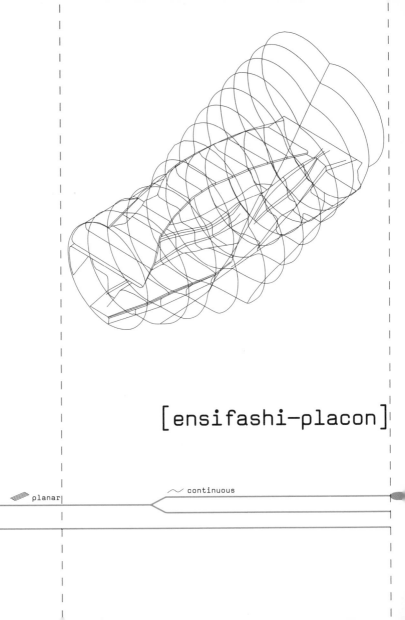

[ensifashi-placon]

planar   ～ continuous

The project involves the construction of a structure which explores the potential of a transportable cylinder that can be opened to provide a home or a research unit for use on the planet Mars. Nasa is currently developing Bioplex units as work and living units for scientists who by the year 2013 will be stationed on Mars for periods of one year at a time.

Our proposal – shown at the Future Homes exhibition, organised in Stockholm – aims to challenge the Bioplex unit, designed as a cylinder as a direct consequence of the internal diameter of the rocket that will transport the Bioplex to the surface of Mars. One of the greatest limitations of human life on Mars will thus be geometrical, as Mars's dwellers will be condemned to develop all their activities inside a cylinder. Each aspect, each dimension of their private and public life will be to contain within that omnipresent radius of conditioned space. As architects, our biggest contribution to life on Mars will be to produce an opening up of that spatial limitation, to propose a technical solution to the unfolding of the basic cylindrical envelop into a variety of topologies, scales and shapes that, without a specific function to perform, will perhaps trigger the imagination of the dwellers into developing new, extra-terrestrial activities.

Having studied many alternatives, such as telescopic, axial pro-liferation and perpendicular deformations in order to geometri-cally unfold a cylinder, we have designed a structure where a series of concentric ribs would unfold in space, changing the extruded and homogenous basic space of the unit into a differentiated and deformed cylinder which rotates in section through 90 degrees along its length. This is combined with openable ribs which, when closed form a full cylinder in cross-section. This is supported on tubular steel struts and has an internal perimeter walkway, which either cantilevers or is sus-pended from the inside of the cylinder.

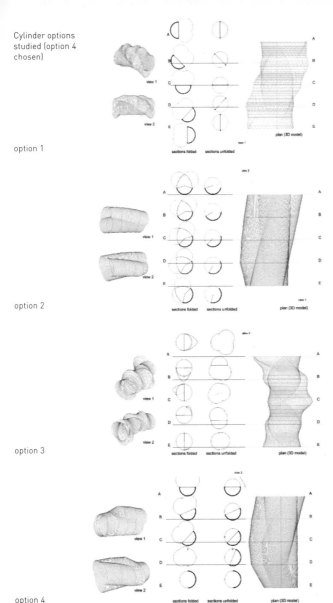

Cylinder options studied (option 4 chosen)

option 1

option 2

option 3

option 4

533

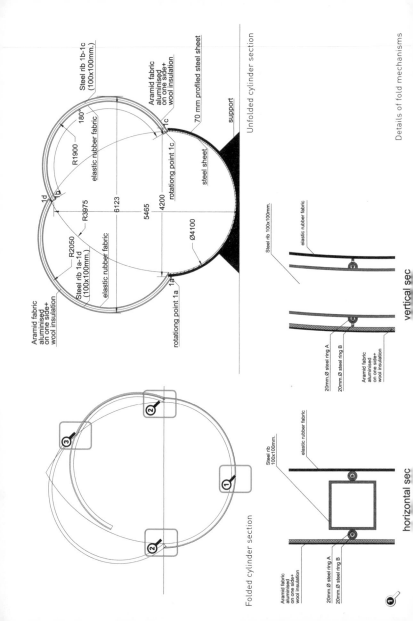

Aramid fabric
aluminised
on one side+
wool insulation

Steel rib 1a-1d
(100x100mm.)

elastic rubber fabric

R2050

R3975

rotationg point 1a - 1d

R1900

180°

1d

6123

5465

4200

Ø4100

Steel rib 1b-1c
(100x100mm.)

elastic rubber fabric

Aramid fabric
aluminised
on one side+
wool insulation

rotating point 1c

70 mm profiled steel sheet

steel sheet

support

Unfolded cylinder section

Folded cylinder section

Details of fold mechanisms

Steel rib 100x100mm.

elastic rubber fabric

20mm.Ø steel ring A
20mm.Ø steel ring B

Aramid fabric
aluminised
on one side+
wool insulation

vertical sec

Steel rib
100x100mm.

elastic rubber fabric

Aramid fabric
aluminised
on one side+
wool insulation

20mm.Ø steel ring A
20mm.Ø steel ring B

horizontal sec

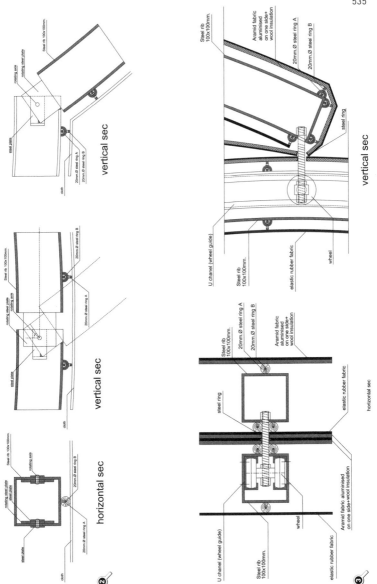

535

Longitudinal section

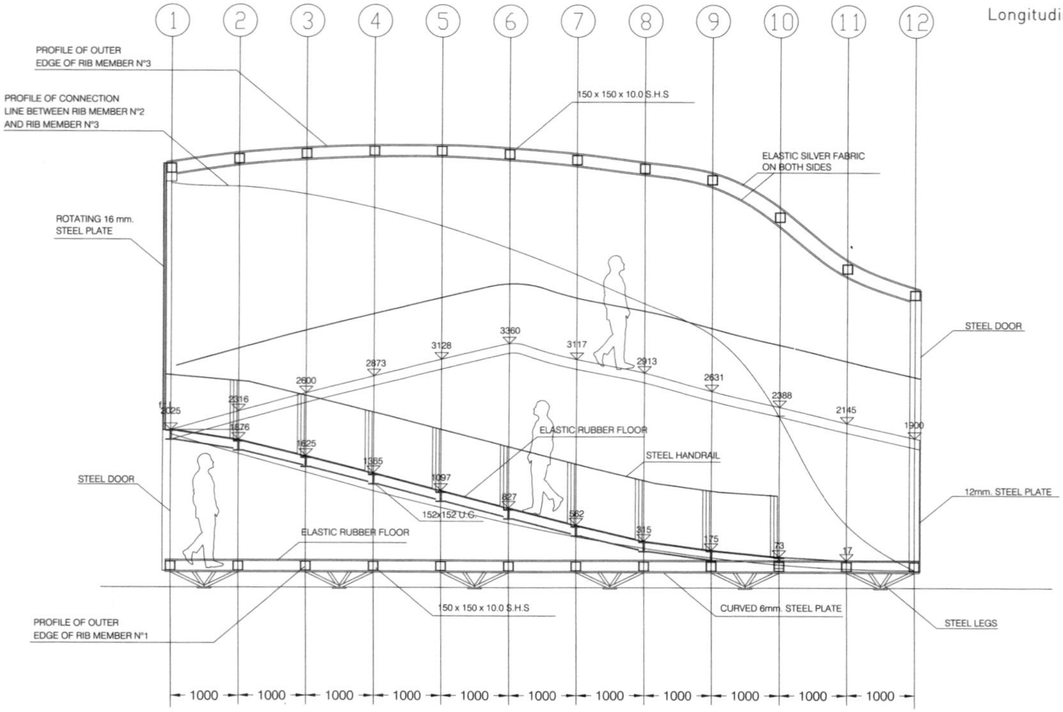
PROFILE OF OUTER EDGE OF RIB MEMBER N°3
PROFILE OF CONNECTION LINE BETWEEN RIB MEMBER N°2 AND RIB MEMBER N°3
ROTATING 16 mm. STEEL PLATE
STEEL DOOR
PROFILE OF OUTER EDGE OF RIB MEMBER N°1
150 x 150 x 10.0 S.H.S
ELASTIC SILVER FABRIC ON BOTH SIDES
STEEL DOOR
12mm. STEEL PLATE
STEEL LEGS
CURVED 6mm. STEEL PLATE
150 x 150 x 10.0 S.H.S
ELASTIC RUBBER FLOOR
STEEL HANDRAIL
ELASTIC RUBBER FLOOR
152x152 U.C.
1000
1000
1000
1000
1000
1000
1000
1000
1000
1000
1000

Plan

Transverse sections

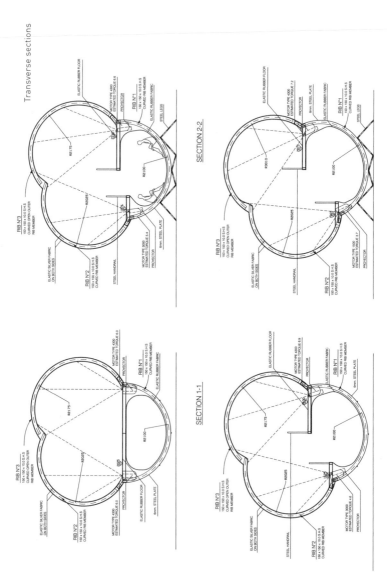

SECTION 1-1

SECTION 2-2

SECTION 3-3

SECTION 4-4

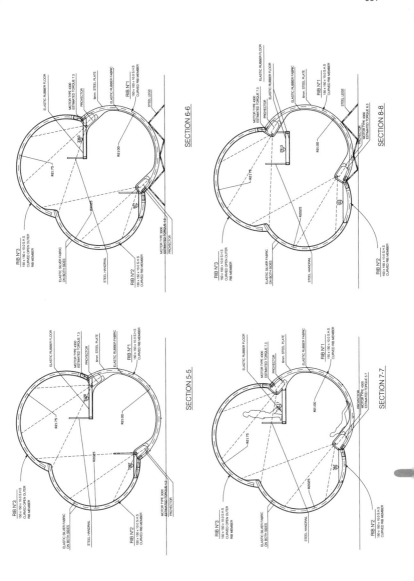

SECTION 6-6

SECTION 8-8

SECTION 5-5

SECTION 7-7

Transverse sections

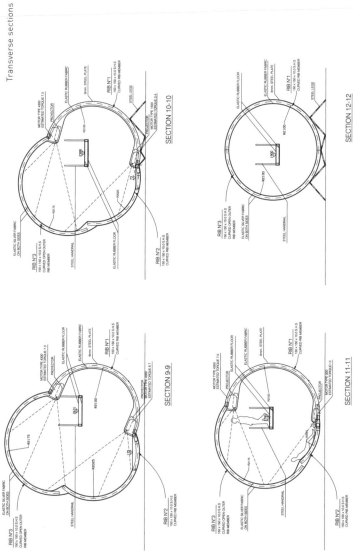

SECTION 9-9

SECTION 10-10

SECTION 11-11

SECTION 12-12

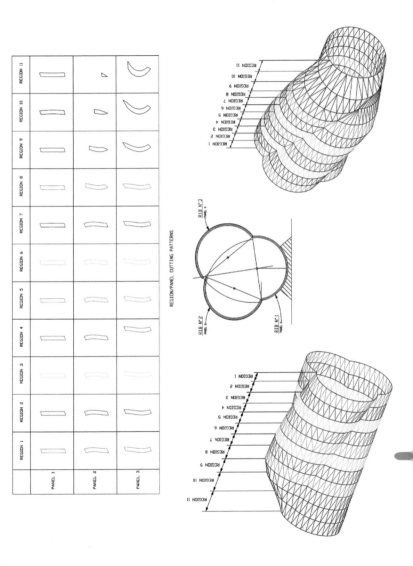

REGION/PANEL CUTTING PATTERNS

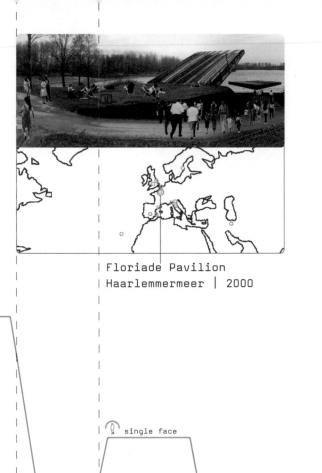

Floriade Pavilion
Haarlemmermeer | 2000

single face

envelope

shifting

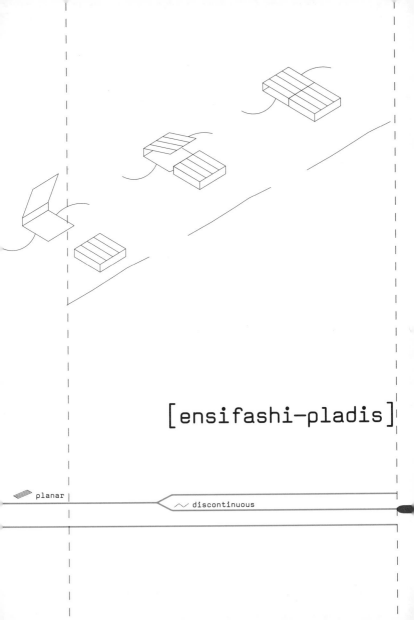

[ensifashi-pladis]

planar

discontinuous

This pavillion, proposed to represent Haarlemermeer at the Floriade 2002 aims at representing and above all synthesising the main constituents of Haarlemermeer's latent identity:
- Schipol as a major infrastructural resource, not only in the Netherlands, but in the whole of Europe, is not only the major economic engine of Haarlemermeer, but also a fantastic source of latent identity, waiting to be exploited.
Despite the environmental disruption it may cause, Haarlemermeerians are also those expanding 37 million passengers, flying through Schipol last year. The local capacity to handle such a flow, and the way of articulating it in the construction of a specific environment is more a subject of pride than a source of regret, most especially in the age of globalisation.
- The Polder nature and its landscape is also a fantastic source of potential identity, and a unique feature of Haarlemermeer. 150 years ago, the ground of Haarlemermeer existed only under the water level. Only through a very sophisticated hydraulic technology, the very ground of the Polder has been able to emerge. Is not only the very particular nature of the Polder's landscape, but also the very artificiality, and the awareness of the instability of the ground that emerges as a fantastic source of local identity in Haarlemermeer.
- The flower market and the tulip fields are last but not least in this list of latent identities of Haarlemermeer that we are attempting to synthesise in this pavilion. The tulip is not a conventional appreciation of nature, but on the contrary another radical manifestation of the possibility of constructing and harnessing nature, this time with a purely hedonistic purpose. The tulip plantations are an extraordinary and extravagant trace of this. Our aim has been to attempt to synthesise all these latent iden-

North Entrance

North Parking

De Groene Weelde

Splotter's Hill

Floriade
2002

Pavilion

Forecourt

Future
entrance

South parking

Future location
of forecourt

tities into a material construct that will bear some of the material traces that characterise these themes. Our models of organisation have been the runways, tulip fields, canal systems and lifting bridges. Our models of performance have been navigation, hydraulics and dynamics.

Our proposal is to use two different building-machines, one for the forecourt pavilion, another for the main pavilion, that we propose as a floating structure in the lake. Both of them have as a purpose to thematise the instability of the ground that characterises Haarlemermeer from its very roots. From the polder construction to the airflight presence, the Haarlemer-meer experience is about the instability of the ground. A ground that is marked by repetitive striations, traces of its function or organisation: tulip lines, channel distributions, runway lights and signs... The striations are not only the plane of consistency where all these organisations coincide, but also the visual structure that serves as an orientation when navigating, flying floating in an unstable milieu. In the Haarlemermeer milieu the presence of material forces is much more present that in the more stable grounds. Either from the ground or from the air, the omnipresence of striations is what allows us to navigate through.

The forecourt pavilion is constituted by a pivoting plane, hover-ing 3m over the ground level on the lake shore level. The pivot-ing plane, planted with tulips on a tarmac surface to synthesise those two materials that characterise the Haarlemermeer expe-rience, can be used as a sun deck or viewing point, but also as a huge advertising board for the qualities of the local ground. It will also provide different degrees of coverage, from complete to none, to the ground surface that lies at the edge of the water.

But most of all, the platform will reproduce in its rotation, those oblique perceptions of striated fields that characterise the Haarlemermeer experience: takeoff, touchdown...
The main pavilion is conceived as an inhabitable piece of drifting ground, this "terrain vague" that characterise the local milieu. A 20x20m floating barge will host the more private functions of the pavilion, being able to locate anywhere in the lake.
By using a hydraulic mechanism, the pavilion can not only displace itself across the lake, but also tilt and submerge to provide different conditions of the ground and different perspectives of the polder horizon. The ground of the two main surfaces of the pavilion will tilt a maximum of 4.5 degrees to shift spatial conditions from those adequate for performances to those adequate for exhibitions or social meetings.
Both pieces can also combine in a multiplicity of arrangements, making them able to host a very large variety of events, from performances to projections, from celebrations, meetings and conventions to contemplation...
The pavilion uses a welded steel plate construction to form this floating object. Cells within the plated form are used to create buoyancy tanks, that provided with a hydraulic pump allow the pavilion to achieve a variety of states of equilibrium for its different uses.

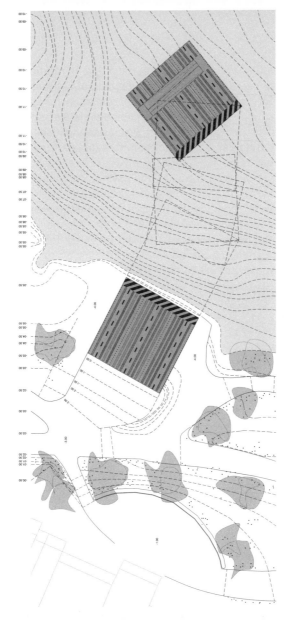

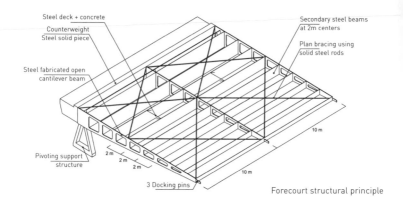

Steel deck + concrete

Counterweight
Steel solid piece

Steel fabricated open
cantilever beam

Secondary steel beams
at 2m centers

Plan bracing using
solid steel rods

Pivoting support
structure

2 m
2 m
2 m

10 m

10 m

3 Docking pins

Forecourt structural principle

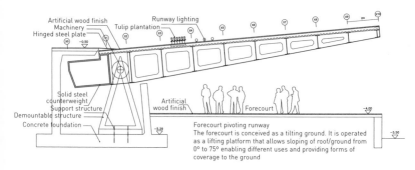

Artificial wood finish
Machinery
Hinged steel plate

Runway lighting
Tulip plantation

2 m

-0.50

Solid steel
counterweight
Support structure
Demountable structure
Concrete foundation

Artificial
wood finish

Forecourt

-4.00

-5.50

-5.28

Forecourt pivoting runway
The forecourt is conceived as a tilting ground. It is operated
as a lifting platform that allows sloping of roof/ground from
0º to 75º enabling different uses and providing forms of
coverage to the ground

Forecourt detailed section

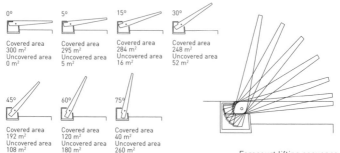

0º
Covered area
300 m²
Uncovered area
0 m²

5º
Covered area
295 m²
Uncovered area
5 m²

15º
Covered area
284 m²
Uncovered area
16 m²

30º
Covered area
248 m²
Uncovered area
52 m²

45º
Covered area
192 m²
Uncovered area
108 m²

60º
Covered area
120 m²
Uncovered area
180 m²

75º
Covered area
40 m²
Uncovered area
260 m²

Forecourt lifting secuence

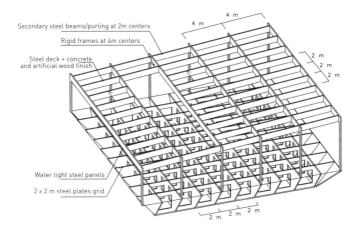

Secondary steel beams/purling at 2m centers

Rigid frames at 4m centers

Steel deck + concrete and artificial wood finish

4 m 4 m 4 m

2 m 2 m 2 m

Water tight steel panels

2 x 2 m steel plates grid

2 m 2 m 2 m

Floating pavilion structural principle

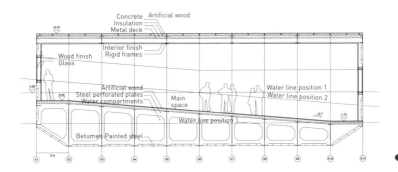

Concrete Artificial wood
Insulation
Metal deck

+3.47

Interior finish
Rigid frames

Wood finish
Glass

0.00

-0.44

Artificial wood
Steel perforated plates
Water compartments

Main space

Water line position 1
Water line position 2

+12.7   -1.73

Water line position 1

Betumen Painted steel

X1 2 m X2   X3   X4   X5   X6   X7   X8   X9   X10   X11

Floating pavilion detailed section

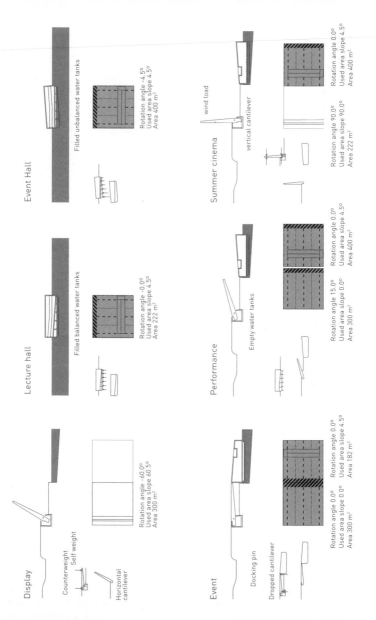

Display

Counterweight
Self weight

Horizontal cantilever

Rotation angle -60.0°
Used area slope 60.5°
Area 300 m²

Lecture hall

Filled balanced water tanks

Rotation angle -0.0°
Used area slope 4.5°
Area 222 m²

Event Hall

Filled unbalanced water tanks

Rotation angle -4.5°
Used area slope 4.5°
Area 400 m²

Event

Docking pin

Dropped cantilever

Rotation angle 0.0°
Area 300 m²

Rotation angle 0.0°
Used area slope 4.5°
Area 182 m²

Performance

Empty water tanks

Rotation angle 15.0°
Used area slope 0.0°
Area 300 m²

Rotation angle 0.0°
Used area slope 4.5°
Area 400 m²

Summer cinema

wind load

vertical cantilever

Rotation angle 90.0°
Used area slope 90.0°
Area 222 m²

Rotation angle 0.0°
Used area slope 4.5°
Area 400 m²

Floating Pavilion sections

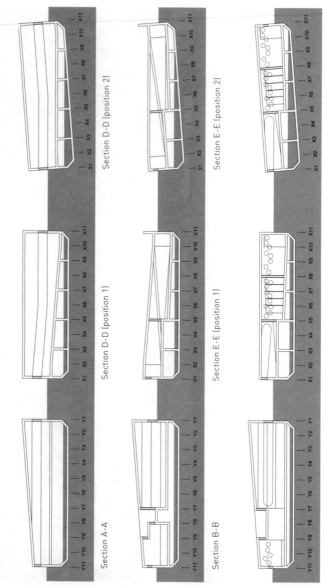

Section A-A

Section D-D (position 1)

Section D-D (position 2)

Section B-B

Section E-E (position 1)

Section E-E (position 2)

Section C-C

Section F-F (position 1)

Section F-F (position 2)

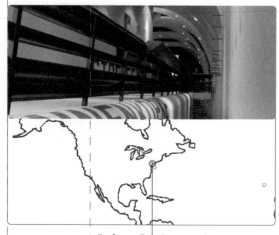

Belgo Restaurant
New York | 1998–1999

single face

envelope

shifting

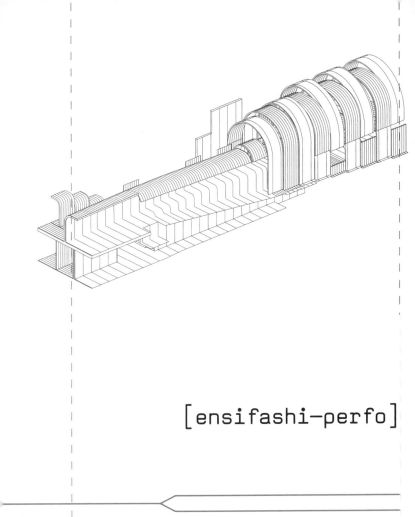

[ensifashi-perfo]

perforated

Belgo New York is located in a former storage building in the east Village in New York City. The space is a typical Manhattan site, occupying the basement and first floor of a 9m-wide by 45m-long plot. Our interest was to exploit the length of the site and the different levels of the floors of the loading bay to distort the Cartesian quality to the typical New York space. The tubular qualities of being in an intestine or a barrel, and its resonance with the experience of the New York Subway, driving along an American highway, or sitting in an aeroplane cockpit were some of the themes that we exploited in this project. The interior structure was totally reconstructed to eliminate the intermediate structural line, so as to emphasise the tubular and directional quality of the restaurant space. A 45m-long, 2m-wide ramp links both levels of the restaurant. The finish of floors, ceilings and walls is always the same, a synthetic resin, sausage-like in colour. The tube proliferates inton a series of transversal bands, from which the lighting and the air conditioning is generated. The kitchen, exposed to the public view, is placed parallel to the entrance tube, contributing to the narrowing of the entrance space. A continuous railing crosses the space longitudinally, as if it were a roadside barrier.

Transverse sections

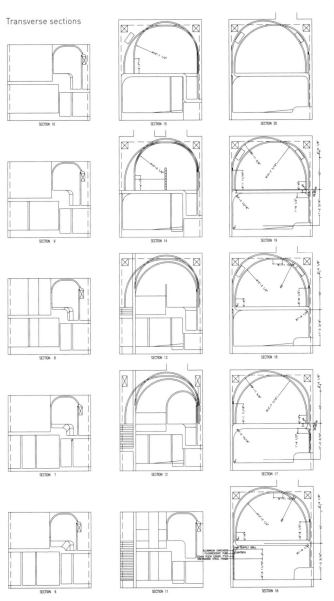

SECTION 10

SECTION 9

SECTION 8

SECTION 7

SECTION 6

SECTION 15

SECTION 14

SECTION 13

SECTION 12

SECTION 11

SECTION 20

SECTION 19

SECTION 18

SECTION 17

SECTION 16

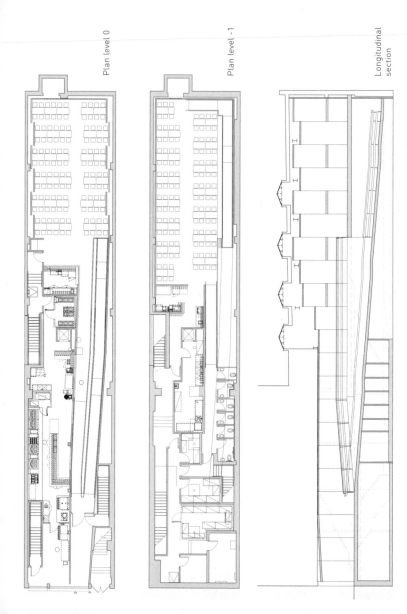

Plan level 0

Plan level -1

Longitudinal section

On the Wild Side
Jeffrey Kipnis

My father was of the sky, my mother was of the earth,
I am of the universe and you know what it's worth."
(Lenin, I mean, Lennon)

Long long ago. When writing about painting and architecture
these days, there are advantages to be gained by starting with
the Big Bang. Despite a pervasive, uneasy refusal to accept
it – it in itself a fascinating feeling – the Big Bang is an
absolute, an indisputable fact of our existence, of all existence.
That makes the BB king, the Big Fact, the only fact in fact,
that big. It is, therefore, very useful for arguments if you can
get it on your side. Of course, the Big Bang was long long
ago and I only have a few thousand words to discuss painting
and architecture, so I am going to have to make a long story
short. Let me draw, then, but three inferences from the BB:
history, matter and ecology, perverting each to an extreme.
History. From the BB, we know that everything, absolutely
everything, even quark, lepton, atom and molecule, every
jot, dot and iota, every being, every sensation, every concept,
every organization, system, network and mesh has a
history; everything began and everything evolved. It is thus
a certainty that consciousness, too, evolved, from primordial
sensate materiality to awareness to consciousness to self-
consciousness, to critical self-consciousness and beyond.
Evolution Rules! Lucky for me, because I want to revisit the
co-evolutions of painting and architecture and consciousness

– as Hegel [and Marx and Darwin and Freud...] did before.
Now, these days, it dawns on us at long last that we
are not in the universe, but of the universe. Thus, as we

are conscious of the universe it must be allowed that the
universe is conscious of itself; allowed not merely as a belief,
not as a point of faith, but as hard reality. Personal
or collective self-consciousness sheds its parochial egoism
to emerge as cosmic consciousness.

I bet you can see where I am going with this already.
Somehow or another, I am going to argue that painting
and architecture are part of this emergence of cosmic self-
consciousness. Sort of. I'll give you a hint. I'm going to
say that even if a particular species – like Us – is the
proximate vehicle for consciousness through our self-
consciousness, much as a small part of the frontal lobe of
each of our brains is the proximate vehicle for each of our
individual experience of self-consciousness, nevertheless,
consciousness itself is an emergent property not of an organ
or an individual or a species or a community or a society,
but or a complex ecology. Painting and architecture are
each species in an ecology that contribute irreducibly and
irreproducibly to consciousness and its evolution.

Like any other ecology, the holistic state of the ecology of
consciousness is intimately dependent on the promiscuous
intercourse that links all of its co-evolved species, and
therefore on the state at any moment of each and every
member species. As a change in local context – the
introduction of a new predator, a comet, the harnessing of
electricity, the tubing of paint, the development of plate glass
– places evolutionary pressure on one species of a
sub-ecology, the entire ecosystem ultimately reconfigures
to some greater or lesser extent in response. Think of what
electricity did to the guitar, and the electric guitar to Jimi
Hendrix, and the two together to music, for example.

In the ecology of consciousness, painting and architecture are two member species among many. Evolutionary developments in one or the other at times initiate reconfiguration in that ecology. In less than a century, the eruption of Collage in and from painting, for example, ripped through all of the species in the ecology of consciousness with as much force as the Yucatan Comet on our biosphere, causing unprecedented mass extinction and new specialifications. At other times pressures felt more immediately in other species – in the sciences, in philosophy, in sports, in the climate – variously reshape painting and architecture. Consider the relationship between Cubism and early 20ᵗʰ century physics, one better understood as a co-evolution than as a representation. The emergence of the species Photography, as another example, had significant, though quite different, effects on every species in the ecosystem; we can see the same kind of evolutionary ripple effects today as the computer, a fascinating new species that evolved from the loom, reshapes the fitness landscape of the ecology of consciousness.

The Big Bang's ultrahistoricity also compels an affirmative answer to another decisive question for art and architecture, "Are there new feelings in the world?" – a way past cooler question than that tired old fart-smelling pus-oozing boil: "Are there new ideas in the world?" Hold it, New Feelings embarrasses you, I can tell. But you must realize that the embarrassment you are feeling at this very instant as you encounter the problem of New Feelings is itself an old feeling, a key policing tactic, a homeostatic feedback mechanism of a certain state of consciousness that is aware of but afraid to let go of its defects. That state stifles the question of New

Feelings, blinds us to its range and power, not with good
Reason, not with Logic or Knowledge, but with a cunning
spell, the feeling of shame. Already, the question of feelings
gets more interesting. That state of consciousness is
Criticality and its correlate mood, Objectivity, crucial moments
in the evolution of self-consciousness. Work that elaborates
criticality must also engender a mood of objective reflection
and vice versa.

The apotheosis of such work in the visual arts and one
of its most far reaching achievements is Collage, to which
we will return.

Having thoroughly migrated to, percolated through and
reconfigured most of the existing niches in the ecology of
self-consciousness, criticality has now stalled – for the
moment at least – as a creative eruption. Compelled to move
with nowhere else to go, criticality transmogrifies into a
social hegemony, an etiquette of doing and talking that is less
productive than courtly, less thoughtful than mean.

In this frustrated humor, criticality suppresses other
moments, other moods, livelier ones, giddier ones, ones
wetter, more freshly, more rhythmic, more transporting, more
creative and much more intelligent. Its potency ossifies into
a regime of manners, a sadistic stultification that, like a
vampire, eroticizes the bloodless ennui it engenders, an ennui
that continues to pose as sobriety, as depth, but is now merely
the ache of unrealized potential.

To be sure, criticality was deeply intelligent, but that
intelligence has begun to sense its own limits. Criticality is
no longer intelligent because as a limb of intelligence,
it is atrophying. Put on a white laboratory coat, sterilize your
instruments, assume a clinical mood, then pick up a white

mouse. Let the mood – itself nothing other that a syndrome
of feelings – let the mood deterritorialize and dematerialize
the mouse from a living creature to a site for a scientific
experiment; you are, by the way, now deep into the psyche of
Collage. Hold its eyes open, put in a few drops of eye shadow
in solution, steel your pity against the subject as it writhes
in agony, then observe it for a week or two to see whether
the eye explodes into weeping lesions. Euthanize it, dissect
it, dispose of it, write down your observations, publish your
results. Or show them in a gallery.

There is no denying it; for over a century, this attitude-process
and those in its constellation have led to an unparalleled
explosion in scientific and medical knowledge of incalculable
benefit. Corollary processes in other sciences and in the
arts and humanities have borne equally abundant fruit.
Now, however, in this cosmetic instance and elsewhere, the
profitable flow of new intelligence subsides: our biochemical
knowledge is so complete, our tissue-reaction models
so effective that we know the results even before we begin.
These days, we undertake such studies more to deflect
product liability claims than to gain new insight. By going
through the motions, we demonstrate earnest intent to
minimize adverse effects, an intent whose value is to be
admissible as a defense in court. Intelligence succumbs to
a regime of manners.

But is the fisc of intelligence available to self-consciousness
through this clinical play with the white mouse spent when
the once fecund violence of critical analysis lapses into
diminishing returns? Or can other, holistic modes of play,
modes that embrace that white mouse as a unique, complex,
sentient, communicating material moment in possession

of a treasure of information/knowledge/wisdom, yield more
intelligence, unimagined intelligence? Like a frightened
bully, the critical state of mind banishes these other modes
and moods from the playground by calling them names.
New Age Sentimentality, for example, Eastern Philosophy,
or sometimes merely Art. But matter is insatiable; in its
essence, as its essence it wants more – more feelings, more
knowledge, more power, more life, and it knows how to get it.
It is no longer just a matter of time; it is the time of matter.
Matter. There were no signs, no ideas, no concepts, no
meanings, no disembodied spirits, no dematerialized
abstractions whatsoever around during the first couple of
seconds after the Big Bang, nor during the first million
or billion years or 10 billion years, or, for that matter, even
these days. Not to say that there was no information nor
communication, there were immense amounts of both – still
are – but that is another story, indeed, the one that will matter
to us most. What there was and all that there was, i.e.,
what there is and all that there is, was and is lots of matter,
always conscious of itself, always organizing itself into
increasingly complex, intelligent arrangements, always
performing new behaviors.
For, like, a really long time, matter has been treated as a
kind of cosmic putty, a mute, ignorant, ultrabland ursstuff
that receives form, vitality, character, spirit, concept or other
infusions of immaterial ideality. But the BB broaches no
ideality, no dematerialized instant, it consists of nothing but
matter and its processes. Thus, the BB requires a radically
different view of matter, one vigilant against the daydreams
of ideality and fallacy of dematerialization in any guise,
one in which trait, form, life, spirit and concept are always

already immanent virtualities of matter, each emerging as manifest material reality in its turn as matter designs itself into ever more sophisticated arrangements.

In simplest terms, the radicalization of matter requires three recognitions: that matter is from the beginning irreducibly sensate and responsive; that at every scale sensate, responsive matter organizes itself hierarchically into discreet, irreproducible configurations with specific emergent behaviors; and that all discreet material configurations at any and every moment and any and every scale further arrange into complex ecologies.

Incarnation of the BB, the BB incarnate, Matter is a primordial trinity: to send/to receive/to organize. Nothing that exists is not matter, nothing that exists does not send/receive/organize. A quark emits/receives gluons; like the beginning of love, it feels another gluon or two emitting/receiving quark(s) and in their sensuous exchange of gluons, they organize into something new, a baryon. A baryon, e.g., a proton, emits/receives photons, an electron emits/receives photons, when they feel one another in their photonic exchange – more a carnal dance than a communication of information – they organize into something new, a hydrogen atom, and so forth into molecules, dust, nebulae, then planets, stars, galaxies, clusters, organic molecules, organelles, cells, organisms. To be continued.

To say "organize into something new", is to say that a new arrangement with new behaviors has emerged. And new behaviors are always nothing more than and nothing less than new ways to send, new ways to receive, new ways to organize, matter taking control of itself for its own pleasure. New materials, new species, new feelings, new thoughts,

all the same. Nothing escapes materiality, but not to worry,
for materiality is no prison. Matter is freedom itself.
An electron has behavioral properties, a proton has behavioral
properties, together they form a hydrogen atom with
behavioral properties of two components, but an emergent
repertoire of new properties. In this repertoire, some
properties are legacies of component properties, some prior
properties are lost, some are manifest for the first time.
The emergent properties of any and every new organization
are typical, i.e., common to every instance of that
organization, discrete, i.e. finite in number, and irreproducibly
specific. Common, discrete and irreproducibly specific,
these are BIG BIG BIG. Nothing else in the universe has
the exact constellation of behaviors of a particular material
organization. Nothing. Only a proton and an electron
configured as a hydrogen atom has its constellation of
properties. To be sure, there are others that have similar
properties – a deuterium atom, for example, is ALMOST
identical to hydrogen EXCEPT that it weighs twice as much...
Other, drastically different material organizations can portray,
represent, or mimic certain hydrogen atom properties, an
emission spectrum photograph for example, or a drawing
of the energy levels or the Schroedinger wave equation, etc.
But nothing else in the universe has all of its properties
and none other. The species hydrogen atom, or gerbil,
or painting, or architecture, or WIMP is a unique mode of
sending, receiving and organizing.
Every new organization possesses new emergent properties;
from molecules to organisms to practices, each typical, each
discrete, each irreproducible. In the history of philosophy,
Hegel, Marx, Darwin and Freud grasped preliminarily the

basic mechanisms of this state of affairs, but the most uncanny anticipation of its consequences, for all of its naivetes and atavisms, is to be found in Leibniz's Monadology, where the catalogue of qualities he attributes to the elusive monad, the most fascinating of which we must omit – like each monad in its finitude the infinity of the universe – are the very qualities we claim for all emergent organizations. Thus, every material organization is monadic.

Emergence is not a renaming of synergy – it is not a matter of a whole greater than the sum of the parts. There are no parts in emergence, only new wholes, though the emergence of a new whole does not simply eradicate the wholes that merge to form it. The properties of a water molecule is irreducibly specific. And a water molecule is not water. Even if you had all the water molecules in the universe, you could not quench your thirst unless they organize into liquid water. The ability of water molecules to organize into a thirstquenching liquid, itself a new material organization other than a sum of water molecules, is one of the unique, emergent properties of the water molecule, one of its new ways of sending, receiving and organizing. And the emergences of liquid water? Not thirsty? Then try some other feelings; savor the exhilaration of a shower, zone out on the surface reflections of a pond, rhapsodize to the hypnotic sound of ocean waves, or reflect on the well-spring of life on earth.

The materiality of BB's Matter, while far from any One, is profoundly common, assuring that the cacophony of sendings, from the gravitons, weakons, gluons and photons to higher order emanations (temperatures, pressures, sounds, smells, pulses, rhythms, beams, modulated waves,

food, images, music, utterances, languages, caresses,
payments, etc.), is more that matched by a robust audience
to feel and respond to them. All material arrangements
to some extent sense all others, sometimes barely, but much
more often through a richly detailed and elaborate palette
of emanations and sensations. Obviously, not every
arrangement can send and receive every emanation.
An electron cannot send a phonon, a hydrogen atom cannot
sense certain photons, a cat cannot smell like a rose, a
painting cannot sing, at the moment, anyway. Moreover,
not every arrangement sense every other arrangement
in the same way nor in total, some arrangements do not
sense others at all.

While the immense commonality of Matter assures a vast
coherence, the differential mesh of send/receive/organize/
taken in concert with the discrete, monadic specificity
of each material organization yields a correspondingly vast
array of differences. These different monadic configurations
at any and every moment and any and every scale arrange
into dynamic complexes that expand the differential
mesh even further, multiplying the species of material
configurations geometrically and connecting those species
into another order of coherent arrangement – Ecologies.
In the Monadology, Leibniz describes this orgy of
organization as the maximum variety with the greatest
coherence; clearly he was Buddha.

Ecology is not a metaphor drawn from the world of biology;
rather it is a fundamental organizational inclination of Matter
whose most renowned example, for the moment, is the
biological instance. By now and at long last, consciousness
begins to hear and sway to the great concert of earth's

bio-ecology, the matrix of all life on earth, a matrix that of necessity exceeds parochial notions of the animate to include the entirety of earth, its geologies, its climates, its gravity, its magnetic field, its rotations and orbit, the fragile precision of its distance from the sun, and so forth. And some few of you will know that the ecological diagram has already emerged in other practices. Astronomers now routinely describe galaxies as complex ecologies and some cosmologists are looking at the universe itself in ecological terms; indeed, a few interesting weirdos are attempting to answer the most intractable questions in physics by imagining that our universe is just one species in an ecology of universes.

But let's not get lost on that byroad. Already these remarks feel like driving to McDonalds by way of Mars. Are we there yet? Huh, are we there yet?

Let me just note that the ecological model of galaxies accounts for the birth, life, death and aftermath of the various species of stars and other galactic flora and fauna.

Now, as you may have heard, the earth itself and every living thing on it, including me and you, are physically made of the material residue of a star that died and blew up. That's right, you are a phoenix of starstuff (as is the sausage you just ate and the fart you just let, lest you wax too poetically on your newfound astral affiliation.) When you look at a star it's kind of like a star looking at itself. Can you not already feel the rumble, the stirring of a new consciousness on the horizon, bound to erupt should such tentative links between these two distinct ecologies – the earth and the galaxy – proliferate until the two are indissolubly knitted?

As the organizational thrust of Matter climbs the hierarchy of complexity, then it passes through levels of monadic arrangements with different, distinct emergent properties, i.e., increasingly luxurious ways of sending/receiving/ organizing. The way an individual member of a species feels the sendings of another of the same species is quite different from the way a member of one species in an ecology feels a member of another. But as new species emerge, and new sub-ecologies cluster, new sendings are sent and new feelings felt. Consider the promiscuous eco-linkages effected by but one of the intricate sendings of a bird, its call. We could just as well have considered other of its material sendings: its image, its smells, its stares, its dances and gestures, its dandruff, defecations and urinations, even its whole body, sent as food. After all, one of the most important modes of receiving and organizing in an ecosystem is Eating, accounting for the ecological significance of predator-prey relationships. But. let's just stick to the call.

However intricate it may be, the call is one emanation, a sound ensemble, specific in pitches, duration, pattern and intensity typical first of that bird's species but further modulated within that typically to be uniquely characteristic of that individual bird. The bird call does not contain, but is intimately shaped by both the history of the species and the history of the individual bird. In the bird's chicks, the call feels like mother, in another member of its species, the call feels erotic or madding, depending on the other's sex; to a nearby hawk the same call feels like an urge to hunt, in a vole panic, in a poet walking in the woods a feeling that cascades into a lyrical turn of language, in a composer into a musical imagination, in a camper background noise.

To a heavy snow bank, the call does not feel like much,
but had it been 10 hertz higher in pitch or 10 decibels louder
in volume, the snow bank might have felt the call enough to
avalanche. A blush of photons, rushing from a tree to reflect
off a pond nearby feels virtually nothing of the call at all,
nor does the call feel much of them. But the air between the
tree and the pond feels some of the photons, heats up and
changes density, an effect the call feels.

Though beyond our scope at the moment, a meditation on
the specificity of emanations and the different types of
feelings induced by an emanation, among individuals within
a species and across species – not just living ones – is
crucial to the materialist recuperation of knowledge, wisdom,
information, communication and consciousness from the
dematerialized-idealist versions fomented by critical analysis,
particularly as semiotics, mathematics, programs and other
wraiths conjured by the cult of ideas. The idea of the triangle,
for example, can never be extricated from the fact that a
sound, or a sight or some other material actuality – is able to
make a wet, grey mass feel slightly differently, albeit in largely
the same way over and over, again and again, though never
exactly the same twice. Nothing, not triangles, not ideas, not
God, exists outside of Matter.

Emanations are themselves material. Specific and detailed,
they are full of information, but they contain no message,
merely the ability to be variously felt. The conversion of
that detailed specificity in part or whole into a message is
entirely in the reception, the feeling. The possibility of a
message, a non-trivial feeling but merely one among many,
grows out of the typicalities of both the specificity of the
emanation and the receiver. When I lift a weight, and my

arm muscle grows larger, has the weight sent me a message? Such a meditation would take shape as a reflection on material resonances and on the orchestration of those resonances into diagrams. It would absorb with respect the achievements of semiotics, mathematics and other idealist approximations, blowing beyond these to astonishing claims and insights. The migration of diagrams through material resonances, reclaimed from such brute notions as signification, learning, programs and memory, would offer a riveting account of how the emanations of an ecology take a nascent organism and reorganize it in such a way as to cause it to recapitulate in a very short period, a matter of months or years, not only the social history of its community, not only the phylogenetic history of its species, not only life on earth, not only the history of the earth, the solar system and the galaxy, but the evolution of Matter since the Big Bang itself! Un-fucking believable!!! Unfortunately, no time to go into at at the moment. Phone's ringing.

... Goddam cocksucking, fucking editors and their goddam deadlines. They say I'm out of time, period. I'm desperate; a million more things to say. man, I really wanted to get into Collage and criticality, see if I could kill that disease once and for all. Fuck it, I'll just get to the point; you will just have to fill in the blanks yourself, or call me.
The Rub is this, Consciousness is not a property of an organ, an individual, a species, a community, or a society. Consciousness is an emergent feeling specific to and existing only in an ecology, the holistic manifestation in any and every material organization of all of the receiving, sensations,

awarenesses and feelings that circulate in an ecology
as the ecology. When a new feeling emerges in an ecology,
it begins to ripple through, to find its specific moment in the
monadic material organization of all of the eco-members.
As each member senses it, it reorganizes itself and manifests
that reorganization in the specificity of its new sendings.
A new state of consciousness emerges in an ecology when
a new feeling finds its specific material moment in all of the
sendings, receiving and organizations of all of its members.
When all of those feelings impinge on a super-sensate
arrangement like your body, it – not just your brain – resonates throughout with all of them. Your self-consciousness,
a monadic member of the Ecology of Consciousness, is the
voluptuous feeling of your body hyperindexing that onslaught
of material information (not signs, not messages, not codes,
not programs, not the cut-outs of a collage). You are in the
shower, a fusillade of warm water droplets rains on you,
each stinging you with its impact and heat. You let it beat
on your head, on your face – mouth open, eyes closed.
You soap your genitals. You tingle, you sing – particularly if
the shower stall resonates. If the light is low, you masturbate,
unless you have a partner. You have ideas about your work,
etc. What's Clean got to do with it?
People are material arrangements unfathomably sensitive
to an immense spectrum of eco-emanations, able to respond
and reorganize with stunning fluidity and to rebroadcast
feelings and new feelings through an amazing catalogue of
sendings – including painting and architecture; they are kind
of like the shower. The problem for the painter or the architect
then is more to develop new techniques of sending than new
messages to send...

Publishing Headquarters
Paju | 2001

envelope

multiple face

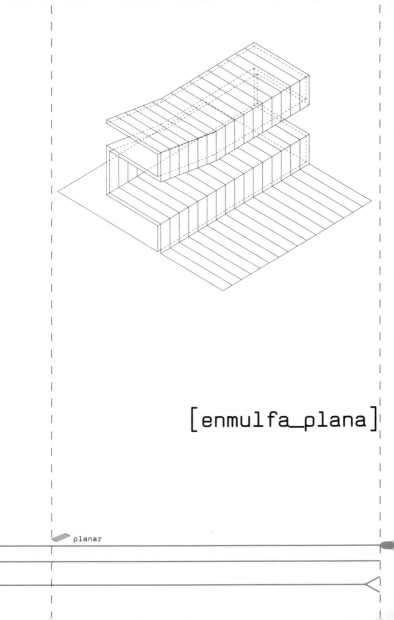

[enmulfa_plana]

planar

This project is a commission from Dulnyouk Publishers to design the facilities to relocate in a centralized form their directive, administrative and editorial facilities in the Seoul area. The building is to be located in Paju Book City, a satellite town of Seoul designed strategically to centralize the editorial business in the region.

The site is a 2000m² lot on the western edge of a hill that towers above the valley where Paju Book City will be located. The regulation of the masterplan enforces the orientation of the built mass on an east-west orientation in order to avoid the blockage of the airflow between the hill and the riverside to the west of the site, and a height limitation of three stories. The program of accommodation includes archive/storage, workspace for the executive and administrative direction and editorial operations, event space and an apartment for guests, for a total area of 1800m².

The building is designed to maximize the potential of its suburban location in Paju Book City, by turning the workspaces into a literal extension of the gardens surrounding the building. Intensifying the qualities of the strong orientation in the masterplan, the building is designed as a folded screen between a south-facing green garden and a north-facing mineral garden, that literally extend into the two faces of the screen, one cladded in wood and the other in stone. The geometry of the folded screen that constitutes the structure of the building is arranged in such a way that every floor is alternatively oriented towards either of the two gardens, producing a constant alternation of landscapes and finishes as one moves across the section of the building.

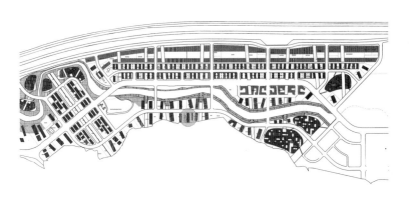

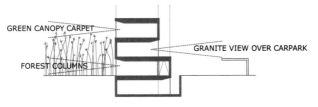

GREEN CANOPY CARPET

GRANITE VIEW OVER CARPARK

FOREST COLUMNS

BAMBOO FOREST | GRANITE

WOOD

ROCK GARDEN

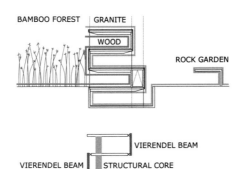

VIERENDEL BEAM

VIERENDEL BEAM | STRUCTURAL CORE

VIERENDEL BEAM

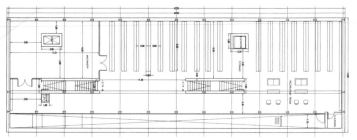

Plan level 0

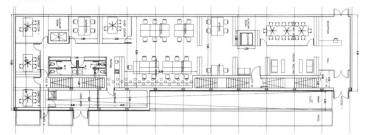

Plan level +1

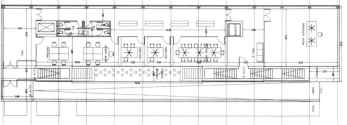

Plan level +2

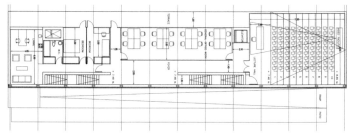

Plan level +3

Transverse section

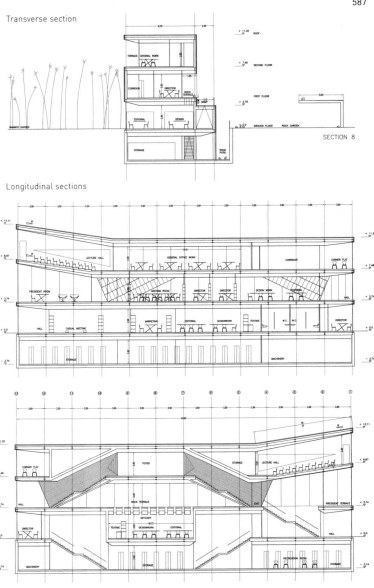

SECTION 8

Longitudinal sections

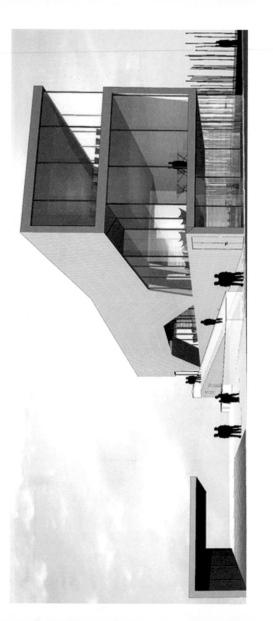

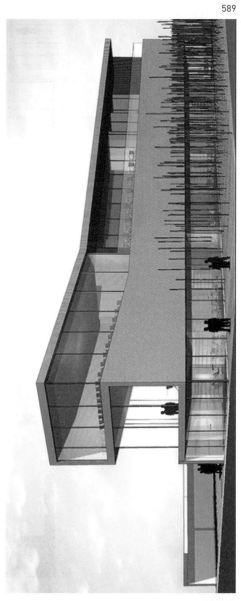

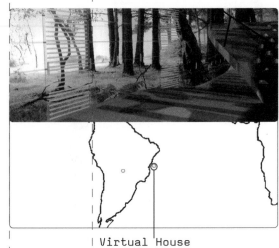

Virtual House
Anywhere | 1997

envelope

multiple face

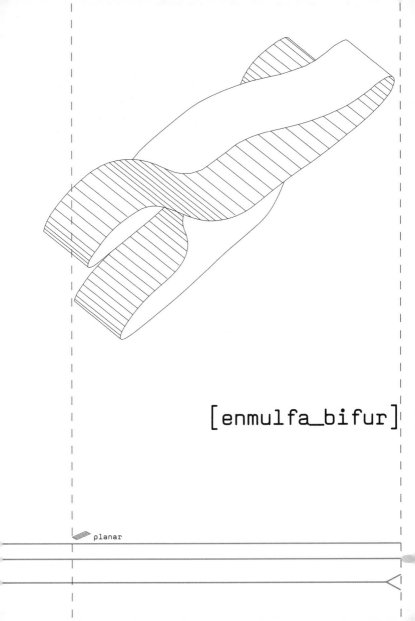

[enmulfa_bifur]

planar

Our ambition for this project was to unfold the effects that a physical structure would produce on the given identities and forms of the dwelling. Our strategy to produce the virtual was not to replace the real with a sophisticated surrogate, like in "virtual reality", but rather to dismantle the complex assemblage of social uses, organisations of space and material qualities that have come to constitute what we generally understand as a house. The virtual is not the better, the future or the past, but what may unfold possibilities or produce lineages. The project emerged from a piece of artificial ground with indeterminate structural strength, supplied with water and energy, and characterised phenomenally as a visually differentiated field: this field of visual singularity was made using Disruptive Pattern Material. DPM is produced by abstracting a given visual field into a differentiated distribution of colour on a surface. DPM is specific not only in terms of its relation to a given visual field, but also in terms of its scale, dependent on the distance at which it should be perceived. This matter will provide our virtual house with a broad palette of abstracted regions, a collection of synthetic landscapes. We could now explore the groundlessness of the house by producing different models of ground, to proliferate the house into a series: the Arizona model, the Kwai model, the Steppe model, the Schwarzwald model... This band of synthetic ground was manipulated to produce the coding of space in a similar form in which a protein band folds to produce a DNA code: the organisation of matter will have precedence over the coding. We manipulated it in order to further challenge some other categories that have been characteristic of the domestic spatial phenomenology, such as the opposition

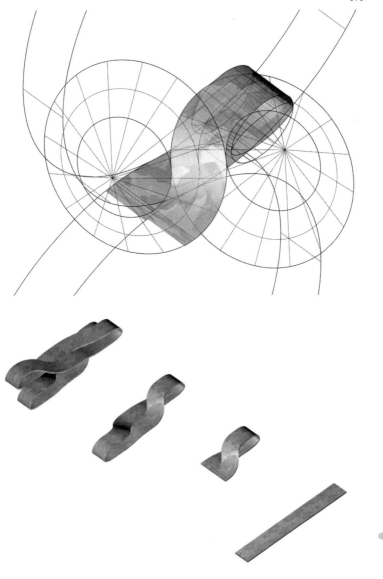

between inside/outside, front/back, up/down, and other cultural constructions of the dwelling.

In order to challenge the conventional categories of inhabitation, each face of the folded DPM surface will shift from a lining condition to a wrapping condition, disrupting the orientation of the relationships between the enveloping surface and the inside/outside opposition. Enclosure and structure are generated by topological handles in the surface. Each room is combined with another room to form a double-sided, double-used band. Each composite band will be combined with other composite bands to produce a more complex organisation of rooms, in which the folding bands will also grow three-dimensionally, as a pile of wafer matter. Rooms are not segmented parts of the structure, but on the contrary, are singular points in a continuous space. To explore the gradients of different conditions occurring on the folded surface, preceding the coding of inhabitation, we had to classify the different areas into three possible qualities of the surface: wrapping/lining, inside/outside, and gravity in/gravity out. The superposition of these three different categorisations will produce the conditions for the use of this topography of inhabitation. The system could proliferate now the body of the house ad infinitum, like as a deep, inhabited, hollow ground, from the room to the city.

Plan level 0

Plan level +1

Plan level +2

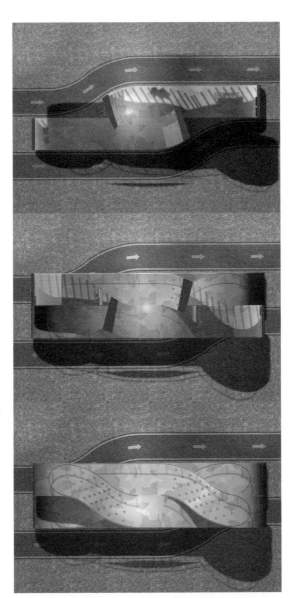

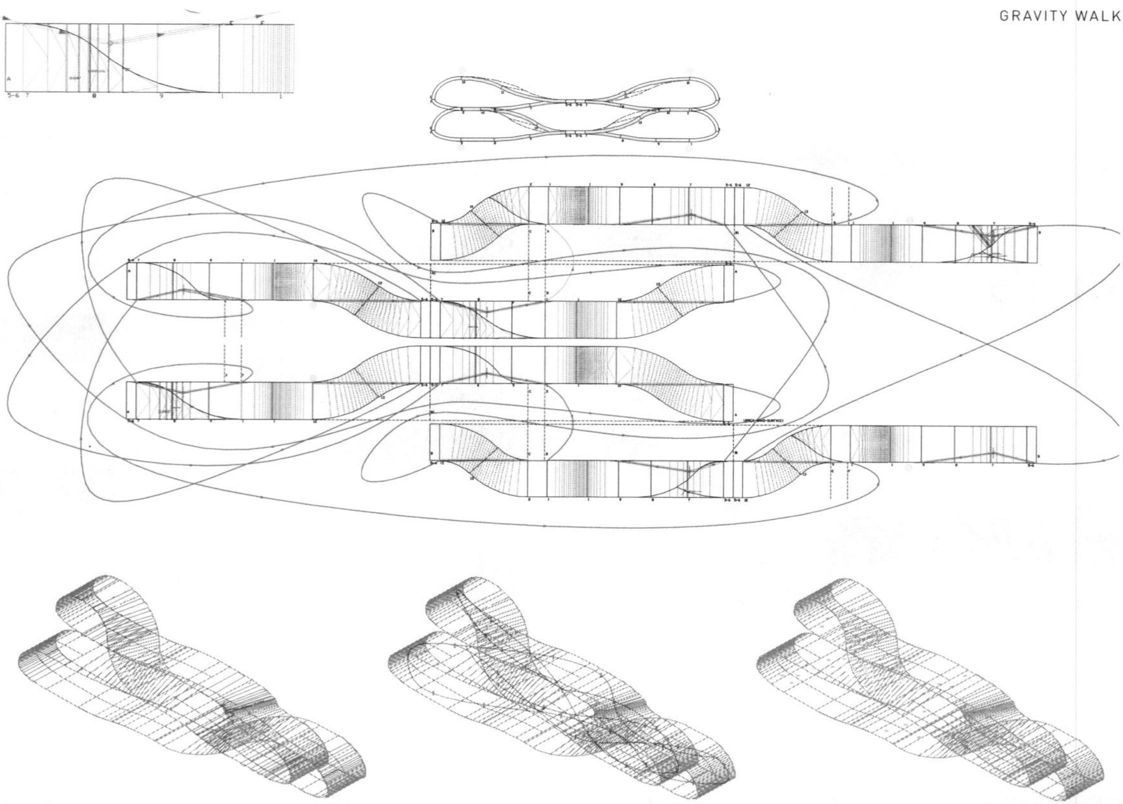

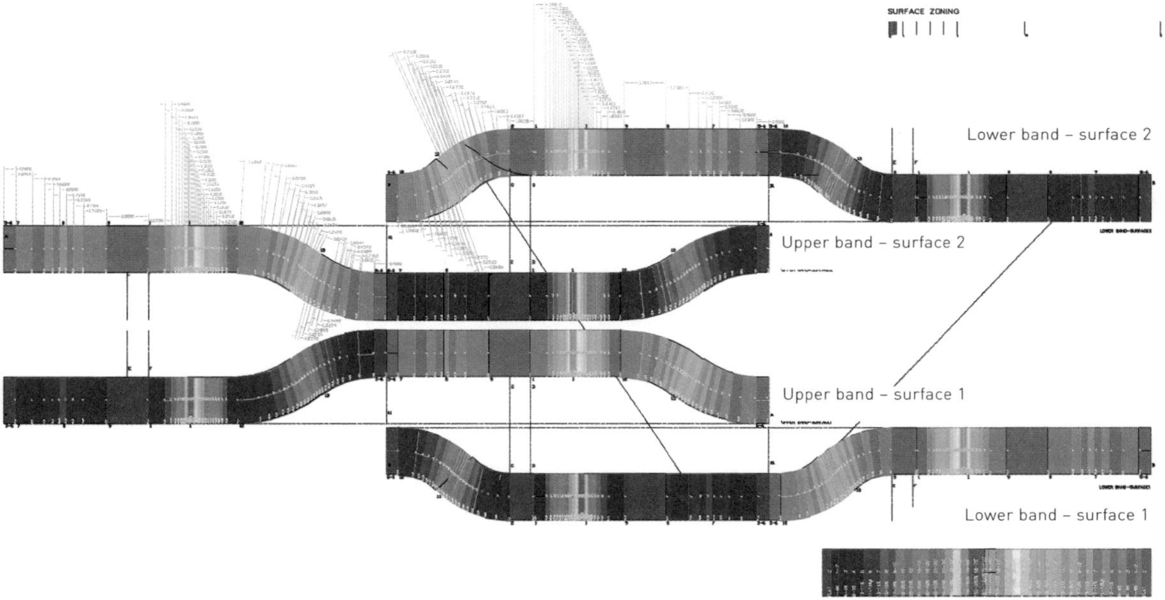

CHROMATOGRAPHIC SLOPE ANALYSIS

Lower band – surface 2

Lower band – surface 1

Upper band – surface 2

Upper band – surface 1

SURFACE ZONING

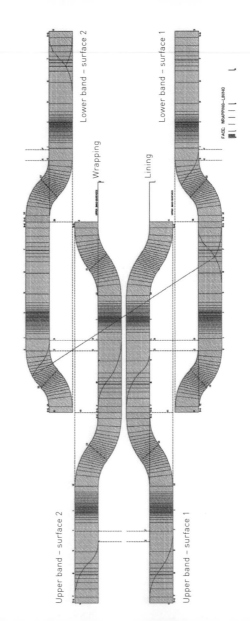

Lower band – surface 2

Lower band – surface 1

Wrapping

Lining

Upper band – surface 2

Upper band – surface 1

599

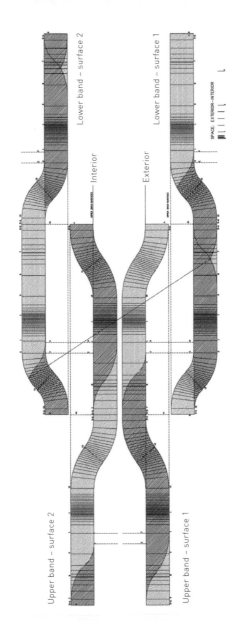

Lower band – surface 2

Lower band – surface 1

Interior

Exterior

SPACE: EXTERIOR-INTERIOR

Upper band – surface 2

Upper band – surface 1

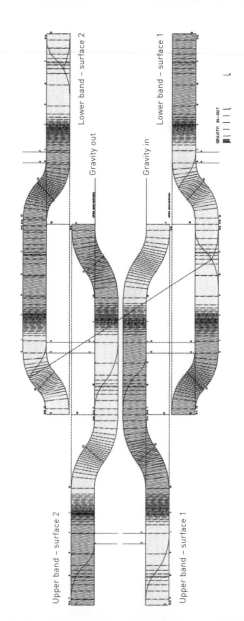

GRAVITY: IN-OUT

Lower band – surface 2

Lower band – surface 1

Gravity out

Gravity in

GRAVITY: IN-OUT

Upper band – surface 2

Upper band – surface 1

MULTIPLE SURFACE CODING:
FACE – SPACE – GRAVITY

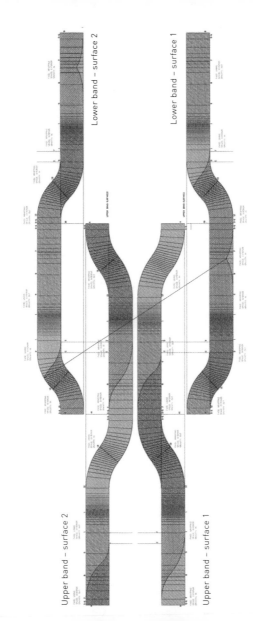

Lower band – surface 2

Lower band – surface 1

Upper band – surface 2

Upper band – surface 1

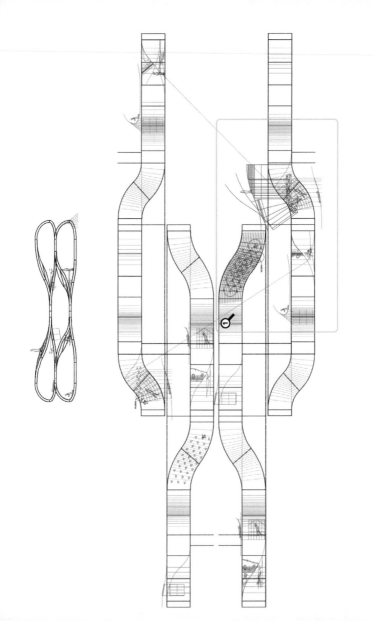

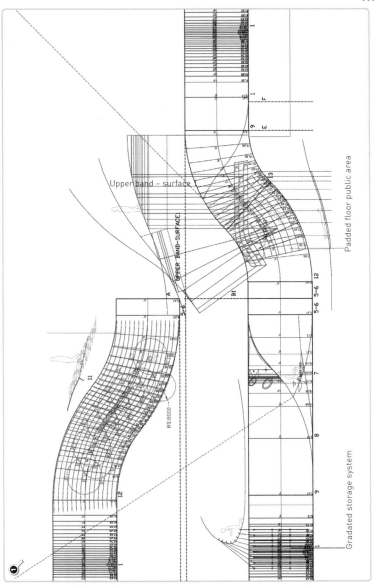

Upperband – surface

UPPER BAND-SURFACE

Padded floor public area

Gradated storage system

R0.8000

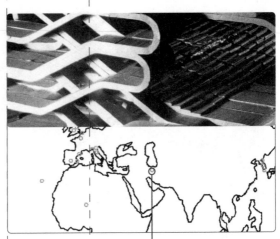

Azadi Cineplex
Tehran | 1996

$\bigcirc$ envelope

$\bigvee$ multiple face

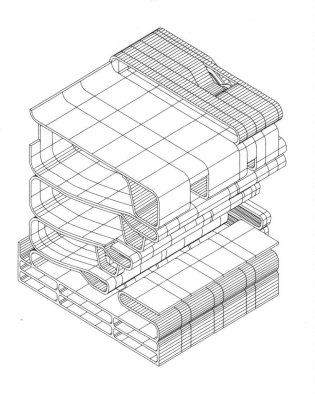

[enmulfa_perfo_azadi]

bifurcated

The main requirement of the brief was the location of seven auditoria of varying sizes — between 150 and 700 seats — together with an area of commercial and cultural spaces, on a 43 x 45 m corner site formerly occupied by the city center's most renowned cinema. Our proposal was to provide a very figurative strategy to this nostalgic and monumental project, turned literally into the formal and organisational device of the scheme. A filmstrip, rising from the ground in several folds, was the image/ organisation we sued. Following this organisation, the different rooms and necessary access and exit routes were piled one on top of the other. In forming tubular beams/ rooms spanning the 43m distance between the edges of the site, the formal structure was also to become the load-bearing structure.

The circulation in the building is organised through a system of differentiated access and exit tubes, located in parallel to the screen, and opening onto a system of escalators located on the West Side of the site. This circulation system connects with the complementary uses above and below the movie theatre, while a fire-exit system on the east and north sides of the site produces a buffer to the neighbouring firewalls. In order to sustain activity beyond the operating hours of the movie theatres, the other services were located around the latter on the ground floor and at the roof level. In this way both zones retain certain dynamism, especially the roof, which offers a splendid view over the city.

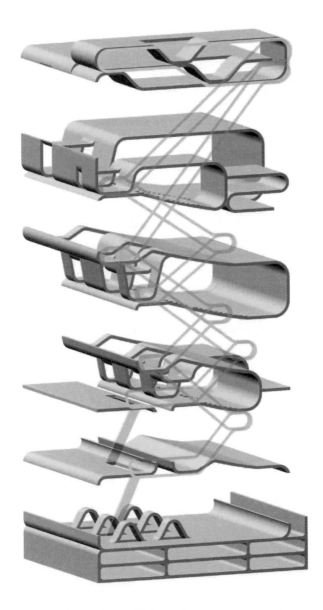

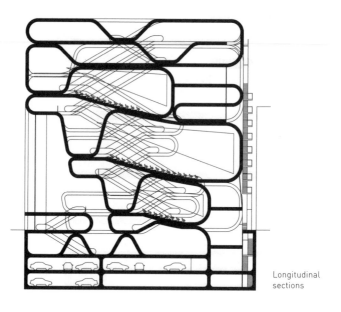

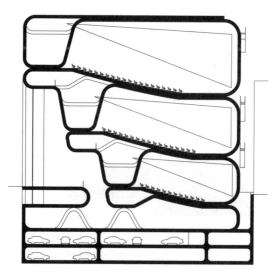

Longitudinal
sections

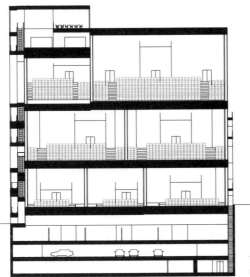

Transverse
section

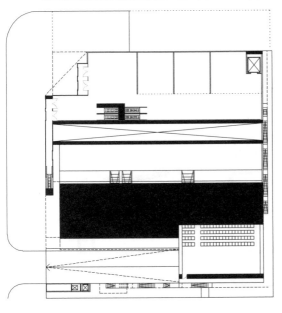

Basement
level

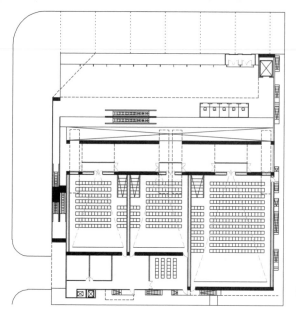

Foyer level

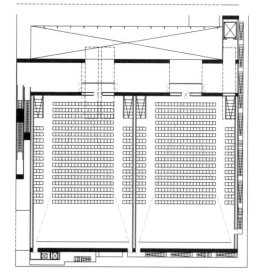

Cinema auditoriums
level 2

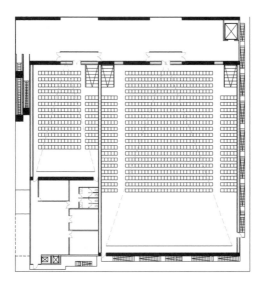

Cinema auditoriums
level 3

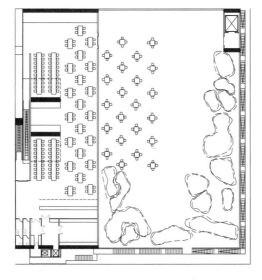

Roof terrace and
restaurant level

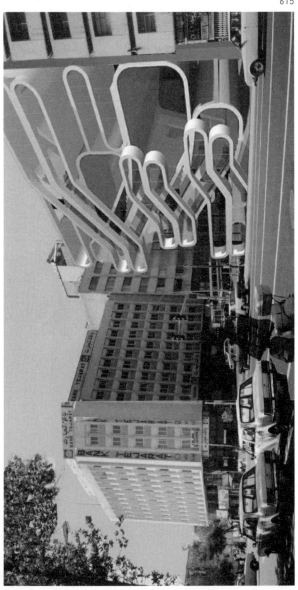

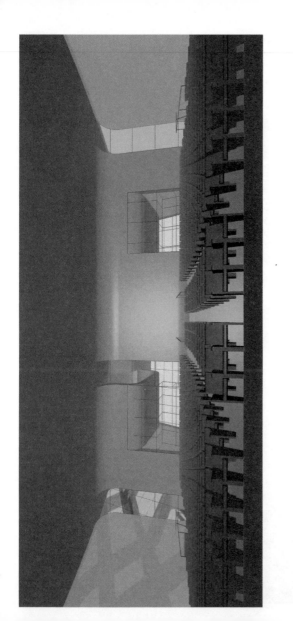

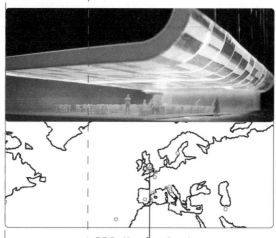

BBC Music Centre
London | 2003

envelope

multiple face

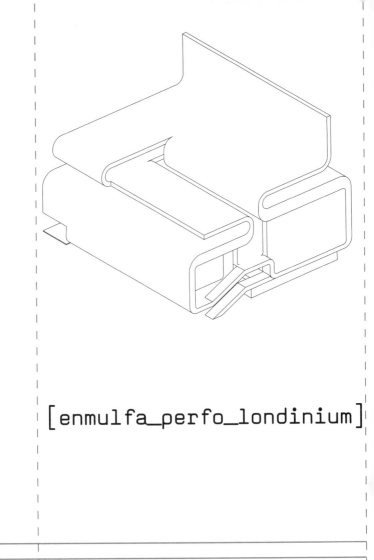

[enmulfa_perfo_londinium]

perforated

We have imagined our role as the enablers of the BBC urban and architectural identities rather than as providers of a prefabricated architectural brand. We have not aimed to deploy forms but to trigger the architectural potentials in the project to communicate the BBC to the public.

Our proposition operates by attempting to engage in the very essence of the BBC as a public Broadcasting Corporation: to visually connect the space of the studio with the space of the city through a glass membrane. What can be a more exciting image of the BBC than a building where you can witness the studios from the street? Like being allowed to enter the backstage of a theatre, the passers-by will be able to contemplate the activities taking place inside the building from outside, and the musicians will be able to perform within the city. Of course that is only one of the possible modes of operation of the studio, and mostly a possibility for the BBC to present itself in public as an open and transparent organization: Simply by lifting the facade-curtain, the conventionally hidden studio is suddenly transformed into a stage.

Music is a sequence of events in time. Its physical notation or registration implies a primarily linear structure: a band.

The Music Centre is like an instrument, constructed by a manipulation of the band. The band is folded in loops that envelope the main spaces in the building, becoming a screen or a diffuser, depending on the adjacent activity. The folded loops organize the spaces in the building, jointly with the public space in a very clear division between screens and windows.

Screens are sides of the loops separating inside and outside, inducing a mediated and distant relationship between the activities in the Music Centre and the public. This opaque side of

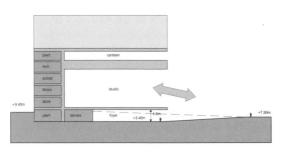

View connectivity.
Relation of studios to street

the bands exposed to the distant view will be treated as a broadcasting device, a piece of film capable of producing coloured,
changing images. This will allow the building to literally reproduce the music performed inside through an audio scan that will
turn pitch, rhythm and volume into changing digital patterns of
colour and light. Windows are sides of the loops that are continuous with the public urban space and induce a direct visual
communication between the activities and the public.

The room acoustic is calculated in order to operate perfectly
with a fully acoustically reflective/ diffusing and visually transparent glass window on one side, depending on the specificities
of use the surface may need to be fully absorbent acoustically
and visually opaque through a wide variety of insulation conditions, seasonal changes and specificity of programs.

In order to provide this flexibility we have designed a system
composed of a series of diaphragms that operate in combination
to produce a range of visual and acoustic effects from complete
visual exposure to full black-out and absorption scenarios.

The complex, just like the BBC, operates constantly in this
double mode of relation between the public and the technology,
between the real and the mediated.

The site is located in central position in respect to the other
BBC facilities in the White City area. One of the particularities of
the other clusters of BBC is that there is no open space capable
of hosting large public events within the campus. The possibility
of breaking the mass into two volumes will allow us not only
to make efficient and appropriate use of the ground, but also to
administer the public space into a series of interconnected
plazas able to react to the multiple facets of this urban setting.
In order to produce the liberation of ground and increase in

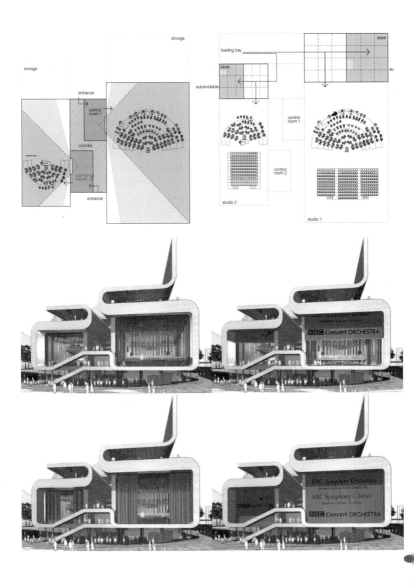

height that will enable us to develop these urban strategies, we have systematically followed a strategy of footprint condensation by choosing typologies and organizations able to compact the ground of the buildings to a minimum, without decreasing their functionality.

The drive towards a more compact plan has a sectional implication by stratifying public areas under, between and above the studio level. It produces a large open space connected to the surrounding landscape at ground level where space for an art gallery, foyer for the BBC cinema, BBC shop and small cafe will be located. By enclosing public space for the musicians in between the studios, rather than wrapping it around them, we are simultaneously compacting the plan while exposing one blank side of the studio to the street, one full opening toward the outside and one side towards storage and service areas. The complex also features public spaces high up in the sections of both buildings, visually connecting the various BBC complexes within White City and establishing another layer of experience across the BBC population.

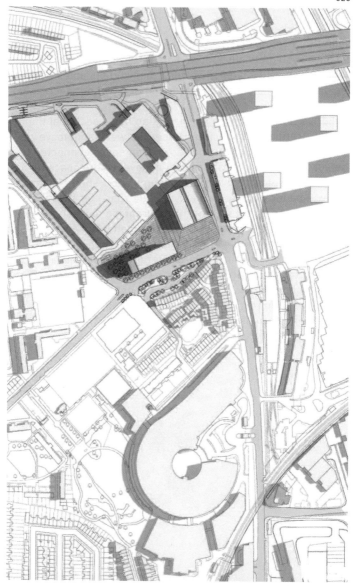

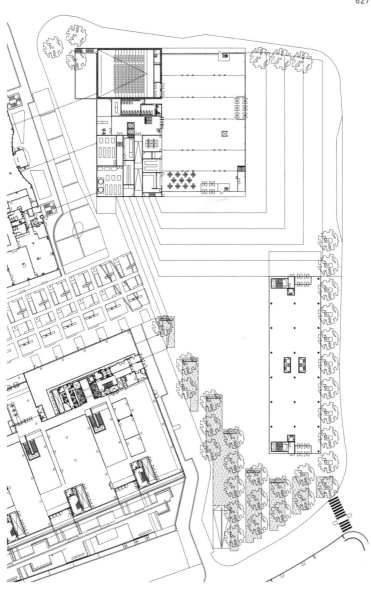

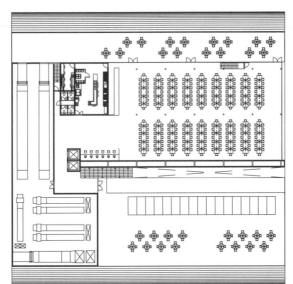

Canteen level +30.6m

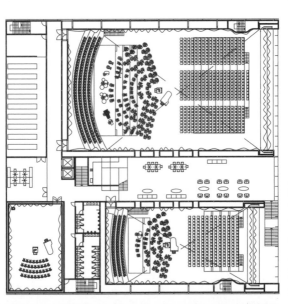

Musician's gallery level +16.2m

Transversal section through studios

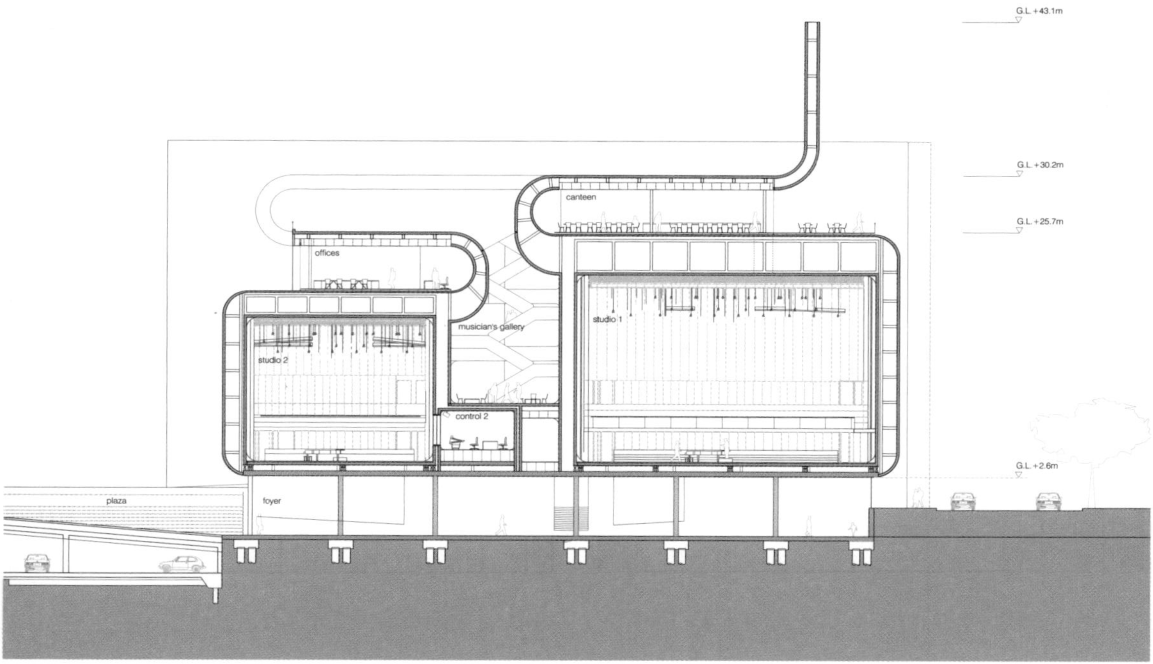

G.L. +43.1m

G.L. +30.2m

G.L. +25.7m

G.L. + 2.6m

canteen

studio 1

musician's gallery

control 2

offices

studio 2

foyer

plaza

Longitudinal section through studio 2

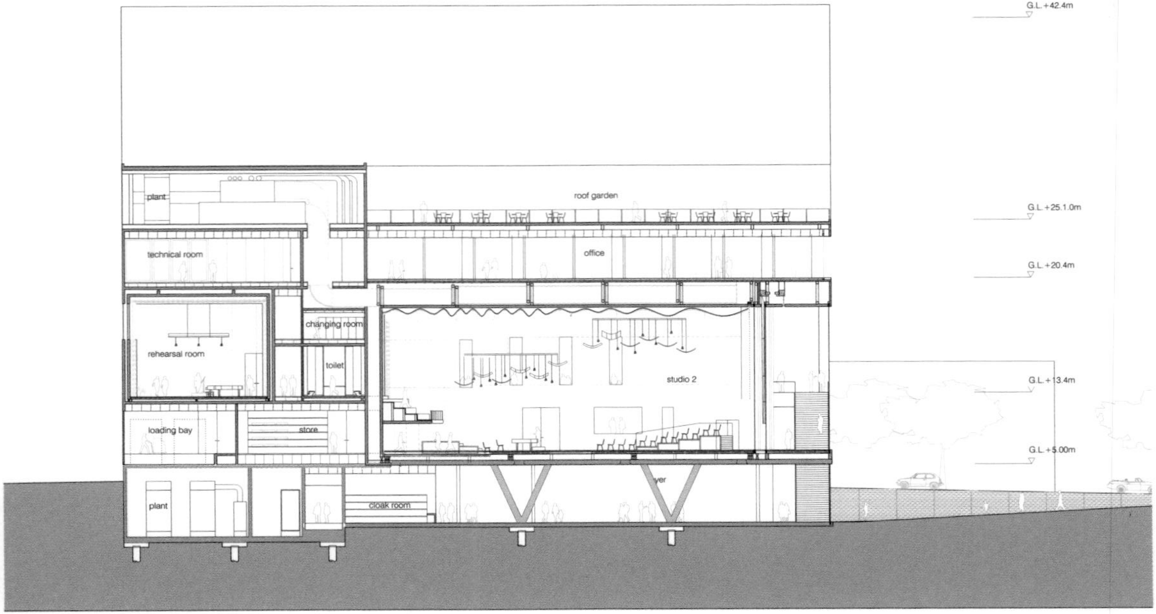

G.L. +42.4m

G.L. +25.0m

G.L. +20.4m

G.L. +13.4m

G.L. +5.00m

roof garden

office

studio 2

changing room

toilet

cloak room

store

plant

technical room

rehearsal room

loading bay

plant

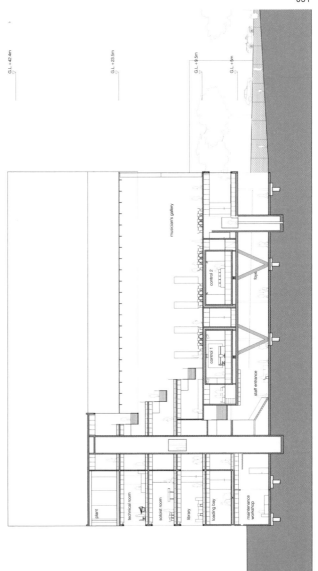

Longitudinal section through musician's gallery

Transversal section through production spaces

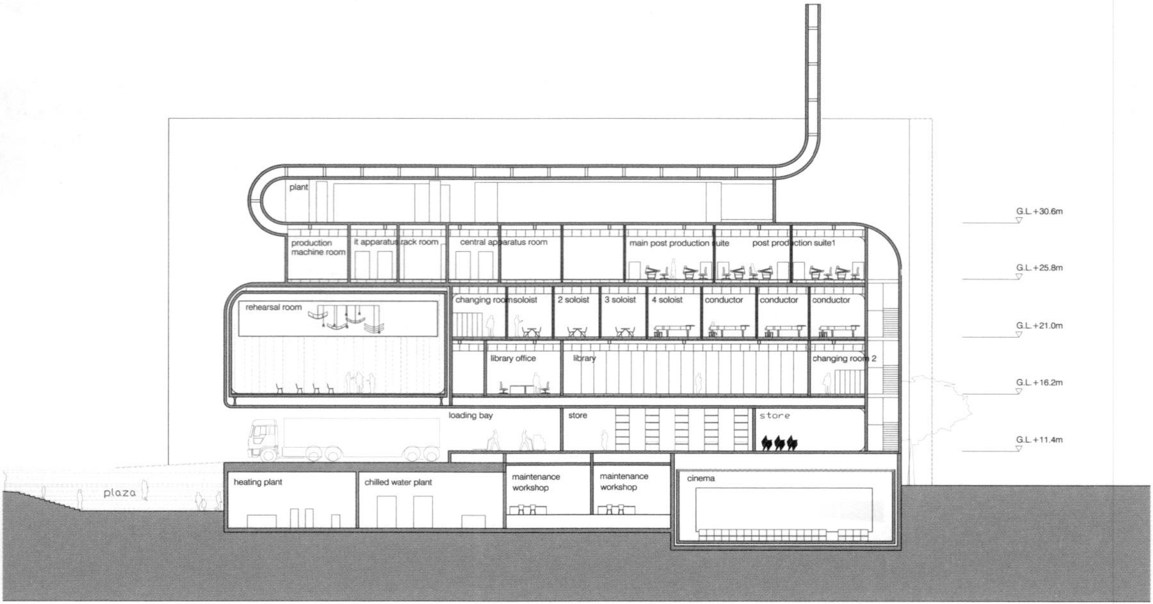

G.L.+30.6m

G.L.+25.8m

G.L.+21.0m

G.L.+16.2m

G.L.+11.4m

plant

production machine room

it apparatus/rack room

central apparatus room

main post production suite

post production suite

plant

changing room/solosoist

2 soloist

3 soloist

4 soloist

conductor

conductor

conductor

conductor

changing room 2

library office

library

rehearsal room

store

store

loading bay

maintenance workshop

maintenance workshop

chilled water plant

heating plant

cinema

plaza

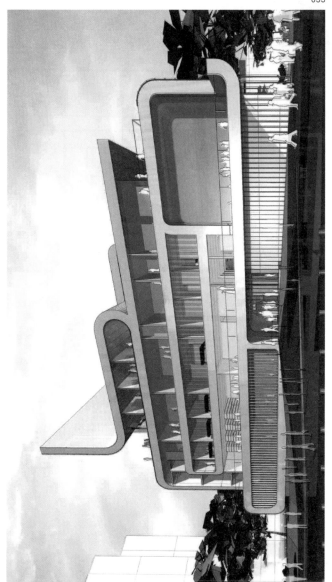

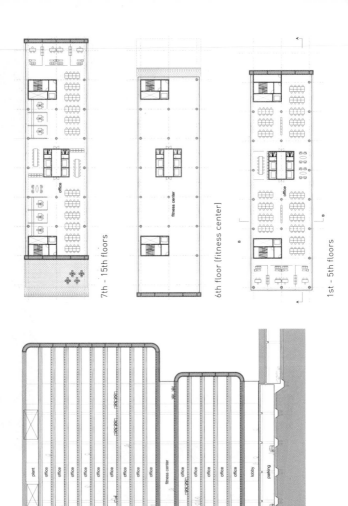

7th - 15th floors

office

6th floor (fitness center)

fitness center

1st - 5th floors

office

Office tower section

plant
office
office
office
office
office
office
office
office
fitness center
office
office
office
office
lobby
parking

Phylogenesis and the Tree of Life
Sandra Knapp

The discovery and description of order in nature has long been at the heart of the human interaction with the environment. The interface between human society and the world in which it operates is mediated through the prism of metaphor. The nurturing arms of Mother Earth, the violent vagaries of the physical forces beyond our control, the helplessness of the human condition, are all ways in which our surroundings have been conceptualised. Today's society is no different; we see our environment through a particular worldview, but one very different from any that has gone before. Despite the apparent distrustful and anti-science attitude of society today, we, as human beings, see the world in which we live through the lens of science. Like it or not, science underpins how we look at both ourselves and at our place in nature. Relationships – us to our fellow human beings, species of life on Earth to other species, humans to their surroundings – are at the heart of modern science. The paradigm for relationships in nature is phylogeny – the genesis of diversity. The powerful and gripping image of phylogeny on Earth is the dichotomously branching tree of life. Rooted in the Earth on which we live, its branches include all organisms that have ever lived on the planet. Scientists today know that all life has historical connections through time; the evidence is overwhelming and compelling. But this was not always so.

The Greek philosophers and their pupils named and classified plants and animals useful to humans, their knowledge was passed down and copied over and over again through the "Dark Ages". Essentialism as practiced by Aristotle and applied to the science of taxonomy (the naming and classifying of plants and animals) was based upon the assertion that organisms had forms or essences, the task of science was to discover these and that the definition of the organism was the description of its essence. Order in nature was revealed by discovering the essence. In the mid-18th century the great Swedish botanist, Carl von Linné, also known as Carolus Linnaeus, devised a system to classify all organisms. He catalogued life on Earth as he knew it. In his system he ordered nature in ever smaller inclusive groups – constructed to encompass all diversity in a set of named boxes that were easy to remember. In constructing his system he invented the naming system we still use today for scientific names – the binomial system, where each smallest inclusive group, today called a species, has two names, the genus name and the species (what Linnaeus called the trivial name) epithet. Thus, the scientific name for our own species is Homo sapiens – thinking man. Funnily enough, Linnaeus' description of Homo sapiens was merely "Know thyself" – good advice, really. Not a single other species was put into the genus Homo – we were a species apart. As were most other species – each placed in a box, connected only by some similarities in structure. But for Linnaeus and his contemporaries, the boxes or categories were really just tools for memorization. In his great catalogue of the plant kingdom, Species Plantarum, published in 1753, Linnaeus devised a system for the logical memorization of the approximately 5500 species of plants he knew, he thought there were probably fewer than 10,000 altogether, so his system could easily accommodate every plant ever created. Created was the operative word, as biologists of his day "knew" that the world had been created and organised by a superior being; all that remained was for us to uncover the order in that creation. But as discovery proceeded and humans began to explore more and more of the surface of the globe, the story just got more and more complicated. The German poet, playwright and self-taught botanist Johann Wolfgang Goethe summed it up eloquently, describing the complexity of life as "the eternal Weaver's masterpiece; look how one press of her foot sets a thousand threads in motion – how the shuttles dart to and fro, the flowing strands intertwine and a thousand interconnexions are made at one stroke!"

The image was no longer that of a nice collector's cabinet with many discrete boxes, each for a single species distinct from all the rest, but rather of cloth, a complex skein of connected forms. At the time Goethe was teaching himself botany. Helped by Linnaeus' recently published works, a general aim was to arrange plant (and by extension animal) families in an ascending and gradually developing progression, as Goethe put it "from the simplest, almost invisible rudimentary manifestations to the most complex and devious." The scale of nature – from the simple to the complex, culminated of course by man – pervaded imagery about the inter-relationships of living things. That individual organisms could change and adapt to their circumstances was clear from the study of life itself – plants growing in cold places were smaller than ones from more temperate climes – but the scale of nature, of ever-increasing complexity, was to be discovered in the study of form itself.

In the early part of the 19th century many systems evolved to describe order in nature – it had become clear that the ladder did not really exist, or if it did, it was twisted and not easy to follow! Circular systems were devised to depict how life was inter-related, such as that proposed by those now known as the Quinarians. Their imagery revolved around sets of interdigitating circles, often based on multiples of the number five. Into this intellectual soup stepped the young man Charles Robert Darwin – who changed forever the way in which we view the world around us, whether or not we acknowledge it. As a young man, Darwin had embarked on the ship the Beagle as a supernumerary ship's naturalist and companion to Captain Robert Fitzroy. Between 1831 and 1836, the ship's inhabitants mapped the coastline of southern South America, stopped off in the Galapagos and eventually circumnavigated the world. Darwin returned to England a changed man –like Goethe, his study of the new stimulated his intellect and he made a tremendous theoretical leap from the intellectual milieu of the day. His ideas on what was termed transmutation were the next logical leap from that made by Goethe and the French philosopher Jean Lamarck – that organisms change in response to their environment. That change in individuals influenced survival and ultimately reproduction led Darwin to his "species theory" – what we now term evolution by natural selection. Darwin worked on his ideas in private, perhaps tortured by the sheer leap into the dark they implied – that species were not created, they evolved and changed. Twenty years after his return from the voyage of the Beagle, Darwin received a letter from a young naturalist in the Malay Archipelago, in what is today Indonesia. The letter, from Alfred Russel Wallace, outlined ideas on "The tendency of varieties to depart indefinitely from the original type" – just the sort of idea Darwin himself was working on. Wallace's letter, written by a younger to a much admired older man, spurred Darwin into writing his 500 page tome (published in 1859) "On the origin of species by means of natural selection, or the preservation of favoured races in the struggle for life ", where he articulated a new imagery of how living things are inter-connected.

The only picture in Darwin's entire book is a dichotomously branching diagram – with time on the vertical axis and biological diversity on the horizontal. This branching diagram shows ancestry and descent for life itself, not just for families of people, where it was well known, but the concept extended to ancestry and descent of all forms of life. No longer could man sit at the top of the scale of nature, created apart from all the rest of the multitudes of species further down; rather, we were now connected to the rest through lines of descent. Darwinism (a term coined by Wallace, who remained a great admirer of Darwin's) spawned much imagery – the ape courting the prim Victorian young lady and the great spiral of diversity beginning with a worm and ending with Darwin himself are both images of the time that have persisted to this day. Janet Brown, in her two-volume biography of Darwin, presents evidence that Darwin was the first scientist to become readily recognisable – as caricature. But for the future, the more important imagery Darwin's ideas engendered was yet to come. Ernst Haeckel, a professor of zoology in Jena, emphatically championed Darwin's theory – vehemently defending the concept of evolution by natural selection against all comers. Through his study of the morphology of single-celled animals, almost crystalline in their symmetry, he constructed genealogies of similar forms – taking the image of descent with modification from the abstract as it appeared in "On the origin of species" and applying it to real organisms

in the real world. Haeckel claimed that all species represented
stages in the developmental process of a unified genealogy
of living things – he called this process phylogeny. He first
coined the word phylogeny – the earliest ever use of the word–
in his 1866 book "Generelle Morphologie der Organismen".
Derived from the Greek – phylum (race), genesis (birth) – the
word for Haeckel became the embodiment of the depiction
of a Darwinian world-view. Phylogeny was the way of looking
at the lines of descent of all organic beings. Haeckel used
incredibly memorable images to depict his phylogenies – his
phylogeny of the plants is a seaweed-like branching diagram,
looking for all the world like a large interconnected kelp bed
rooted from a single holdfast. That of the pedigree of Man
– all life on Earth - is a gnarled oak. The image of the tree of
life has its roots in Haeckel, and it is inextricably linked with
the concept of phylogeny.

Constructing the phylogeny required careful examination of
the structure or morphology of the organism – the symmetrical
organization of life-forms was for Haeckel the ultimate proof
that evolution did exist. By studying morphology in detail,
the lines of descent - the phylogeny - could be drawn and
known with certainty. Neither Darwin nor Haeckel knew what
mechanisms drove evolution by natural selection worked –
for biologists in the late 19th century the study of morphology,
of the form of organisms, was the ideal way to discover the
phylogeny or interconnections between them. When the
principles of heredity were discovered and genes were shown
to be the fundamental units upon which natural selection
worked, the study of morphology and with it phylogeny, fell,
if not exactly disrepute, certainly into the doldrums.
Speculation about the totality of evolutionary history had

involved arguments about descent. That is after all what Haeckel meant when he coined the word phylogeny – the lines of descent. But how can we know the history of the past – reconstructing a complete narrative is an impossibility, how can we know all of history? A way around this conundrum is to use "relativity rather than narrative" (a phrase borrowed from Richard Fortey's book "Life: an unauthorized biography"). Rather than focusing on the arguments about descent itself, it is more profitable to focus on theories, hypotheses and about relationships – about how one type of organism is related by descent to another. On the face of it this is much like Haeckel's phylogeny, but this new way of looking a phylogeny does not require complete knowledge, it is enough to know relative common ancestry.

The re-emergence of phylogeny as a metaphor for our view of life and its inter-relationships is due primarily to another German biologist, Willi Hennig. Working in the early 20th century, Hennig developed a new way of practicing systematics – the science of classifying the natural world. Hennig's methodology – now called cladistics – involves using morphology to group species. For cladists, the fact that wombats and humans share a backbone, four limbs and fur unites the two in a clade –in an inclusive group. It does not imply that humans have descended from wombats, or vice versa – it only states that wombats and humans share characters not shared with fish, for example, or insects. A cladogram is a branching diagram depicting these nested sets of shared characteristics – a modern phylogeny. Hennig's book, published in 1950 and entitled "Grundzüge einer Theorie der phylogenetischen Systematik" (a modified version of which was translated into English

and published in 1966 as "Phylogenetic Systematics")
united evolution and taxonomy (systematics) in a new, more
scientific way of looking at nature – through the individual
characteristics themselves. The deconstruction of an
organism into a bag of characters may seem counter-
productive, but in fact it is logical and forms the basis for the
construction of testable hypotheses about evolution itself.
We know that some things have arisen more than once
in the history of life – take wings for example. The wings
of butterflies and bats are not structurally the same; rather,
the two types of organisms have independently arrived
at a "solution" – flight. The distribution of this character,
wings, on a cladogram or phylogeny, allows us to make
that hypothesis and to use other characters to test it.
Each phylogeny then becomes not the truth, but simply a
hypothesis about relationships of living things – subject to
change and modification as new evidence is found. Both
new organisms and new characters can falsify (a term
popularized by the philosopher Karl Popper) a phylogenetic
hypothesis. New fossils of feather-bearing dinosaurs found
in China showed that Archaeopteryx was not only not the
"missing link" between the birds and non-birds, but also that
feathers and flight followed different trajectories in evolution
– feathers having arisen first and independently from flight.
The discovery of DNA in the mid-20th century, and the ensuing
ability to read its sequence of nucleotide bases with ease has
provided us with huge numbers of new characters with which
to construct phylogenetic hypotheses. Some of the results
are surprising indeed; elephant shrews are closely related
to elephants, waterlilies are quite close relatives of irises and
fungi are more closely related to animals than to plants.

Each new character however does not represent revealed truth, we now know better than that. Hennig's new phylogenetic systematics articulated more than just using characters to examine relationships about the memberships of clades, as he also emphasized the importance of what he called "reciprocal illumination" –always going back to examine the evidence again. Reciprocal illumination showed that the scaly skins of reptiles and dinosaurs were merely shared ancestral characters – dinosaurs in fact share many evolutionarily derived features with the feathered birds. One of the great defenders of the principles of cladistics (Hennig's phylogenetic systematics), the fish taxonomist Gareth Nelson, once said that systematics was the "study of character conflict" – not all characteristics evolve at the same rate. Phylogenetic systematics (or cladistics) has been the subject of as much scientific controversy as that which surrounded Darwin's original formulation of evolution by natural selection, but has now become the prevailing paradigm with which we represent the relationships of the organisms of the world in which we live.

Phylogenies – hypotheses about the relationships of living things – allow us to predict the distribution of new characteristics. That humans and the great apes (today represented by chimps, bonobos, gorillas and orang-utans) are members of a single clade – more closely related to each other than any are to other animals – means that, for example, we can predict a new disease emerging in one of the great apes might also affect us.

A chemical compound found a particular plant – say the cancer-beating chemical taxol in the Canadian yew Taxus baccata – is more likely to be found in other members

of the Taxus clade than in the snapdragons. A phylogeny
also provides the framework with which we understand
nature, and by analogy our place in it. The most recently
published phylogeny of all of life – based in the DNA
sequence of ribosomal genes – clearly shows that
vertebrates, including humans, are but a tiny bud on an
incredibly diverse tree of life.

We are quite insignificant. But a phylogeny is only a
hypothesis, it is not static or fixed, nor is it linear–
Darwin's diagram of an ever-dichotomously-branching
ancestry with descent is, as he intended, merely a caricature
of the reality we are discovering. Bacteria apparently
exchange genes among each other, making the tracing
of a species genealogy in a linear or even dichotomously
branching fashion impossible. Hybridization is a
common theme among plant species, both straightforward
crossing and polyploidy (doubling of chromosome
numbers) are amazingly widespread. The tree of life
clearly has some interconnecting threads – reticulations
– linking some of the branches.

The constructing of phylogenies using DNA sequences
has shown that these phenomena are more common than
perhaps we previously thought – a DNA phylogeny is
the phylogeny of that gene, not of the species themselves.
Does this mean that we should throw up our hands and
give up, admitting that we can never know the "true"
form of the tree of life? The image of the tree of life as a
regularly branching, sturdy structure is seductive;
phylogeny is more interesting than that.

A phylogeny is a hypothesis about how characters are
distributed in nature – a moving metaphor.

1. Downsview Park, Toronto 2000
Farshid Moussavi and Alejandro Zaera-Polo with Lluís Viu Rebés, Enrico Buonanno, Jordi Mansilla
Associate architect: KPMB Toronto
Landscape Architects: Tom Leader+James Haig-Streeter, PWPLA San Francisco

2. La Gavia Park, Madrid 2003
Farshid Moussavi and Alejandro Zaera-Polo with Bernardo Angelini, David Casino, Nacho Toribio, Daniel Valle.

3. South—East Coastal Park and Auditoriums, Barcelona 2002–2004
Client: City of Barcelona
Schedule: Completion 2004
Site area: 50,000m²
Budget: 12 million euros
Competition design team
Farshid Moussavi and Alejandro Zaera Polo with Lluís Viu Rebes
Landscape architect: Teresa Galí, BCN
Structural engineers: Obiol, Moya y Asociados SL, Barcelona
Basic design phase design team:
Farshid Moussavi and Alejandro Zaera Polo with Niccoló Cadeo, Danielle Domeniconi, Marco Guarnieri, Sergio López-Piñeiro, Terence Seah, Daniel Valle, Lluís Viú Rebes
Landscape architect: Teresa Galí, Barcelona
Structural engineers: Obiol, Moya y Asociados SL, Barcelona
Detail design phase design team:
Farshid Moussavi and Alejandro Zaera Polo with Marco Guarnieri,

Sergio López-Piñeiro, Pablo Ros, Lluís Viu Rebes, Juanjo González
Landscape architect: Teresa Galí, Barcelona
Structural engineers: Obiol, Moya y Asociados SL, Barcelona
Mechanical and electrical engineers: Proisotec, Girona
Quantity surveyors: Tg3, BCN

4. Prototype for a Rural High-Speed Terminal, Perafort 2002
Farshid Moussavi and Alejandro Zaera-Polo with Jordi Pagès i Ramon

5. High—Speed Railway Complex, Pusan 1996
Farshid Moussavi and Alejandro Zaera-Polo with Denis Balent, F.Benedito, Young Yoon Kim, J. Lundberg, Kenichi Matsuzawa, Tae-Hong park, Santiago Triginer
Local Architect: Nam-San architects & engineers, Seoul
Structural Engineers: Dewhurst Macfarlane, London
Mechanical and Electrical engineers: Flack & Kurtz, London
Traffic Consultants: Logan associates, Hereford

6. Masterplan for the Enlace Pier, Santa Cruz de Tenerife 2003
Farshid Moussavi and Alejandro Zaera-Polo with Kenichi Matsuzawa, Lluís Ortega, Luis Falcón, N. Ninomiya, Ch. Ag-ukikrul, J. Galmez, M. Ansari, L. Jensen
Services Engineer: BDSP, London
Structure Engineer: AKT, London
Landscape Architects:

Karres and Brandt, Hilversum
Traffic Engineer: Halcrow Fox, London

7. Concorso internazionale Ponte Parodi e la città di Genova, 2000–2001

Farshid Moussavi and Alejandro Zaera-Polo with Nicolò Cadeo, Peng Chua, Ueli Degen, Daniele Domeniconi, Marco Guarnieri, Jordi Pagès i Ramon, Sergio López-Piñeiro, Terence Seah, Daniel Valle, Lluís Viu-Rebes
Structural Engineer:
Adams Kara Taylor, London
Services Engineer:
BDSP Partnership, London
Quantity Surveyors:
Davis Langdon & Everest
Local Architect: Sergio Zampichelli

8. South Bank Centre, London 2001

Farshid Moussavi and Alejandro Zaera-Polo with Ueli Degen, Friedrich Ludewig, Terence Seah, Daniel Valle,
Services Engineer: BDSP, London
Quantity Surveivor: Davis Langdon Everest, London
Structural Engineer: AKT, London.

9. Technology Transfer Centre, La Rioja 2003

Farshid Moussavi and Alejandro Zaera-Polo with Kensuke Kishikawa, Jordi Pagès i Ramon, Pablo Ros
Technical consultants
Structures: Brufau, Obiols, Moya y Asociados (BOMA), Barcelona
Costs: J/T Ardèvol i Associats, Barcelona
Installations: Juan Gallostra Isern/ Ramon Cos
Local technician in la Rioja:
Jesús Alfaro Lafuente
Landscape architect:
Teresa Galí, Barcelona
Models: Luis Montiel
3D animations: Werner Skvara

10. High-Speed Railway Complex, Florence 2002

Farshid Moussavi and Alejandro Zaera-Polo with Edouard Cabay, Nerea Calvillo, Marco Guarnieri, Kensuke Kishikawa, Jordi Pagès i Ramon, Lluís Viu Rebes, Chu Ka Wing Kelvin
Structural Engineer: SDG (Structural Design Group), Tokyo
Services Engineer: BDSP Partnership, London
Traffic Engineer: Ninian Logan, Radlett
Cost Consultant: Davis Langdon & Everest, London]
Model: a-models, London

11. Hortus Medicus: Novartis Underground Car Park & Gate, Basel 2003

Farshid Moussavi and Alejandro Zaera-Polo with Nerea Calvillo, Kelvin Chu Ka Wing, Kazuhide Doi, Marco Guarnieri, Kensuke Kishikawa, Friedrich Ludewig, Jordi Pagès i Ramon, Ines Tabar
Structure: Walter Mory Maier, Basel
Services: Waldhauser Haustechnik, Basel Fire Strategy: Prof. Mario Fontana, Zurich Landscape Architect: Fahrni + Breitenfeld, Basel

Medical Consultant:
Prof. Axel Fenner, Lübeck
Model: Andrew Ingham, London

12. Yokohama International Passenger Terminal, Yokohama 1996–2002

Client: The City of Yokohama Port & Harbor Bureau Construction Department Osanbashi Passenger Vessel Terminal Maintenance Subdivision
Architects: Foreign Office Architects (FOA) / Farshid Moussavi and Alejandro Zaera-Polo with:
Competition: Ivan Ascanio, Yoon King Chong, Michael Cosmas, Jung-Hyun Hwang, Guy Westbrook
Basic Design: Felix Bendito, Victoria Castillejos, Dafne Gil, Jordi Mansilla, Kenichi Matsuzawa, Oriol Montfort, Xavier Ortiz, Lluis Viu Rebes, Jose Saenz, Santiago Triginer, Julian Varas, Thomasine Wolfensberger
Detailed design: Kensuke Kishikawa, Yasuhisa Kikuchi, Izumi Kobayashi, Kenichi Matsuzawa,
Tomofumi Nagayama, Xavier Ortiz, Lluis Viu Rebes, Keisuke Tamura
Construction Phase
Shokan Endo, Kensuke Kishikawa, Yasuhisa Kikuchi, Izumi Kobayashi, Kenichi Matsuzawa, Tomofumi Nagayama, Keisuke Tamura
Quantity surveyor: Futaba Quantity Surveyors Co., ltd. / Shohei Obinata
Structural engineer: Structure Design Group (SDG) / Kunio Watanabe
Services engineer: P.T.Morimura & Associates, Ltd / Masanori Sodekawa,
Takao Kawauchi
Main contractors
1st division: Shimizu Corporation
2nd division: Kajima Corporation
3rd division: Toda Corporation
Other consultants
Disaster prevention consultant: Akeno Fire Research Institute / Hideo Nakajima
Acoustic: Nagata Acoustics Inc. / Yasuhisa Toyoya
Traffic: Urban Traffic Engineering / Takayuki Suzuki, Michiyuki Arai
Lighting: Kado Lighting Design Laboratory / Yasuo Tsunoda
Subcontractors and suppliers
Steel: Kawasaki Heavy Industries, Ltd. / Masaaki Hashimoto
Steel: NKK Corporation / Yasuhiro Otani
Stainless steel nail fastening:
HILTI (Japan), Ltd. / Tom Fujiyama
Glass: Asahi Glass Building Conponent Enginnering Co., Ltd. / Kanji Yamasaki, Kazuomi Kagami
Waterproofing polyurethane: Mitsui Chemicals Industrial Products / Masashi Nozawa
Wood (IPE): Isolite Insulating Products Co., Ltd. / Motohiro Kojima
Wood (IPE): Maeda Environmental Art Co., Ltd. / Takanori Maeda, Kojiro Katsuta
Handrail metal work: Kanematsu Devices Corporation / Toshiaki Yoshida, Kimihide Kodama
Mesh: Koiwa Kanaami Co., Ltd. / Senji Nishimura
Low-temperature metal spraying system: Metal Spray Engineering Co., Ltd. / Tadashi Kitada
Artificial soil: Toho LEO /

Akihiro Nishiyama
Elevator: Yokohama Elevator /
Mitsuhiro Tozaki
Conveyor: Toyo Kanetsu K.K. /
Shigeru Yagi
Tender date: February 2000
Start on site date: March 2000
Contract duration: February 2000
to November 2002
Gross external floor area: 438,243m^2
Total cost: ¥ 23.5 billion

13. Myeong-Dong Cathedral, Seoul 1995-1996

Farshid Moussavi and Alejandro Zaera-
Polo with Ivan Ascanio, Yoon King Chong,
Pablo Heredia, Lee Dong Ju, Jong Jin
Kim, Kenichi Matsuzawa, Guy Westbrook
Local Architect and engineer: Beyond
Space group, Seoul

14.Bluemoon Tent, Groningen 2001

Client: City of Groningen
Farshid Moussavi and Alejandro
Zaera-Polo
Associate Architect: ARTES, Groningen
Structural Engineer: Adams Kara Taylor,
London
Area temporary dwelling: 210 m^2
Area temporary market: 900 m^2
Total Budget: 450,000 euros

15. Prostneset Ferry Terminal, Conference Centre and Hotel, Tromsø 2003

Farshid Moussavi and Alejandro
Zaera-Polo with Edouard Cabay, Nerea
Calvillo, Kelvin Chu, Manuel Clavel Rojo,
Marco Guarnieri, Friedrich Ludewig,
Jordi Pagès i Ramon, Lluís Viu Rebes
Services Engineer: Battle McCarthy,
London
Structure Engineer: AKT, London
Quantity Surveyor: Davis Langdon Everest
Traffic Engineer: Logan Associates

16. T'Raboes Harbour Facilities, Amersfoort 2003

Farshid Moussavi and Alejandro
Zaera-Polo with Kensuke Kishikawa,
Lluís Viu Rebes

17. National Glass Centre, Sunderland 1994

Farshid Moussavi and Alejandro
Zaera-Polo with Jung-Hyun Hwang

18. Olympic Aquatic Sports Center, Madrid 2002

Farshid Moussavi and Alejandro
Zaera-Polo with Manuel Clavel Rojo,
Marco Guarnieri, Kensuke Kishikawa,
Jordi Pagès i Ramon, Lluís Viu Rebes
Services Engineer: Battle McCarthy,
London
Quantity Surveyor: Manuel Iglesias,
Madrid
Structural Engineer: Adams Kara Taylor,
London

19. Belgo Zuid, London 1998-1999

Farshid Moussavi and Alejandro
Zaera-Polo with Chotima Ag-Ukrikul,
Luis Falcón, Kenichi Matsuzawa,
Mathew Morís, Naomi Ninomiya,
Lluís Ortega, Xavier Ortiz, Lluís Viu Rebes

Industrial engineer: John Brady
Associates
Structure: Adams Kara Taylor, London

20. Kansai-Kan Library, Kyoto 1996

Farshid Moussavi and Alejandro Zaera-Polo with Kenichi Matsuzawa, Santiago Triginer, Guy Westbrook, Akira Yamanaka
Technical Consultants:
Kajima Design, Tokyo

21. Municipal Police Headquarters, La Vila Joiosa 2000-2003

Farshid Moussavi and Alejandro Zaera-Polo with Jorge Arribas, Nicolo Cadeo, Daniele Domenicone, Sergio Lopez Piñeiro, Jordi Pagès i Ramon, Natalia Rodriguez, Daniel Valle, Nuria Vallespin, Lluís Viu Rebes
Associate architect: Antonio Marquerie, Torrevieja
Structural Engineer: NB35, Madrid
Services Engineer: Ángel Garrido, Madrid

22. Bluemoon Hotel, Groningen 2001

Client: City of Groningen
Structural Engineer:
Adams Kara Taylor, London
Area temporary dwelling: 210 m^2
Area temporary market: 900 m^2
Total Budget: 450,000 euros
Design Team
Farshid Moussavi and Alejandro Zaera Polo with Marco Guarnieri, Xavier Ortiz, Lluís Viu Rebes
Local Architect: Artes, Groningen

23. Sociopolis, Valencia 2003

Farshid Moussavi and Alejandro Zaera-Polo with Ines Tabar Rodriguez, Jordi Pagès i Ramon

24. Eyebeam Museum of Art and Technology, New York 2001

Farshid Moussavi and Alejandro Zaera Polo with BCNSWS: Juan Carlos Castro, Santi Ibarra, Toni Montes, Lluís Ortega, Xavier Osarte
Multimedia: Straddle3 - Joan Escofet, David Juarez, Roberto Soto
Acoustics: Pedro Cerdà
Structure: GIDJ

25. Municipal Theater and Auditorium, Torrevieja 2002

Farshid Moussavi and Alejandro Zaera-Polo with Jorge Arribas, Marco Guarnieri, Clara Jorger, Sergio López Piñeiro, Natalia Rodriguez, Daniel Valle, Nuria Vallespin, Lluís Viu Rebes
Associate architect: Antonio Marquerie, Torrevieja
Acoustics: UPV, Dpt. Física Aplicada, Jaime Llinares Galiana
Installations: Consulting de Ingeniería ICA SL, Leandro Feliu Maqueda
Structure: NB35
Stage equipment and acoustic ceiling: Audiotec Sistemas

26. Glass Enclosure Prototype, U.K. 2001-2002

Farshid Moussavi and Alejandro Zaera-Polo with Marco Guarnieri, Friedrich Ludewig, Terence Seah
Structure: Adams Kara Taylor, London

Services: BDSP Parternship, London
QS: Davis Langdon & Everest

27. Department Store, Bristol 2002

Farshid Moussavi and Alejandro Zaera-Polo
with Kazuhide Doi, Kensuke Kishikawa
Structure: Adams Kara Taylor, London
Services: Peter Hammond, Cameron
Taylor Brady

28. The Bundle Tower (WTC I), New York 2002

Farshid Moussavi and Alejandro
Zaera-Polo with Daniel Lopez-Perez,
Erhard An-He Kinzelbach, Edouard
Cabay, Chu Ka Wing Kelvin
Model photos: Valerie Bennett

29. Special Plan for Cabo Llanos, Santa Cruz de Tenerife 2003

Farshid Moussavi and Alejandro
Zaera-Polo with Nerea Calvillo, Laura
Fernández, Kazuhide Doi
Developer: Gestur Tenerife

30. Zona Franca Office Park, Barcelona 2002–

Foreign Office Architects with
Arata Isozaki
Farshid Moussavi and Alejandro
Zaera-Polo with Nerea Calvillo, Marco
Guarnieri, Izumi Kobayashi, Ksk Tamura,
Jordi Pagès i Ramon, Pablo Ros

31. Bioplex, Mars 1999–2001

Farshid Moussavi and Alejandro Zaera-
Polo with Friedrich Ludwig, Xavier Ortiz

Structure: Adams Kara Taylor, London

32. Floriade Pavilion, Haarlemmermeer 2001

Farshid Moussavi and Alejandro Zaera-Polo
with Nicolo Cadeo, Danielle Domenicone,
Marco Guarnieri, Sergio López Piñeiro,
Lluis Viu Rebes.
Structural Engineer: SDG (Structural
Design Group), Tokyo
Services Engineer: BDSP Partnership,
London
Traffic Engineer: Ninian Logan, Radlett
Cost Consultant:
Davis Langdon&Everest, London

33. Belgo Restaurant, New York 1998–1999

Farshid Moussavi and Alejandro Zaera-
Polo with Kenichi Matsuzawa, Lluís Viu
Rebes Guy Westbrook
Local architect: Michael Zenreich
Architects, New York
Industrial engineers: Helmut Fenster,
New York
Structure: Rodney Gibble Structural
Engeneers, New York

34. Publishing Headquarters, Paju 2001

Farshid Moussavi and Alejandro
Zaera-Polo with Jorge Arribas, Natalia
Rodriguez, Nuria Vallespin, Lluís Viu
Rebes, Xavier Ortiz, Marco Guarnieri,
Pablo Ros
Associate architect: Iroje architects,
Young Yoon Kim
Structural Engineer: SDG
(Structural Design Group), Tokyo

Services Engineer:
BDSP Partnership, London
Traffic Engineer: Ninian Logan, Radlett
Cost Consultant:
Davis Langdon&Everest, London

Service Engineer:
Cameron Taylor Brady, London
Facades: Waagner Biro
Model: FOA and Andrew Ingram, London
Animation: Werner Skvara

35. Virtual House, Anywhere 1997
Farshid Moussavi and Alejandro Zaera-Polo with Mònica Company,
Kenichi Matsuzawa, Jordi Mansilla,
Manuel Monterde, Manuel Pérez

36. Azadi Cineplex, Tehran 1996
Client: City of Tehran
Area: 8,500m^2
Budget: $5,000,000
Farshid Moussavi and Alejandro Zaera-Polo with Ivan Ascanio,
Yoon King Chong, Kenichi Matsuzawa

37. BBC White City Music Centre and Offices, London 2003
Farshid Moussavi and Alejandro Zaera-Polo with Nerea Calvillo, Kelvin Chu Ka Wing, Kazuhide Doi, Eduardo Fernández-Moscoso, Laura Fernández, Kensuke Kishikawa, Friedrich Ludewig,
Jordi Pagès i Ramon
Structure: Adams Kara Taylor, London
Acoustics: Sandy Brown Associates, London
Lighting: Speirs and Major Associates
QS & Project Management:
Davis Langdon & Everest, London
Theatre Consultant: Ducks Sceno, Vaulx-en-Velin

In November 2003, FOA is:
Farshid Moussavi
Alejandro Zaera-Polo
Friedrich Ludewig
Kensuke Kishikawa
Kenichi Matsuzawa
Kazuhide Doi
Nerea Calvillo
Jordi Pagès i Ramon
Pablo Ros

Lluis Viu Rebes
Lorena Camisuli
Eduardo Gutiérrez

Javier Monge
Lys Villalba

Publisher: Actar
Edited by Michael Kubo and Albert Ferré
in collaboration with FOA
Book design concept: Ramon Prat
Editorial assistance: Anna Tetas,
Tomoko Sakamoto
Graphic design: Rosa Lladó, Estela Robles
Graphic design assistance:
Montse Sagarra, Max Weber
Digital production: Oriol Rigat, Carmen Galán,
Leandre Linares

Texts:

Sanford Kwinter, "Who's Afraid of Formalism",
1994. Originally published in *Any Magazine* no. 7/8.
Mark Wigley, "Local Knowledge", 1999. Originally
published in a catalogue of studio work of the
architecture class at the Städelschule Frankfurt
(www.staedelschule.de).
Detlef Mertins, "Same Difference", 2003
Patrick Beaucé and Bernard Cache
"Towards a Non-Standard Mode of
Production", 2003
Translated from French by Paul Hammond.
Manuel de Landa, " Deleuze and the Use of
the Genetic Algorithm in Architecture", 2001.
Originally presented at the conference E-Futures:
Designing for a Digital World, held at the RIBA,
London and published in Neil Leach, ed.,
Designing for a Digital World (London: Wiley-
Academy, 2002).
Jeffrey Kipnis, "On the Wild Side", 1999.
Originally published on the occasion of an
exhibition on Fabian Marcaccio and Greg Lynn
at the Wiener Secession, Association of Visual
Artists, Vienna (www.secession.at).
Sandra Knapp, "Phylogenesis and the Tree
of Life", 2003

All texts are published by courtesy of their
authors.
Translation of project texts on pages 330
and 420 by Edward Krasny.

Photographs:
Valerie Bennett pp. 346-347, 352-353, 492-493,
Cristóbal Palma pp. 373, 384, 385
Ramon Prat pp. 76-81, 250-257, 376-383, 386-389
Christian Richters pp. 285-287, 414-417

Special thanks for their help to Neil Leach,
Cristóbal Palma, José María Flores,
Marquería Asociados, and Casa de Cultura
de La Vila Joiosa.

Printing: Ingoprint
Distribution: Actar
Roca i Batlle 2
08023 Barcelona
Tel: +34 93 418 77 59
Fax: +34 93 418 67 07
info@actar-mail.com
www.actar.es

This book was published in collaboration
with the Institute of Contemporary Arts
on the occasion of the exhibition
*Foreign Office Architects:
Breeding Architecture*, London,
29 November 2003 – 29 February 2004.
www.ica.org.uk